Carrier Air Group 86

Schiffer Military History
Atglen, PA

Cover artwork by Steve Ferguson, Colorado Springs, CO.

CURE FOR KURE

When Air Group 86 went aboard the USS *Wasp* in March of 1945 to relieve AG 81, they inherited all of the latter's combat aircraft replete with unit markings. The Hellcats, the F4U-1D Corsairs, the Avenger torpedo-bombers and Helldiver dive-bombers all bore the black three-digit number foiled on the broad white tail band. Several of these aircraft displayed white forward cowl markings used during the March-era task force operations. After the *Wasp* was hit on March 19th, the aircraft remained with the carrier for the voyage to Seattle. Back in the States, VBF-86 would exchange their 1D-model Corsairs for the new F4U-4, distinguishable by its larger powerplant and four-bladed propeller. Just prior to the second voyage, air group geometric designator markings were changed service wide to single letter symbols. In the case of AG 86, they adopted the letter "X" on the tail as well as the upper right and lower left wingtips for all of their aircraft types. During the second combat cruise, the aircrews of VBF-86 quickly proved the worth of their upgraded Corsair fighter-bombers. The increased power of the F4U-4 allowed for a great payload in their ground attack roll, and fully paid off in the interceptor sorties. Of the nineteen aerial victories officially awarded to AG 86, their Corsair squadron would claim twelve of them. The improved altitude performance of the bent-wing birds had given them the tactical edge for running down the kamikazes threatening the fleet. Depicted are two VBF-86 wingmen in their rocket armed F4U-4s descending on enemy ships harbored at Kure naval station in Japan's Inland Sea.

Copyright © 1997 by Schiffer Publishing Ltd.
Library of Congress Catalog Number: 96-70841.

Printed in the United States of America.
ISBN: 0-7643-0221-3

We are interested in hearing from authors with book ideas on related topics.

Published by Schiffer Publishing Ltd.
77 Lower Valley Road
Atglen, PA 19310
Phone: (610) 593-1777
FAX: (610) 593-2002
Please write for a free catalog.
This book may be purchased from the publisher.
Please include $2.95 postage.
Try your bookstore first.

CARRIER AIR GROUP
EIGHTY-SIX

They . . .
Were young,
And life is dear when you are young;
Saw little,
Yet lived so much without the seeing;
Were mortal,
But knew the clouds and sky so well;
Were lost,
But flew with us before, and always will.

This book is dedicated to the officers and men of Air Group Eight-Six who have given their lives for their country . . .

Lt. Cmdr. Sheldon Ellsworth Prentice, USNR
Lt. James Elijah Burk, USNR
Lt. Albert Theodore Harshbarger, USNR
Lt. Robert Alan Ogden, USNR
Lt. Robert Elliott Plaut, USN
Lt. (jg) Arthur William Anderson, USNR
Lt. (jg) Charles Herbert Case, USNR
Lt. (jg) Leonard Joseph Hose, USNR
Lt. (jg) Robert Johnson, USNR
Lt. (jg) John Gold Shirley, Jr., USNR
Lt. (jg) James Edwin Tolle, USNR
Lt. (jg) Richard Weldon Turnbo, USNR
Ens. John Abernethy, USNR
Ens. William Arthur Bartling, USNR
Ens. Andrew Charles Butko, USNR
Ens. Robert Charles Cregar, USNR

Ens. John Frederick Gafner, USNR
Ens. Willis Grimes Howie, Jr., USNR
Ens. Charles Newton Lund, USNR
Ens. Harris Raymond Romer, USNR
Ens. Wendall Orvin Spauer, USNR
Ens. Walter Stepahin, USNR
Harold Newton Taylor, ARM1c, USN
Charles John Johnson, ARM2c, USNR
Bernard Patrick McGovern, ARM2c, USNR
Thomas Oscar Russell, ARM2c, USN
Gilbert Elroy Austin, AMM3c, USNR
Richard Curtiss Bryan, ARM3c, USNR
Keith Wayne Gordon, ARM3c, USNR
Robert Joseph Guariglia, AMM3c, USNR
Arthur Milton Jenkins, ARM3c, USN
George Thomas Melleney, ARM3c, USNR

Stanley Clay Morris, ARM3c, USNR
William McReynolds, ARM3c, USNR

. . . and to those who are missing in action . . .

Lt. Harold Russell Keller, USN
Lt. (jg) Warren Seth Anderson, USNR
*Lt. (jg) Joseph Donald Brown, USNR
*Lt. (jg) Harold Raymond Eyer, USNR
Lt. (jg) "T" "E" Jenson, USNR
Lt. (jg) Thomas "H" Morton, USNR
Ens. Leo Henry Ahern, USNR
Ens. Sylvan Anthony Cabrials, USNR

Ens. Richard Gould, USNR
Ens. Clarence Roder Johnson, USNR
Ens. Ralph Stites Webber, USNR
*Frederick Charles Lockett, ARM2c, USNR
Robert Lee Sayre, ARM2c, USN
David Lowell Hancock, ARM3c, USNR
William August Hemenway, AOM3c, USNR

*Repatriated after cessation of hostilities.

Commander George Robert Luker, USN
Born: 15 June 1908
Graduated U. S. Naval Academy 1932
USS COLORADO 1932-36
Flight Training—Pensacola 1936-37
VS-41 USS RANGER 1937-38
VP-9 USS WRIGHT 1938-40
Pensacola, Instructor 1940-43
CO, Hedron 11 1943-44

COMMANDER LUKER possesses those rare qualities, which combine daring leadership and devotion to duty with the ability to understand and inspire all those who work under him. Under his leadership the Air Group has been welded into an efficient and effective organization that has gained praise and prestige from all with whom they have worked. In combat, as in training, the Commander has personally led the Air Group in its major strikes against the enemy and at all times has provided that aggressive type of leadership which has made navy pilots famous. Equally famous among the pilots are such excerpts as " I was only doing 2100 RPM at 33 inches. Where the hell were you?" and "I never run my wingman out of gas. He had fifteen gallons left didn't he?"

The Commander with his warm smile and ready laugh has an appreciation for social moments as well. Always encouraging group parties, none were really under way until christened by the Commander's presence whether it was one of the barn dances at Otis, the wienieless wienie roast at Paia, the Hula Luau at Wailuki or that ultra ultra at Sands Point.

A firm believer in physical fitness, Commander Luker excels in most sports and generally finds time during a busy day to indulge in a little relaxation, tennis, swimming, skiing and hunting being but a few of the ones in which he takes a special interest. No talk of hunting would be complete without mentioning "Duke", the Commander's much beribboned and much traveled pointer. It is rumored that Duke is not yet fully cognizant of his responsibilities since Duke is hunted far more often than he is hunting. What he really needs is a regular canine S.P. to which the sentries at Atlantie City will attest.

Born in Staunton, Illinois, in 1908, Commander Luker attended Illinois University three years before entering the Naval Academy with the class of 1932. His midshipman cruise aboard the USS UTAH was the start of our midwestern skipper's saltwater career.

Married to Margaret Stewart Luker, who is charming and gracious, the Commander has two fine children, Ann, age 7 and Ned, age 5 all of whom reside at the family's home in San Francisco, California.

It will be a sad day in the hearts of all when we must bid adieu to such a gallant leader. We may all be thankful for his courage and inspiration, and for the opportunity of having served under him on our tour of duty with Air Group EIGHTY-SIX.

GEORGE ROBERT LUKER
COMMANDER USN
COMMANDER AIR GROUP EIGHTY-SIX

Wilbur B. Davis
Born: 20 March 1906
School: Washington State, Harvard School of Law
Naval Indoctrination School, Quonset Point, R. I.

LIEUTENANT COMMANDER DAVIS is the efficient and capable Administrative Officer to Commander Luker charged with all the pleasant duties involving monthly reports, etc. Much of the Air Group smooth operation is a direct tribute to Wilbur's diplomacy and foresight.

Wilbur, a cosmopolitan New Yorker, Gin Rummy player extraordinary and memo writer without end—amen—really deserved the purple heart for that smashed finger in the door.

Originally from the cow punching country of Montana, Idaho and Washington, Wilbur graduated from Harvard Law School and remained in New York to practice corporate law. Entering the Navy via the first class at Quonset Point, he attributes much of his success as a Naval Officer to its sterling training program (yea, brother!). After helping to commission the Navy Pre-flight School at Chapel Hill, N. C., Wilbur served a tour of duty as OinC Cadets and Assistant to the SAT at the Primary Training Station, Bunker Hill, Ind. After which he became active in squadron work serving as administrative officer with VC-6. Wilbur, the mighty atom of the CAG staff, has, by his astute judgment and sage advice in administrative matters, contributed a real factor in the efficient functioning of the Air Group.

Wilson T. Cann
Born: 12 May 1912
School: Westminister College
Previous Stations: NIS Quonset Point, R. I., PFS
    Athens, Ga.

BILL is the Air Group Recognition Officer. Any time you walk into one of the squadron ready rooms, you may find Bill combining the acrobatics and fervor of Billy Sunday, the showmanship of Billy Rose and the vociferous delivery of the Little Flower to point out why it's better to shoot at a Jack or Jill rather than a P47 or Firefly. In civilian life Bill turned his hand to many and varied activities. Exercising his education as an engineer, he turned to salesmanship. He sold many of the luxuries and necessities of life in carload, or maybe trainload (we forget which) lots, including shoe polish—all colors, and toilet paper—assorted sizes. In Hawaii, he earned the title "Cann of the Maui cans." Despite numerous promises, he has failed to alter his rotund figure since joining the air-group. "I'll get around to that later." Whenever the CAG has an odd job to perform . . . a party to arrange . . . money to collect, or somebody is needed to brow beat somebody into something, he usually says, "Let's get Cann on that."

Ricardo Angelo Mestres
Born: 8 January 1910, Tampico, Mexico
School: Princeton, 1931
Previous Stations: ACI School, Quonset Point
  NAAF, Amchitka, Alaska
  Advanced Intelligence Center, Adak, Alaska

DICK, the CAG ACI Officer (meaning, of course, Able, Capable and Intelligent) is the man who supplied all the answers to Who? When? Why? and Where? Assistant to Commander Luker in planning operations and other matters, Dick had a responsible part in the planning and execution of all tactical orders. He has ACI "ed" against the Japs from Adak to Ulithi.

Married, Dick has two Navy juniors to his credit. A resident of New York City he entered the Navy via the Indoctrination and the ACI school at Quonset Point, R. I. from which he was immediately assigned to Amchitka, Alaska.

During his leisure hours, which were not often, Dick was often to be found oogling at the octopodes or cavourting in through the coral on some tropical isle. Seeing a strange creature out on the reef will probably just be Dick and his goggles.

Serious and hard working, Dick's post war plans consist of arriving at LaGuardia Field in the shortest possible time and away from last minute cancellations, changes in Op orders and "prepare to operate" on five minutes notice. Regarding these, Dick has no printable comments. Famous as any saying aboard is Dick's "Where's the CAG?"

Charles Herbert Gilliland
Born: 26 September 1911, Melrose, Iowa
Schools: B.S., University of Florida, M.D., University of Iowa
Previous Stations: NTS, Great Lakes, Ill., NRS, St. Louis, Mo., Flight Surgery Training, Pensacola

"DOC" the Air Group Medic, has had more jobs and done more things than the village blacksmith. Popular, cheerful, and dependable "Doc" was always around to give you a typhus shot, an aspirin for your hangover or a first class surgical job with casts, pink ribbons and all the trimmings. Of course, if you had to report to sick bay to use the ophtholmometroscope he only wanted to check your eyes or if he asked about your dermatomocasomyositis or your dontohyperesthesia he is only asking about that tooth that needs filling or that sore throat, but if he says he has to do a gonadectomy, well brother, you had better start running.

Married to a Captain's daughter as befits a navy man, Herb has found time to launch two offsprings, one a navy junior—naturally—and the latest a girl.

Being the only USN man on the CAG's Staff Doc plans on hanging around awhile now that the shooting has stopped—we hope (the shooting, we mean), but when the time comes, it's kinda figured that he will be heading down Florida way for keeps.

Will Hal Rhodes
Born: 8 May 1912, Siloam, Georgia
School: Georgia Tech
Navy Training: NSI, Dartmouth
    Pre-Radar, Bowdoin College
    Radar, M.I.T., Boston
    CVE, CAPE ESPARANCE

"DUSTY" another Gaw-ja lad has traveled a long road since, as a child of one, he slipped out of the Georgia reddog into Atlanta. A "Johnny Come Lately" to the Group, Dusty, a radar countermeasures expert, was welcomed by all members of the Air Group with open arms.

"Dusty" furnishes one of those rare cases in the navy where a man pursues an activity for which he is trained. Charged with both the maintenance of equipment and the training of the operators, Dusty, a former air conditioning man, had a real job in putting the Jap radar gear on ice. We are grateful for the swell job that he did. Dusty's greatest concern was that some crew would accidentally turn their new found gadgets loose on the "Bull' just to listen to the roar. In such case the explosion of an atomic bomb would be definitely in the peanut class.

His present tour is not "Dusty's" first contact with the enemy, having gotten within shooting distance of a Jap torpedo on a previous tour of duty.

The proud father of two girls, Dusty awaits patiently his release, when he can return again to his family, the air conditioning business and fishing in north Florida.

Raoul Adrien Jacques
Born: 14 February 1917
School: Worcester Tech: 1939
Previous Stations:
    Fort Schuyler Indoctrination
    NATTC, Jacksonville, Fla. Ordnance School
    NAS, Honeywell Field, Minneapolis

BUD, the "Wooster Wonder" from Worcester, Mass., the CAG Ordnance man is of no ordinary talent. Just in case the rockets didn't rock, the bombers didn't bomb or the guns didn't make with the noise, Bud was the man to see. Efficient, cooperative and well-liked by all, Bud's greatest concern was, "Who put fuses on the water-fills?" or "Now, for gawd sakes don't bring back *that* Tiny Tim!"

When Bud wasn't agunning or something, he assumed the responsibility of the No. 1 Tourist of the outfit. If there was any place to go, and anyway to get there, Bud would be on his way. It was rumored in the Hawiian Area that he was going to put in for (KFC) Kamaiina First Class.

Married, proud papa of two children, one a he, and one a very recent she, Bud is very social minded. No matter where he be, at home or on land or at sea, Bud's final words will always be ."That last bar looked mighty good to me."

Frank Edward French, Jr.
Born: 8 December 1922, Cincinnati, Ohio
School: BS, M.I.T., Boston, Mass.
Previous Navy Experience:
    NTS Fort Schuyler, N. Y.
    NTS (Pre-Radar) Princeton Univ., N. J.
    NTS (Radar) MIT

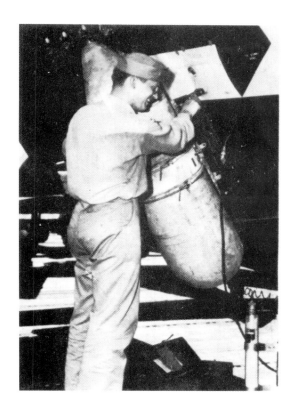

JERRY, after finishing the above grand tour reported as Radio-Radar Officer to CAG at Atlantic City. Fearing the competition of La Chateau Renault, Jerry eventually centered his full time nocturnal duties at the Jolly Whaler in New Bedford after a short fling at Arnolds in Wildwood. It was at the Jolly Whaler that Jerry achieved new heights and became famous as the green eyed Lothario. One could always detect a Jolly Whaler night by the appearance of the dark glasses. Incidentally Jerry did do a swell job of maintaining the squadron Radio-Radar equipment and fathering the aircrewmen in his leisure hours.

Jerry was probably one of the greatest promoters of the Air Group. If he needed an admiral's barge or a gig, a jeep or a rig, well we don't know how he did it but he did. The only time he really overdid it was, when he tried to make a Greyhound bus out of a command car and then played tag with a bakery truck. Arcata's a nice place to be from isn't it, Jerry?

Sincere, hardworking and ambitious, Jerry's immediate postwar ambition is to obtain his PhD in chemical engineering and get on in the world.

Robert Hugh Yeatman
Born: 25 April 1922, Washington, D. C.
School: Maryland University: 1943
Navy Training at:
    M.I.T., Boston, Mass.
    Princeton Univ., N. J.
    Fort Schuyler, N. Y.

BOB, one of the junior members of CAG Staff has proven himself extremely capable in keeping in order the histronic matters concerning all radionics and other complicated gadgets beyond the scope of normal men.

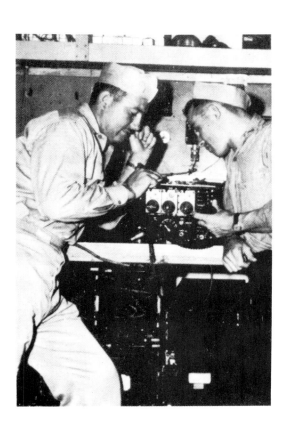

Probably as terrifying as the more technical duties of his profession, are the responsibilities of keeping the communications programs in order and making sure that no one is homing on Radio Tokyo instead of the right ship, especially the Commander.

The quietness of his manners and the youthfulness of Bob's ways belie his efficiency and his capacity for work. All of the responsibilities are bringing on a more mature countenance, or is it the receding hair line or perhaps the Clark Gable mustache. Yes, Bob, it does give one the look of experience.

Bob, although a recent graduate of our education institutions has already set himself up a definite five years plan for a post war future and all five of them concern a rendezvous with the trout and bass of the streams of Frederick County, Maryland.

Thomas "E" Dillard
Born: 21 April 1924, Buena Vista,
    Georgia
School: Georgia Tech.
Flight Training, Corpus Christi, Texas
    and Olathe, Kansas.
Previous Stations:
    LSO School, Jacksonville, Florida
    ComFAir, Quonset Point, Rhode
    Island.

TOM, our tall amiable CAG youngster, our blond lad from East Point, Gaw-ja was the real flag waver of the outfit. Some he waved in fast, and others he waved in slow, some high, and some low, but if they really had to get in, Tom could bring all of his chicks safely back to roost. Never did find out if he had had any previous experience as a bee keeper or hawg caller, but any time Tom got out and started waving paddles, the planes just seemed to swarm.

The Air Group was fortunate in having Tom with them throughout most of the training period. He will always be affectionately remembered by all members of the outfit for his cheerful grin and his calm demeanor at all times, especially during landing operations. Tom was in no small manner a contributing factor in the excellent carrier operations record made by the Group.

WALKER, Charles William, CPhM, is an old time Navy man from Healdton, Oklahoma. If you want to get stuck, well; Chief's the man to see. Capable assistant to "Doc" Gilliland, Chief Walker's nightmares consisted of having to retype all of the Air Group's health records and his daydreams of having his leave. We hope it isn't all daydreams Chief. He has practiced his needlework on practically all of the members of the Air Group with a purposeful gleam in his eye.

WHITELY, George Robert, ART1c, who is from Hood River, Oregon could always be depended on to have things just right. Always cheerful and eager to help others, WHITELY kept the radionic equipment in tip top shape all of the time. Of course, if things did go wrong, explaining the trouble to the Commander was a show, well worth the price of admission.

GIBSON, James Harry, PhoM1c, from Chicago, Illinois, is the real CAG "contact" man. An East Pointer (enough points to go East) GIBSON is soon heading back to a wife who waits for him and that Printing Shop, not sader, perhaps a little wiser but definitely more rotund. In charge of maintenance and operations of the combat photographic equipment, GIBSON had a real responsibility in Air Group operations.

McWATERS, Myron Walter, Y1c, able, slow-drawling CAG assistant office manager from Newman, Georgia says that 15 October will be V-Day for him, V as in going home to that sweet Georgia wife and poached eggs, ham and grits for breakfast. "This Navy's alright" says Mac, until they mix up the clatter of the 20MM with clatter of the typewriter. Then it's time to go home."

STEFFEN, Delmar Dee, AMM1c, plane captain to the Commander and CAG "Mech" hails from Burdett, Kansas and is proud of it. Having made "first" since on the present combat tour of duty and also having his first child since joining the Air Group, STEFFEN ranks first among the first. Genial and able, he is charged with the important duty of keeping the Commander's plane in tip top shape.

DRESSLER, Warren, ARM3c(CA) CAG'S youngest man hailing from New York and a "fly-boy" specializing in Radar Countermeasures, didn't join the outfit until late, but not too late to see action over the enemy's homeland. Bill's one desire is to get back to the "Big City" and to the one and only who has been writing him very sweet "smelling" sugar reports.

HOSIER, Wayne Franklin, ARM3c(CA) is the other combat aircrewman radar countermeasures specialist who joined CAG late. HOSIER calls Kankakee, Illinois home and is a valuable man to have around for any job though he is more than willing to "turn-to" when icing beer—did I say ICING?

Also in the office is John Joseph "on the spot" KOWALSKY, S1c from Bethel, Conn. Johnnie will always be remembered by his ready grin, his eagerness to help and his humorous ways and sayings. Jack-of-all-trades and handy man of CAG Staff, Johnnie could always be depended upon to fix a watch, put out the cat or carry an important message to the Captain.

SKETCH OF AIR GROUP COMMANDER AND
SQD. COMMANDERS IN "CAG" OFFICE

FIGHTING SQUADRON
EIGHTY-SIX

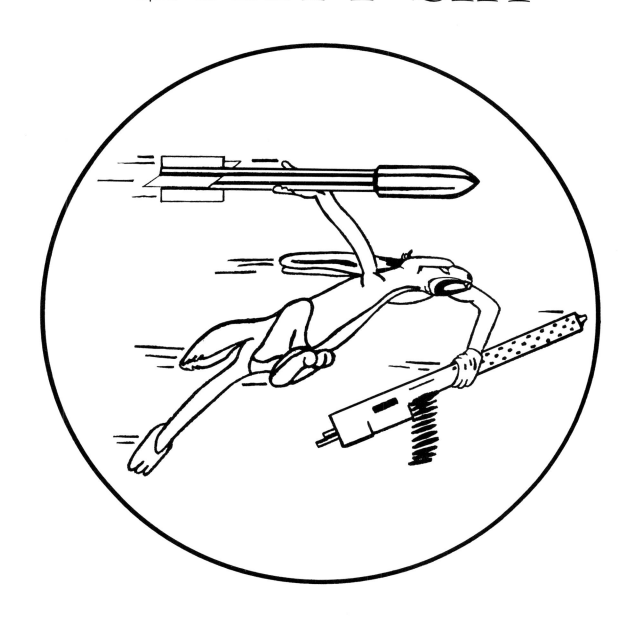

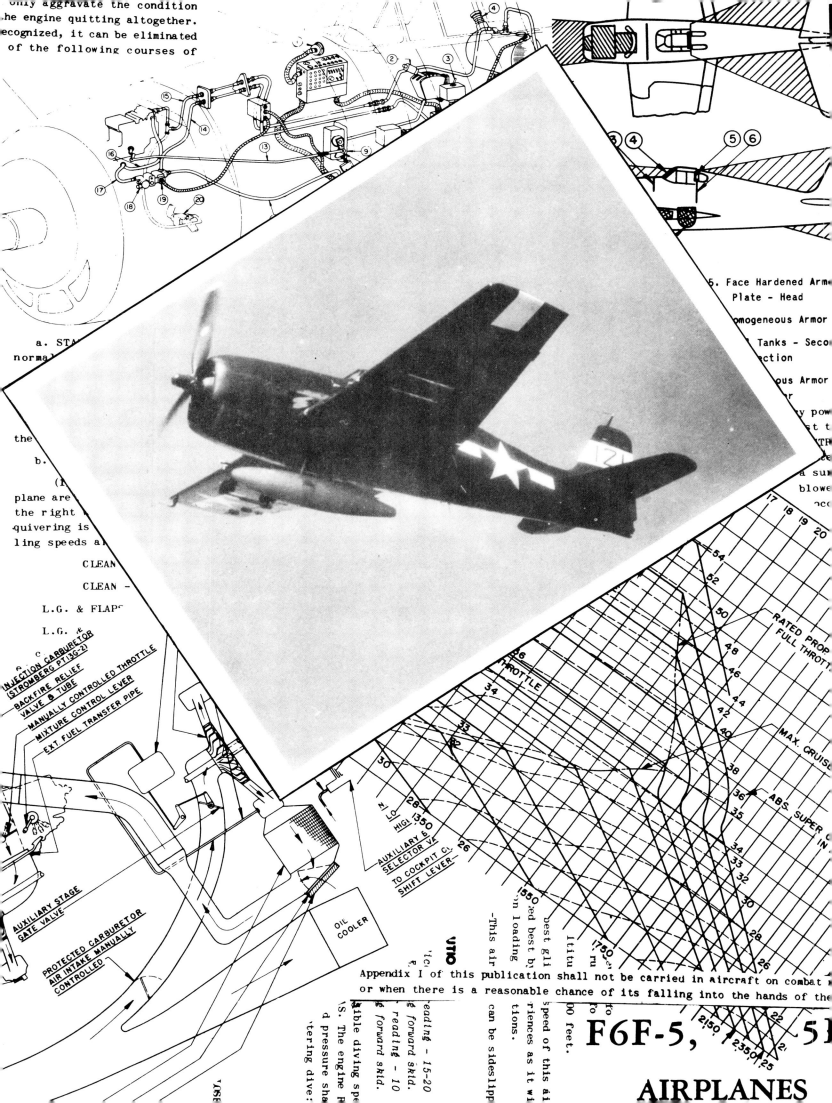

THE SQUADRON

These men were brought together from all sections of the country and from all walks of life. In a short time, through constant training, they were molded into a smooth-working, capable unit. They were just a group of ordinary Yanks. . . .

THE OFFICERS AND MEN OF FIGHTING SQUADRON EIGHTY-SIX

Front Row (Left to Right):

Shuptar, Lawton, Morton, E. T., White, Harris, Ogden, Myers, R. P., Lowrie, Grover, Morrison, Gunn, Jones, Sargent, Drew, Bouchet, Curnayn, Lautz.

Second Row

O'Bryan, Morton, T. H., Leland, McCoy, Ahern, Baker, Brown, Hawke, Datte, Bellinger, George, Bartoloni, Metcalfe, Myers, O. E., Farmer, Smith, Kurfis.

Third Row

Lansing, Stauffer, Peterson, Camp, Harlan, Thompson, Hamilton, Dobson, Holderman, Rothenberg, Wilson, Hill, Anderson, Bahn, Hopkins, Mellin, Richmann, Thomas, Vannatta.

Fourth Row

Clements, Pfeifer, Schwartz, Barron, Wolfard, Cuthbertson, Morris, Trycinski, Scholl, Couch.

On Wing

Pinkham, Woodruff, Ward, Huckins, Klippert, Lightbody, Heller, Tinnirella, Ross, Moye, Williams, Edwards, White, Conger, Nelson, Albright, Klima, Mumpower, Noon, Goetsch, Steele, Crice.

LIEUTENANT COMMANDER C. J. DOBSON

COMMANDING OFFICER

FIGHTING SQUADRON EIGHTY-SIX

LIEUTENANT COMMANDER CLEO J. DOBSON went from Oklahoma A & M to Pensacola where he entered Flight Training in December '38. He received his wings on 1 November '39. He went aboard the USS ENTERPRISE with VS-6 in January '40. He was on the ENTERPRISE when war broke out and flew into Pearl from the ENTERPRISE between waves of the Japanese attacks on the morning of 7 December '41. His being in the air at the start of the war was to have a curious consequence as he was also in the air to shoot down the last Nip to attack the Third Fleet. He participated in nine of the first battles of the war, including the Marshalls and Gilberts, Wake, Santa Cruz, Marcus and Guadalcanal. He left the ENTERPRISE with his squadron and spent the following two years as a Landing Signal Officer in Florida. He came to Fighting 86 as exec in September '44 and became skipper of the new Fighting 86 in January of '45. In this capacity he has led us for nine months. Being proficient in everything he taught us, he won the admiration, respect and love of all of us.

AHERN, Leo H.
Born: October 12, 1922
School: Loras College, Dubuque, Iowa
Trained at: Corpus Christi, Tex.
    Melbourne, Fla.
Address: 202 Hayes Street
    Burlington, Iowa

LEO was the handsomest of the Rover Boys. Youthful and gay, he helped furnish the squadron with the spirit that wins wars. He came to the outfit as a "boot Ensign" fresh from operational. He flew hard, took up his various duties, zealously and quickly became one of the boys. He helped attack Molokini, dove for fish at Maui Beach and became a standby in Boy's Town. He had a delightful sense of bravery and even when the bombs were falling close aboard the carrier or when the flak was crowding his plane, he always found a breath for a wisecrack. This cross section of American Youth did not question the causes of war, he simply helped eradicate the source. He had a duty, saw it and performed it well.

ANDERSON, Warren Seth
Born: January 19, 1921
School: Chicago Art Institute
Trained at: Corpus Christie, Tex.
    Sanford, Fla.
Married
Address: 6635 Yale Avenue, Chicago, Ill.

ANDY was one of our more mature pilots. He was serious in all of his undertakings, and yet he had an adjacent sense of humor. He did his job consistently well without question or reservation. Andy was a thinker with a taste for the esthetic; he seemed to be struggling for an ideal or a particular brand of philosophy. His way of living, if practiced, would obviate wars forever. He wanted to live and let live and was convinced that religion was not necessarily a practice but as he said, "a condition of the mind." Our squadron discussions, with or without alcohol, would always provoke an acceptable theory from Anderson. He dabbled in art; his surrealist drawings brought unique observations from the squadron . . . from Ensigns, "I don't get it" . . . from jaygees, "I see it" . . . from Lieutenants, "Where?" Tomorrow's world has much to learn from Andy; we have prayed that he'll be there to help form and reshape it.

BAHN, William S.
Born: June 5, 1916
School: St. Louis University
Trained at: Pensacola and Jacksonville, Fla.
Previous Squadron: VB-7
Married
Address: 1215 Claytonia Terrace
  St. Louis County, Mo.

BILL, the legal mind from St. Louis, by his own admission, was not run out of town; he strolled out just ahead of the tar and feathers. "By all the statutes the Navy should release me; of course I haven't enough points, but I wanna go home to Pinky." Bill took care of the death-dealing attachments to our planes and it was a great relief when he'd tell us the bombs would *never* go off until we dropped them. We always believed him . . . we had to believe something. An abetter to the reservists, he was a frequent guest at Mrs. Henderson's and Mr. Camp's cocktail hour and he'd tell us gently, but in a legal way, that "the Air Group will be relieved in ten more days." Confused at times with the helmsman of the ship (the helmsman never got out of the sack, either) Bill played a red-back game of tennis at Barber's Point and was an intense wader at Waikiki, and at times was found reading. One book, "The Abdominal Criminal", was prob-ably his favorite. A worshipper of fresh air and sunshine he was often found on the flight deck in his brief shorts. He would look, legally, down his nose at himself and say "Hey, I am losing weight, aren't I fellas?"

BAKER, Carl Willis
Born: November 9, 1921
Schools: Amarillo Jr. College
  South Western Oklahoma State
Trained at: Pensacola and Sanford, Fla.
Address: 809 Buchanan Street
  Amarillo, Texas

CISCO tried to enter the bathing beauty contest while we were in Atlantic City, since then we have all wondered just what fool trick he will try next. Just what kind of exercise he can do while in the sack to get all those beeootiful muscles is . . . Is it a pastime for him? When "I'm-so-mean-it-hurts" Baker organized the parade and paid the band to do his "send off" from Amarillo up brown, little did he realize how his weak, skinny competitors gave a sigh and that his future life was not going to be just a bed . . . The Body hasn't done half bad, though. While at Otis he had two broken hearts painted on the side of his airplane and while coming across the country in one of Hawke's International Harvester combines he reaped things that couldn't be repeated. Although good in a fast game of "Oh Hell" (for funsies) he is quick, if losing, to offer, "What's your file number, Junior?" Then he flexes a muscle, quietly, "Ho-hum, I've been up over an hour. Guess I'll hit the sack, fellas."

BARRON, William Davis
Born: March 25, 1922
School: Georgia Tech.
Trained at: Corpus Christi, Tex.
  Deland, Florida
Married
Address: 1245 University Drive
  Atlanta, Georgia

DAVIS, the kid with the nervous throat muscles that are constantly opening his mouth, is, they say, in love with two things . . . a convertible Buick and a shy maiden from his native alligator land. Barron left the alligators when he found out they had more lip than he did, and started a flight career which had two major incidents in it. The first at Otis when, with the firm ambition to do better than anyone else in field carrier landings, he made a wheels up landing and was caught stealthily lowering the landing-gear handle while waiting for the crash truck. The second on the ship in the Pacific when he was in the sack while the rest of his division shot down two Jap planes. Claiming to be a champion in the field of acey-ducey he still doesn't understand why some of the checkers are red, the others black. After a particularly long run of bad luck in the game he turned up with a cut on his chin. When questioned about it he would only answer, "A-ah, I fell down the ladder, you damned Ya-a-a-ankee."

BARTOLONI, Larry Neal
Born: July 25, 1922
School: La Salle-Peru Jr. College
Trained at: Pensacola and Deland Florida
Address: Cedar Point, Illinois

BART to the fellows in the squadron and Larry to the twelve occupants of LaSalle, Illinois. This guy has considerably more hair on his chest than on his head—as a matter of fact, he's got more hair on his chest than a fellow who really has some hair on his head. Shy and modest, he readily admits that he was both the outstanding athlete and lover of Cedar Point. He's a pretty fair card player— Cuthbertson owes him his flight pay for the next four months. At the mention of cards, he nonchalantly pulls a deck from his pocket, shuffles them like a pro, and says, "Why yes, I just happen to have a deck with me." Bart's a fair troubadour well known for his rendition of "eric canero something". He is convinced that dice have replaced the Gallup Poll and that slot machines will ultimately replace baseball. About his forthcoming baldness, "I only worry because maybe the fellows sitting across the table will be able to see my cards reflected on my high forehead."

BELLINGER, Frank Howard
Born: December 7, 1920
School: Wheaton College, Illinois
Previous Squadron: VF(N)110
Address: 44-05 60th Street
    Woodside, N. Y.

BELL is a featured performer in Allan's Aerial Artistes, known at the Bureau as Night Fighters . . . they sleep all night and all day, too. Bell was distinctively honored by being allowed to fly occasionally in the daytime . . . to the nearest bad weather. "Cobra Base, this is Bell 6-9000, flying conditions above average . . . I can't see nuttin' and it's closing in." So he flew under a couple of Nip Luggers to keep from getting wet and when they had escorted him to good weather he returned the gesture with some friendly strafing runs. "I'll get the one to sta-hbud for Josephine." He has tried to navigate by means of that little radar gadget the Night Fighters are always claiming they know how to use, but all he has ever been able to see in it is the fuzzy outline of above mentioned Josephine. "Well, that's what they get for taking us out of our stand-by condition."

BOUCHET, Robert
Born: October 2, 1921
Schools: San Francisco Jr. College
    University of California
Trained at: Pensacola and Melbourne, Fla.
Married
Address: 1042 Venture Avenue
    Albany, California

BUCKET is the squadron's one man intelligence bureau. Right or wrong he is always willing to give you the word on anything . . . the war, flying, or sex. But Bucket, without his Plymouth, just wouldn't be Bucket. He drove it across the country, and with all respects to Horace who called it that "thing", got there in time to board the ship. When Bucket left it, the Plymouth cried and tried to come aboard the ship, too; weary of its life of perpetual evasion of the junk-man . . . but the two were separated, by necessity, and Bucket went westward to the Moana hotel where he started the evenings drinking out of glasses and ended them with the words, "What the hell do I need a glass for, this bucket here is ok," and he methodically mixed the rest of the drinks in the ice bucket. In the daytime he read "Forever Amber" and talked. "Gee I sure wish they lived that way today." And talked, "But, O-B, you're not going in your swimming trunks."

BROWN, Kenneth M.
Born: June 27, 1921
School: Conemaugh Township
Trained at: Pensacola and Sanford, Fla.
Address: Washington Street
　　Hyndman, Pa.

BROWNIE, or K-M, is Pennsylvania's athletic adviser and Parker's Monopoly expert, lend-leased to the Navy Air Corps for reasons unknown. You greet him with a smile and he says, "Yes, I know, I remind you of Lou Costello." And he winds up for a mashie shot, still dreaming of breaking eighty. We remember the day he had engine trouble and had to land "right away right away" . . . so he landed back on the Wasp from which he had taken off; but when they asked him his position he gave the puzzling reply, "Some carrier gave me a Charlie so I landed on it, I don't know which one it is though." Then he walked into the ready-room and saw all the old familiar faces, "Anyway, I wasn't long in the groove this hop." A.B. Thompson says Brownie has been lost on every type flight from bounce drill to a strike on Japan and the only words he has ever said over the mike are, "Where the hell are you guys, A.B.?"

BUTKO, Andrew Charles
Born: July 5, 1920
School: McKeesport High School
Trained at: Pensacola, Fla.
Address: 819 Evans Street
　　McKeesport, Pa.

ANDY came to the Air Group from VF-44 which was then stationed in Sanford, Maine. He was first assigned to the Bombers and then later was transferred to the Fighters. He was an extremely popular lad, well liked by all who knew him. He was perpetually gay; if he ever had a sad moment while he was with us, he camouflaged it well. He laughed heartily and often and, what is more important, sincerely. A lover of popular music, he was usually singing or whistling the latest song. He had a fine singing voice and went about trying to recruit a quartet to "try out" a new one. He fitted in well, and was always eager to help carry out all our plans. Like most young boys, he spoke much of his parents and while it is most difficult for parents to offer a son to the just completed conflagration, it is some consolation for them to know that it was people like Andy who restored peace to the world.

CAMP, Robert Clifton Jr.
Born: October 27, 1910
Schools: St. Albans, Washington, D. C.
    Yale University
Trained at: NTS Columbus, Ohio
Address: 920 E. 5th Street
    Ocala, Florida

BOB, EL CAMPO, the Campo Camp . . . thus the levious pilots would call him as he changed the charts on the wall every ten minutes, after the arrival of a new dispatch. Hoppy titled his briefing lectures "Up front with Bob Camp" and we all sat breathlessly, as he talked, expecting a Yarp to peer out of his left ear at any minute. And he briefed us and he briefed us and then they changed the targets. A connoisseur of the finer things, from the Cross Creek country to Ahbiggerwan, he is an outstanding artist and has illustrated many books. And he briefed us and briefed us and then they changed the targets. Mr. Cramp has been in every war since the Boer affair in Africa, and doesn't look a day over sixty-two. And he briefed us and.

briefed us . . . "Then you will proceed to Tokyo, and if all the girls who attend the Yale Prom were laid end to end . . . I wouldn't be a bit surprised."

CLEMENTS, Billy Franklin
Born: April 29, 1921
School: Elgin High School
Trained at Pensacola and Melbourne, Fla.
Married
Address: 606 Grace Street
    Elgin, Illinois

CLEM, number two man in Ham's team, carried the burden of captain of the team's car pool in Arcata, and saw to it that they showed up within a reasonable period of tardiness for their hops. In combat he holds the first-time distinction of ever changing the color of a Hellcat while in full flight. He returned from the Japanese homeland, after neutralizing a beautiful little rice pattie, with a mud-brown plane instead of a bright blue one. "I

must have gone a little too low on that run." But he acquired a very personal liking for Grumman and a firm belief in the law of averages. At his very very noisy Luaus he entertained us, spacing our songs with impromptu imitations of Donald Duck and introducing himself to anyone who came within talking distance . . . "My name's Cle-em. What's yours?"

COUCH, Edwin Grant
Born: August 20, 1922
School: Greensboro High School
Trained at: Pensacola and Deland, Fla.
Married
Address: Greensboro, North Carolina

GROUCH, flat on his back in the North Atlantic ("but I saved the tail-hook, they **can** build a new **plane** around that"), was going to get us all a private jeep at Barber's Point, until the army sent his brother to Bima Jima. A person of definite opinions, Grouch hates crowds, a phobia which has caused him to return from almost all group hops by himself. One of our leading authors, he is planning a new book, "The Massage in Honolulu, and Where to Find It", or, "Follow Lowrie, The Steam Will Make You Beam". Grouch mystified us all by his meagre appearances at the squadron in Arcata until we met his pretty wife . . . "You wolves, I'm going to get a house as far from the base as I can." And they finally did teach him to land on a carrier, although they have to soup up the signal officer with vitamin pills before he can swing the paddles fast enough to get him aboard. And there he was, flying by himself, eating his diet of two apples per mission . . . and the unanswerable explanation . . . "Gee. I wasn't out of formation, T. R. I was flying a relative position on the leader."

CURNAYN, Robert William
Born: May 13, 1922
School: Elder High School
Trained at: Corpus Christi, Tex.
  Melbourne, Fla.
Address: 842 Kirbert Ave., Cincinnati, Ohio

BOB is a fair beer guzzler . . . for a Rover Boy. He says he is a mere amateur beside his grandmother who is known as "Budweiser Bess" in her sewing circles. He hails from Cincinnati, that Dutch settlement on the Ohio (I think). Bob has learned how to bounce since we were at Maui; that splash he made could be heard in Frisco . . . and he doesn't want another. Bob has a tavern in his home town and his ambition is to congregate all the Rover boys in front of the bar for free drinks, " 'Tain't no risk," he says, "they can't drink a dozen beers between them." He wants to hurry home to marry Peg before she runs off with some Army "driver". He persists in shaving all four whiskers nightly in hopes of cultivating a fifth. "If you're ever in Cincinnati drop in; every 75th drink is on the house."

CUTHBERTSON, Richard Eugene
Born: November 22, 1923
School: North Kansas City High
Trained at: Pensacola and Miami, Fla.
Address: 2009 Erie Ave.
    North Kansas City, Missouri

UNCOUTH-CUTH, the fellas call him, and his familiar "ah-hahs" have echoed in all the taverns from the Omar Room in Kansas City to the De Luxe Club in Eureka. There's quite a story, along with legal correspondence, which comes out of one of his visits to the Omar Room . . . "How did I know she was married?" His life long ambition is to make one join-up without over-running. If he only had something besides his wheels and flaps to drop we think he could do it. We've known a lot of revengeful wingmen, but never one who took a shot at his division leader. Cuth is a talented singer and at many squadron "beer-busts" one could clearly hear his fine tenor voice doing justice to the "Beer Drinker's Medley". This lad has a great abundance of energy—always on "the go"—and always up to something. There's never a dull moment with Cuth in shouting range. "Ah-hah ee-hee oh-ho how to go."

DATTE, Hugh John
Born: August 7, 1918
School: Drexel Tech.
Trained at: Corpus Christi, Tex.
    Sanford, Fla.
Address: 417 Lincoln Ave.
    Collingdale, Pa.

RED, to his intimates, insists that he is from Collingdale, Penn. He is outstanding in the squadron if for no other reasons than his pretty red hair and old age. His buddy, Sam Jones has been conducting research on Red's age for over a year now and has decided that "Red's pretty old—somewhere between 26 and 40." Jack has been in all departments of the squadron and curses the day he was drafted into Flight because since then he has done nothing but draw huge charts which nobody looks at save himself. He's all tied up with some home town gal whom he insists is going to marry him because she has known him for Mm-mmm years. He still beefs about the CAP he missed last March when the Nips were sprinkling the ocean and he didn't get a shot. Says "Hawke, throw out the stick, you can fly this machine with the throttle" and "I may be Irish but it's the lace curtain variety."

DOBSON, Cleo John
Born: November 3, 1913
School: Oklahoma A & M
Trained at: Pensacola, Fla.
Previous Squadron: VS-6
Married
Address: Box 255, Coyle, Oklahoma

DOBBIE (where the wind comes sweeping cross the plain), our Skipper, has held the squadron in check by dint of a big frame, a lot of pounds, a get-things-done personality, a great amount of ability, high qualities of leadership, and a file number better than anyone else's. Dobbie was the outstanding squadron athlete until, while playing basketball, he broke his leg tripping over an F6F on the number one elevator . . . after which, until he got the brace off, he kept the squadron flying from the Ready Room, Ward Room, Hangar Deck, Flight Deck, and Radar Control . . . which only proved what we already knew, his sincere interest and devotion to the squadron. Except for an inaptitude in the game of cribbage, he is proficient in everything we have needed to know, and has guided us with a firm hand, and well, for he has the loyal following and love of everyone in the outfit. His bulk and voice at the front of the Ready Room will always be remembered and his familiar words when someone has done something not quite right, "Well goddamit, you guys, well goddamit . . ."

DREW, Henry
Born: September 3, 1923
School: Armstrong Jr. College
Trained at: Pensacola, Fla.
Previous Squadrons: VF-100, VT-100
Address: Royal Palm Nurseries
    Oneco, Fla.

HANK is from Florida, land of high prices and long alligators. He had seen most of the western hemisphere when this here new war broke out so he swaggered into the nearest Naval Recruiting Station and asked for a ticket east . . . and got it. We picked him up at Barber's Point along with the rest of Hill's Hotrocks. When Hill became materiel officer succeeding fatigued Jim Lansing, he promptly made Hank his assistant. "Assistant, hell . . . I do all the work. Hill doesn't even know where aviation issue is." Hank has some original philosophy on life. "The airplane will never replace sex." "A fighter pilot is, by necessity, a cross between a tom cat and a Don Quixote." "Hill is a jerk." Hank is supposed to have been an outstanding student in flight training and after his second hop was convinced that, "Hell, there aren't many people who can land on three points everytime, two wheels and a wing tip."

FARMER, Lewis Turner, Jr.
Born: July 28, 1922
School: Middle Georgia College
Trained at: Corpus Christi, Tex.
  Daytona Beach, Fla.
Previous Squadron: VF-81
Address: 401 West Eighth St.
  Louisville, Ga.

SPIDER developed those legs (and hence the nick-name), he says, racing for those Georgia peaches. However, he's more often called L.T. or Lt. and answers to either, but it takes the latter (and you have to have a certain lilting tone in your voice) to get his heart to release that drop of blood and allow him to stir. Generally, though, he lets that drop lie dormant and wanders off into the fairy land of red hills, pine trees, and pigs . . . and has accepted the night fighter tradition that the only happy man is the one in the sack. His shins are covered with scars from his inability to lift those web-weaving legs over the hatch sills in the passageways . . . so you ask him what the trouble is and he gives you a misleading, affable grin and says, "What the hell did you expect, a broken-field runner."

GEORGE, Milton DeWitt
Born: February 1, 1922
School: University of Georgia
Trained at: Corpus Christi, Tex.
  Vero Beach, Fla.
Married
Address: Blakely, Ga.

PAPPY hails from some insignificant town in Georgia, the population of which he stoutly main-tains is 3500 when everyone comes home and brings a friend. Why he ever strayed into a Navy recruit-ing station is anybody's guess (we imagine Local Board #2 was close behind) and why he chose to win his laurels as a night fighter is an even deeper secret. Pappy, as you have probably imagined, is a family man. He never ceases to amaze his room-mates with stories of his off-spring's exploits, some of which have even awakened his fellow night fighters from their perpetual slumber. Junior, unlike his father, will probably turn out to be a perfect blend of Charles Atlas, Rudolph Valentino, and a hot fighter pilot. The latest stateside communique says that Junior, the one man air corps, is going to be our relief; but we earnestly hope this is a mis-print for he was last reported still wearing his three cornered sarong. "Boy, you ought to see that kid, he's blub . . . blub . . . blub . . . etc."

GOULD, Richard
Address: 65 Winslow Ave.
Somerville, Mass.

DICK was one of our night fighters and like all our night fighters (a thing which must be instilled in them in their training) was an advocate of a lot of sack-time and was always engineering a big deal. He was a notorious talker on all subjects and could keep people interested in what he had to say because of his keen sense of humor. This sense of humor was well brought out in the incident of the bomb hitting the Wasp. When Dick was awakened and informed of the hit he said "Well, it didn't hit me" and went back to sleep. This was like him, this and his favorite expression, "Not this kid, Jock". But he tossed this lightness away the minute he had a job to do, whenever he was in the air he was working hard every minute and whenever he had a job to do on the ground he did it efficiently and well. All these things, and more, made him the all-round, capable, pleasing person that he was.

GRADEL, Philip E.
Born: August 7, 1922
School: Northeast Catholic High
Trained at: Pensacola and Melbourne, Fla.
Previous Squadron: VF-99
Address: 7763 Cottage St., Philadelphia, Pa.

GRIDLEY is called Gridley only by his intimates. The origin of this nickname is just a bit ambiguous and Gradel is mum. Born and bred in Philly— three years of Navy life have broadened his geographical aspects to a point where he now realizes that the world does extend beyond the Alleghanies. Gridley refuses to talk about his early social life, "the world began with Annie." His clean cut handsomeness and his hose nose are the rage of the Philly bobby soxers, but "I only want Annie." Gradel is a personable chap having two hobbies— drinking whiskey and drinking beer. He was recently fished out of the Pacific by a British Destroyer and after having only been aboard for twenty minutes, picked up a limey white uniform and an accent. "Iye say there, the English were deucedly nice to retrieve me, don't you know."

GROVER, Leon R.
Born: January 21, 1924
School: Moorefield High School
Trained at: Corpus Christi, Tex.
    Deland, Fla.
Previous Squadron: VB-86
Address: Moorefield, West Virginia

GROVE is the outstanding (and only) West Virginian in our squadron. He is a constant devotee to flat-hatting, from a scientific angle, of course. He and Tom Dillard, our USO (I mean LSO), were showing the residents of a lake-side cottage some of the fine points of the art. Grove says that they were really good. The Admiral who lived in the cottage thought differently. "I almost became a signal officer, myself," Grove says. He also explains, "Don't go buzzing Daytona Beach on a Sunday afternoon . . . especially on a *Sunday* afternoon." In Hawaii this escapee from a mountain feud really went hillbilly and was seen out in a pineapple patch teaching the Polynesians how to cut down the size of their population by the process of "elimination with the pineapple". Grove brought back all the used pineapples and served them at our luaus with the exciting news, "Say . . . uh . . . say fellas, I'm standby for another feud tomorrow."

GUNN, Clifford Paul, Jr.
Born: April 21, 1922
School: Technology High School
Trained at: Corpus Christi, Tex.
    Melbourne, Fla.
Address: 406 Inmal Street
    Atlanta, Ga.

BUBBER would rather sit around admiring the beauty of a peach from the "City of Flowers" than have the chance to go all through flight training again. He claims that he's seen Georgia girls prettier than Sweetie Wilson, and he seemed quite infatuated with Sweetie when we were fighting the War of Maui. As a matter of fact, he was the only person ever to complete ten missions to the Wilson "Don't Think—Drink" manor without cracking up a jeep. For this they let him make another strafing attack on Molokini Rock. Bubber is the only acey-ducey player in our records who has always rolled less "names-of-the-game" than his opponents, but he says he's saving his luck for something else. In combat he was hot on the tail of a "Frank", but the plane managed to land on an airfield before he could flame him. "Anyway," Bubber says, "I'm the only guy who ever checked a Jap out in formation approaches to a landing."

HAMILTON, Alfred Gunnar
Born: December 20, 1921
School: Hofstra College
Trained at: R.A.F.
Previous Squadron: VF-18, VJ-15
Married
Address: 15 Washington Place
    Northport, L. I., N. Y.

HAM, our refugee from Ye Olde Boar Inne, colorful ex-RCAF pilot ("The Spits a sweet ship their grogs nice over there") . . . Promised us all a case of Scotch back in Atlantic City, arrived on board without any even for himself, "Well, I stopped for a cocktail and . . ." . . . Taught us the difference between The Stinger (a cocktail) and The Stinger (a gun shooting out the back of a plane) . . . And the difference between The Triple (a drink with three shots of something) and The Triple (a play made in baseball, by the catcher, I think) . . . Led half the squadron in the air, did a tremendous job, and indoctrinated us with the rudiments of slipstream flying . . . Showed us that you can fight a war and still have a good time, if you take the war seriously only when you have to . . . Explained some of the intricate ways of the Navy to us, and laughed . . . Proved that anchovies were highly edible and that a car will run on old canvas and a shoe stamp . . . Taught us the correct way of saying, "Aye sigh there old chawp . . . another . . . ?"

HARLAN, George Monroe
Born: February 13, 1918
School: Westmenister College
Trained at: Corpus Christi, Tex.
    Melbourne, Fla.
Previous Squadrons: VS-ID-14, VS-16
Married
Address: 1734 Fourth Street
    Madison, Illinois

DODE is our hard working (God forgive us) flight officer. He was busy from G. Q. until late at night, devising ways to make that-goddamned-Hawke make out the next day's schedule. Thus has Dode come to be known by many as The Whip. Schooled at Westminster (that's in Missouri) the Whip was a sensational basketball player in a class of eight men. After this he went after a long record of sea duty in the Pacific; he was out there when there were still some airborne Nips to shoot at. He spent several months on Tarawa where he acquired many odd habits . . . drinking warm beer was not the least peculiar of them. Apparently having seen something that we haven't . . . Dode is going regular Navy. "That's all right you guys, when you're all selling apples I'll still be polishing them."

HARRIS, Albert Kenneth
Born: September 21, 1923
School: Edgewood High School
Trained at: Corpus Christi, Tex.
   Melbourne, Fla.
Married
Address: 1921 Merida Street
   San Antonio, Tex.

AK-AK is the only one of the Rover boys who is married . . . poor girl. He made his fiancee leave her dolls at home and lied about his age and the ceremony was completed without challenge. Although he has many times been tempted by wine, women and song so far he has only yielded to the wine and song and has never wavered from his devotion to the little one. Some of the boys suspected Ak-ak was in the employ of his Imperial Majesty because of the number of planes he has committed to the deep. He's a dandy flier but just a little rough in the groove (high and fast, they say) . . . this he attributes to "skipper", his San Antonio rose. Ak-ak wants to hurry home and start a little something running around the house other than a fence. "Don't bother with the jiggers, I'm a man now. Wait 'til I get back to Texas. Yippee."

HAWKE, Harold, Jr.
Born: September 26, 1919
School: Iowa State College
Trained at: Pensacola, Fla.
Married
Address: 2246 North Eleventh Street
   Terre Haute, Indiana

HAWKEY-TALKEY, the big wind from Terre Haute, makes more noise than a two dollar victrola. Hal talked his way out of night fighters and into 86 while in Atlantic City. He's allergic to night unless he's alongside his wife. He tried to scare his wife into giving him a son by requesting, and getting, a couple of "I-wanna-be-there-for-the-birth" leaves. She was completely unimpressed by his presence and waited until he got to Pearl Harbor, whereupon she delivered him a daughter, "The cutest little thing you ever saw." This fugitive from International Harvester Tractors has been our schedule maker, and has literally worked his way into all the pilots' hearts by scheduling them for pre-dawn takeoffs, G.Q. stand-bys, and towed spar attacks. They affectionately call him "That-God-damned-Hawke". But little impression do their bitter words make on Hal. He still stubbornly declares, "Well, it wasn't my fault that 86 didn't take Molokini Rock."

HILL, Donald Raymond
Born: July 9, 1917
School: Sioux Falls College
Trained at: Pensacola, Fla.
Previous Squadron: VT-27
Address: Winnebago, Minnesota

D. R., the boys who fly with him call him "Center-line", is built so much like a cowboy that rather than fly the Hellcat he rides it. They say he has it almost saddle-broken, and late one night it was seen actually eating out of his hand. He does the same things with automobiles and practices shyster-ism on the side. The story . . . a car, wrecked twice, square wheels, driven across the country inverted, sold for twice what he paid for it. So we gave him the materiel department. He immediately became efficient by throwing everything overboard except "stuff we really need, and the pilots certainly can't carry spare sparkplugs, they don't even know where they go." D. R. was out here jipping the Nips even before A. B. Thompson took Rabaul "when we didn't have anything. Now it would be like Child's play if they would only fill the rubber boats with popcorn. I miss popcorn."

HOLDERMAN, Armind Talbott
Born: November 10, 1917
School: Sacramento Junior College
Trained at: Pensacola, Fla.
Married
Address: 160 Covina Street
    Long Beach, Cal.

HOLY JOE, our Executive Officer, hails from Napa Valley, California where the giant Redwoods grow and trout jam the streams (Northern California Chamber of Commerce advertisement). Joe was a member of ship's company on the old Lex when she went down. However Joe put on a couple extra sets of officer's bars before abandoning ship and wound up in his own private raft reading a copy of *Good Housekeeping*. Armind Talbot (catch that, it sounds like a new after-shave lotion) has a hell-uva swell wife and she has three children, two girls and Joe. "How now, Brown cow" gets most of his education from his daughters who restrict much of his activity. When Joe grows old and is still trying to catch something other than a cold with his rod and reel, he can most probably be found in one of those California wineries telling how he shot down those two Nip planes, etc., etc.

Says the old salt "Why I've worn out more sea bags than most of these kids have socks."

HOPKINS, Jesse Reuben
Born: June 1, 1921
School: Hampden Sidney College
Trained at: Pensacola and Miami, Fla.
Previous Squadrons: VF-18, VF-4
Address: 3636 Fort Ave.
   Lynchburg, Va.

HOPPE, old fleet pilot and expert at cribbage, daring driver of a car whose hood's always locked in the UP position, came out of Virginia with Stonewall Jackson and startled the world with a new ivory-cube technique. For the sheer ecstatic pleasure, he toyed with the ownership of an apartment in Atlantic City, an Inn and a Studio in Massachusetts, a mountain ranch on Maui . . . gave them all up, with an inaudible sigh, whenever the squadron issued him a new set of orders. Long since Yankeeized, he took Boston by storm . . . and Boston took him, a situation he didn't fully understand until he got a bill for the installation of a new motor in the Merry Go-Round Bar. He thought, he said, that "the girls were brass rings". In the air he taught his boys to handle the stick like southern cotton and the throttle like a hot Virginia peanut, but could never teach them to say, "The ship's aboot here, oot." And one morning in the sack he mumbled,

"There wasn't any question of who got the best. In Massachusetts they're all horrible."

HOWIE, Willis Grimes, Jr.
Born: 1921
School: Texas A&M
Trained: Pensacola
Address: RFD 2, San Benito, Tex.

MONK enjoyed life to the fullest extent. He really lived every minute, wasting little or none. His mirth was contagious and consequently was a welcome addition to any of the pilots "batting the breeze" sessions. His generosity knew no bounds and he made friends at every turn. His ability to talk his way out of some pretty trying situations eased his travels through flight training and all of its rigors. He knew how to laugh at his own mistakes and come up smiling as it were; this certainly kept him on the brighter side of life. His death, coming as it did just when the squadron began to click, was a set back to everyone. In his sacrifice, we could only see the loss of a real guy. And yet it was he and thousands just like him that helped form combat units. And even though they did not get to participate in the final victory, they helped mould the combat units that brought peace to the world on the eve of it's own annihilation.

JONES, James Clyde, Jr.
Born: January 13, 1922
School: Ohio State University
Trained at: Corpus Christi, Tex.
　Jacksonville, Fla.
Previous Squadron: VF-44
Address: Oak Hill, Ohio

JIM alias SAM or "What is it? I'm against it Jones" takes the greatest amount of pride in his knowledge of the proper method of smoking cigars. Sam without a cigar is like Coney Island without hot dogs. The scuttlebutt has it that "What is it? etc." will conduct classes on the finer points of kibitzing or how to get the most out of watching some hapless soul slowly succumb to your unwanted counsel. Our erstwhile son of Oak Hill and Ohio State U. is the possessor of many talents: pianist for example.

Many renditions of the classics were so well slaughtered that I fear the great maestros turned over in their graves. The thing that has been puzzling our boy Sam for months is how a Mack truck gained access to a room on the second floor of the Moana Hotel in Honolulu. His shout of "Get that Mack truck's number" will no doubt go down in history as one of the great utterances of all time. How about that Sam? His answer. "MMMMM I reckon."

KURFIS, Robert Frederick
Born: February 21, 1923
School: Case School of Applied Science
Trained at: Corpus Christi, Tex.
　Vero Beach, Fla.
Previous Squadron: VF(N)-75
Address: 4364 West 146th Street
　Cleveland, Ohio

KURF . . . a tall lanky crewcut set off by a pair of Clark Gable ears. His pin-up collection bristles like his hair and is the envy of all. This is confirmed by the many who make the daily trek to his glamorously decorated room . . . and the Kurfis arrow points to the coolest sack on the second deck in which he is usually found comfortably dreaming, much to the chagrin of his sweltering roommates . . . Kurf is not a person to take a back seat from anyone. When a difference of opinion arises he lowers his head and charges, invariably coming out with no broken china and a gold nugget in

each hand. When at home Kurf is a great one for visiting the homes of his old friends . . . their homes usually being the nearest bar. After one New Year's Eve party he was seen sneaking aboard with as much finesse as a bull-dozer. In his possession were two cow bells and a paper hat in as rare a condition as Kurf was . . . a bottle of champagne was slung under each arm. His thoughts were of flying and he was mumbling all the way up the gangplank, "What do you mean why didn't I stay closed up. Jeeze, Roth, I couldn't tell if you were flying formation or giving me a primary acrobatic check."

LANSING, James Samuel
Born: September 16, 1919
School: Fordham University
Trained at: Pensacola and Jacksonville, Fla.
Previous Squadron: VB-16
Address: 125 Mayflower Ave.
    New Rochelle, N. Y.

JIM came out of old Bombing Six to give the word to the fighter pilots in young VF-86 and all we can remember of the early days at Atlantic City and Otis was the continuous mumbling . . . "Lansing has a division . . . Lansing doesn't have a division" . . . like pulling petals out of Navy Regs. However, he taught us the Fordham swagger, the Fordham Ram, the Fordham cheer, and a song about O'Malley . . . or O'Bailley . . . yeah, O'Reilly. Then he went away to photo school and was never heard of again until he vacationed from our first cruise in Los Angeles and we all had to chip in and help pay Arturo de Cordova off when he sued Jim for stealing his stuff. Jim steamed out of there to Arcata, where he chopped some wood, and then climaxed the peace convention in San Francisco by holding a small one of his own and acquiring an honorary membership to a spook of the month club from which he gets . . . books. His job as manager of materiel is a thing of the past we know, but we can't forget . . . "I'm not going to issue you any more goddamned gear. Get up front and mill around."

LAUTZ, Louis Romeo
Born: November 13, 1923
School: La Crosse State Teachers College
Trained at: Corpus Christi, Tex.
    Daytona Beach, Fla.
Previous Squadron: VF(N)-110
Address: 2014 Main St., La Cross, Wis.

LOU is another of Rothenberg's Roving Redhots. He has a variety of nicknames but Lou is the only one printable. He has had a complete night fighter syllabus which qualifies him for standing by in the ready room, lying down in the ready room or just lounging in the ready room. Occasionally they did launch Lou in the daytime to seek out some bad weather so that the task force could head into it and knock the bow off some ship. Lautz used to be a happy little day fighter in AC until some Commander came through recruiting night fighters. Lou said the Commander started burning matches under his nails and he decided that he had better "volunteer." Lautz wants to hurry back to LaCrosse for the duck hunting season, "Boy, you give those Bluebills fifty mills and you can splash them every time."

LAWTON, Lawrence Wells
Born: February 14, 1925
School: Annapolis High School
Trained at: Pensacola and Miami, Fla.
Previous Squadrons: VF-100, VT-100
Address: R.F.D., Newcastle, Pa.

LAWT came to Fighting 86 along with Hill's Hotrocks. He's from Annapolis, Md.; that's where a file number and a man are blended into a Naval Officer. No doubt the proximity of the Naval Academy beckoned Lawt toward the Navy when the war broke out — that and Annapolis Selective Service Board #4. One of his favorite hobbies is sailing (with sails). This is done by putting a sail upright in a boat, the wind then hits the sail and blows you and the boat over into the water. It seems kind of silly, but he's crazy about it. There is no one in the Air Group more photogenic than Lawton. He takes an especially good picture as a Saturday afternoon athlete tossing women and babies around. It isn't that he doesn't trust Grumman and his boasts, but he just likes to wear that rabbit's foot. "This isn't Rabaul, Hill, you don't go down to fifty feet here."

LELAND, Benjamin Towne, Jr.
Born: February 15, 1920
School: Union College
Trained at: Corpus Christi, Tex.
    Jacksonville, Fla.
Married
Address: 33 Coleman St.
    Bridgeport, Conn.

BEN is our flying wonder. We wonder what he thinks about most of the time. It's the general concensus that when his mind isn't on the actual mechanics of driving his Helltruck he is dreaming up a design for a new bridge . . . or maybe the load limits on a double bed. Blondie is one of the squadron's most talented musicians. A true wizard of the harmonica. You name the tune you want to hear and he'll play "Tiger Rag". To us one of the things that makes him no one else *but* Ben Leland is that incinerator he carries around between his teeth. When it is all fired up the odor of burning fabric drifts into every nook within fifty feet. We are all certain that pipe has something to do with this business of smashing atoms. The one thing that Ben wants to do more than anything else in this squadron is to successfully complete a night rendezvous. We think that if he removed his red glasses after take-off it might be done. "Which way did he go, Schwartz?"

LOWRIE, Richard Easton
Born: October 2, 1922
School: Michigan State College
Trained at: Pensacola, Fla.
Previous Squadrons: VF-44, VB-86
Married
Address: Clarkston, Michigan

LO-OWRIE, the only man to ever spend his honeymoon on a CVE. He had himself changed from bombers to fighters so that he wouldn't have to wear a throat mike, then found out that all navy mikes had gravel in them. He traveled easily with the squadron through all of its migrations, his only complaint being that the minute he got rendezvoused with his wife the Navy sent him someplace else. It didn't take him long to learn the intricacies of formation flying and as soon as he accomplished same he explained readily that he only flew wing on TR because it was easier to lead the division from the number two spot. And then one day he slowly unwound himself from the barrier on the flight deck. "How did you do it?" everyone asked. Lowrie smiled, looked at the wrecked airplane and drawled " 'Twasn't easy."

McCOY, Robert P.
Born: February 28, 1923
School: Texas A & M
Trained at: Corpus Christi, Tex.
    Melbourne, Fla.
Address: 2410 Las Palmas
    Port Arthur, Texas

MAC is the patrol leader of the Beaver Patrol of the Rover Boys. Coming from the swamplands in a slightly better part of Texas, he became web-footed at an early age and has never wavered from his belief that Texas is first in everything. Although born a landlubber, he quickly picked up the language of the sea . . . wait until his father hears him bellow "Goddamit, pass the potatoes" like he does in the wardroom. "Stud" McCoy tamed a few fillies during our stay in the redwoods and is considering another visit after the war . . . there's still one he didn't tame. He'll probably go home telling sea stories that will never be matched and if he ever becomes the veterinarian that he wants to be we can hear him on the open plains of Texas now, "Easy, boy, now a little more to starboard. Whoa, lift up your port bow leg."

MELLIN, John Lloyd
Born: November 15, 1919
School: Wazata High School
Trained at: Pensacola and Jacksonville, Fla.
Married
Address: R.F.D., Minneapolis, Minn.

JACK is the second heaviest man in AB Thompson's Division. His greatest pleasure is to grind down a few highballs and pick an argument with Joe Holderman (everybody picks on poor Joe). On game nights as he calmly turns the pasteboards, he can be heard to say, "I've got mine you see, I'll raise." Brown says Mellin is a good man to owe money to; he really watches you when you are over enemy territory. Jack has been in the Navy for six years; before taking flight training, he was a mech and he is convinced that this aviatin' is just a passing fad. " 'Tain't safe," he says, "I'll do all my driving in my Mercury in the future." Mellin wants to hurry home and teach his new born baby girl to beware of Navy Fliers. Jack used to break up the games at Otis (when he was ahead, of course) by saying, "this is the last hand fellows, I've got to get Lowrie and Morton home to their wives."

METCALF, Edwin Jack
Born: December 3, 1923
School: Charleroi High School
Trained at: Pensacola and Jacksonville, Fla.
Married
Address: 410 Washington Ave.
   Charleroi, Pa.

MET, weighting in at 145 pounds, is a giant in his family. The boys say he's skinny, but he stoutly maintains that "I'm the wiry type." That's fine as long as someone doesn't short circuit a couple of wires. "Honest E. J." is very popular in party circles; principally, of course, as a mainstay in our dance review . . . this latent talent having been brought out when he danced for the kings and queens of Eureka. Said to be the guiding light in Cuth's pinochle life, he has schooled Cuth until he can now count meld at the drop of an "Ah-hah". And Cuth has returned the favor by teaching him how to give his division leader the word and still keep out of hack. Met learned well, he even dared stray far enough away from Pete to shoot down a plane and become the hero of Charleroi. And he came back and gave Pete the word, made with a wide friendly grin and said, "Never mind Pete, youse is a good boy."

MORRIS, James Bruce
Born: May 18, 1924
School: Searcy High School
Trained at: Corpus Christi, Tex.
    Deland, Fla.
Previous Squadron: VB-86
Married
Address: Searcy, Arkansas

JB is better known to the boys as Hot JB or better yet, as just plain Hot. This tired looking character lounged around the Ready Room for the past six months only moving to allow the sweepers to get under him. He has a youthful winning smile but absolutely no, repeat no, energy. They say a couple of drinks limber him up considerably—he talks then. As a matter of fact he says things about himself that even he didn't know about himself. He's kind of a good-looking guy in a repulsive sort of way, and a pretty fair aviator in a loose sort of way. He was a relentless warrior and his attack cry still echos in our ears, "You're tough Molokini, but damnit we'll take you yet." JB's only real exercise is repulsing the Bear who constantly picks on him. "Go away Fatty, I don't wanna play. I'm tired."

MORRISON, Mahlon Jack
Born: December 17, 1923
School: Everett High School
Trained at: Corpus Christi, Tex.
    Melbourne, Fla.
Married
Address: 1322 Oakes Street
    Everett, Washington

JACK is the original outdoor man from Washington, and still persists in coming out on the flight deck daily and catching two big breaths of fresh air before collapsing. Jack's a pretty fair gunner and was in on one of the last kills of the war. He forever talks about his long canoe trips across Lake How-shouldiremember — his wife paddled and he navigated. The boy is quite versatile, drives a Hellcat like a roadster and a roadster like a Hellcat. The Skipper says he flies a close wing trying to edge his wing tip into the cockpit. "Boy, when I fly wing on 'em, I can reach over and change their tab settings." Morrison is president of the Junior Officer's Bunk Room Association and claims that if they send any more officers up there they will have to sleep in the washbowls. Tell-me-more Morrison couldn't understand why the fellows wouldn't listen to his treatise on the wing loading characteristics of the F6F at Maui. "They seemed more interested in making noise, drinking beer and chasing little girls on the beach, I wonder why."

MORTON, Earl Thomas
Born: November 10, 1923
School: Yakima Valley Junior College
Trained at: Corpus Christi, Tex.
    Miami, Fla.
Previous Squadron: VB-86
Married
Address: R.F.D. No. 7, Yakima, Washington

MORT is from Yakima, Washington but he talks more like he's from Van Buren, Arkansas. He claims to have come from a family of bootleggers, horse-thiefs, and poachers. To prove this he cites the fact that his brother paid his way through high school by selling fire water to the Indians. Their favorite sport was shooting the Indians' chickens out of the trees with their rifles. He did go to school, but always on a borrowed horse; we won't say stolen because they could never prove it. His Navy career has been rather dull. He did bring himself into the light at Otis by joining a tail chase with a 500 pound bomb on his rack . . . he got a week's bomb rack inspection duty out of it. He also managed to miss the boat when the squadron transferred to the Wasp. No one knew where he was; after catching a mail boat at the last minute he admitted he had been playing chess and just didn't get the word. His supreme military endeavor was the strafing of a large greenhouse in an attack on Kanoya. "Boy, you should have seen those pansies flame."

MORTON, Thomas H.
Born: November 15, 1920
School: Princeton University
    Carnegie Tech
Trained at: Pensacola and Vero Beach, Fla.
Address: 99 Hawthorne Ave.
    Albany, N. Y.

TOM was one of the most intelligent pilots in the squadron and was always in on any of our discussions, whether they were light or serious. He had an open outlook on life, not knowing what he wanted from it or what he expected it to give him, so he talked about it, hoping by doing so to find a lead and a goal that would be suitable for him. He was always popular in our "bull sessions" because he had a highly affable nature and a distinctive personality, and he kept his individuality and never lost his sense of humor. We remember how he loved to sing, and how he used to turn every gathering into a real song fest, taking so much interest in it that when we got tired of the songs we knew he made up or sought out others. These were, among others, the things that made him so much one of us.

MYERS, Ora Edwin
Born: April 5, 1924
School: Emlenton High School
Trained at: Pensacola, Fla.
Previous Squadron: VB-86
Married
Address: P.O. Box 16, Emlenton, Pa.

CORK is the nickname given Myers by the studs and fuds of Fighting 86. There is some doubt as to whether the name comes from his ability to lie right down beside his work and doze gently (just to prove of course, that he is not afraid of it) or whether he becomes affected when he smells one. The lover can be remembered as occupying a small part of heaven in the Holmes Motor Court with several pages of the book, "Is Sex here to Stay" laying around in shreds. Whether the target is Molokini Rock or Kisarazu, one pilot can be seen making his approach and retirement doing anything from a split S to a slow roll. "Flash" Myers really gave the Nip AA gunners kinks in the neck.

When he joined the squadron he could be distinguished by his helmet which contained many charms including galloping dominoes and queens' garters. Out here, "Corky got his Zero" which was in keeping with his early academic career; when called upon to render an opinion, he feebly stirs and says, "Who—me?"

MYERS, Russell Phillip, Jr.
Born: May 8, 1923
School: New Kensington High School
Trained at: Pensacola and Melbourne, Fla.
Address: 606½ Fifth Street
   New Kensington, Pa.

RUSS . . . also called FATTY, if you don't want him to do anything for you. Saw sun light for the first time much later than most of us . . . at nineteen, when he left Pittsburgh to go to pre-flight. Graduated with honors from the home town where he was greeted on the street with a familiar, "Hiya shy, handsome, unassuming, maulin' Monk Myers". Proud winner of a popularity contest in which he was the only contestant. Gin rummy expert, "I should have went down on yuh." Receives mail from more different sources than June Allyson. A

natural athlete, he has applied his ability to flying, is now seeking a job as adviser for Thatch on fighter tactics, "That target coordinator didn't have the word did he." Quietly munches his ration of two apples as he takes pictures of Jap airfields, "Have I got my five missions yet?" And is a firm believer in logic. After being forced to land at some strange airfield in Oregon. "Well, I wouldn't have gotten lost, T.R., if I hadn't been trying so hard to keep you from getting lost."

O'BRYAN, Basil Eugene
Born: January 12, 1924
School: Reitz Memorial High School
Trained at: Pensacola and Melbourne, Fla.
Married
Address: 116 Harriet Street
    Evansville, Indiana

O-B, we claim, is the only person who ever got his wings by charming the Navy with smiles and soap. He, somehow, back in the old days on the boardwalk, teamed up in the air with Ham and on the ground, somehow, with the Gold-dust twins and a group of people who are usually talking about the Yarp. The Yarp's mysterious presence, and O-B's, has always been felt in the squadron. O-B's liking for good literature and classical music might be misleading, but he can prove his physical ability with a Casu survival certificate, and we've all seen him in his swimming trunks . . . yes, we've all seen him in his swimming trunks. O-B sings in a clear screech and recites ditto, often heard saying, "Romeo, Romeo, wherefore art thou, Romeo?" . . . and answering himself, "Hyar ah iss." And then laughing, "Well, I don't know why the Navy keeps me out here."

OGDEN, Theodore Roosevelt
Born: December 30, 1919
School: Middlebury College
Trained at: Corpus Christi, Tex.
    Miami, Fla.
Previous Squadrons: VC-70, VF-18, VF-4
Address: Middleton, Mass.

RUDOLF, the Mole, our golden boy from Middlebury, really belongs among the moonlight cobwebs instead of subterranean dives and Stork Clubs. As whimsical as Ariel and as mischievous as Puck, he is sort of a modern Robin Goodfellow with a Grumman fuselage and a Pratt and Whitney Engine to get him around. Armed with a cherubic countenance and a BA he set out to revolutionize mankind and the world ("mankind" also includes womankind). Incensed at the Nips and a 1A draft classification, he joined the Navy and became a fighter and photo pilot. His daring reconnaissance hops are flown so low that they often reveal B-29s flying at 35,000 feet. However TR always makes up in narrative what his pictures lack in coverage. He has learned the empire school schedules and times his hops to allow him to buzz the Tokyo High School girls during recess. "Hot dog. They don't *look* any different to me, rally they don't."

O'SHEA, Maurice Vern
Born: July 18, 1924
School: Ward High School
Trained at: Corpus Christi, Tex.
    Daytona Beach, Fla.
Previous Squadron: VF-99
Address: 721 North 17th Street
    Kansas City, Kansas

MOE is not the only nickname that this boy has. Because of his almost perpetual visits to the land of Nod he is often called Horizontal, Sacktime, and Sacko. Of course this love of the Winken and Blinken can be attributed to Moe being just a growing boy, and it is a known fact that a certain Kansas City Chick can keep him awake . . . what she has that we don't Moe won't tell us. Speaking of Kansas City, there are two of them you know, Moe comes from the other one . . . and so his dealings in spirita fermentae have probably been a little on the shady side. It's a good thing that his Irish luck holds out, for his ability for getting into aerial predicaments is unsurpassed. His last experience ended with a splash and the deep sea swallowed his plane. Holding true to his luck, Moe escaped with only the loss of his Zippo lighter, and a used handkerchief. "And I would have saved the plane only I couldn't hold it up with my shoes on."

PALUS, George Russell
Born: April 19, 1914
School: U. S. Naval Academy
Trained at: Pensacola, Fla.
Married
Address: 3166 Maple Street
    San Diego, Calif.

PINKY was the Academy's only off-spring to haunt our happy little throng. But we never held this against him. We treated him just like an ordinary human being, and under our considerate attention he blossomed forth and became one of us. Our executive officer, until he deserted us to become Cag of Air Group 26, he made sure that we read all Memos and Orders and that we had a good party at least twice a week. A man of discretion, they say, he was even discreet when he nastied up Ding Dong (whom he mistook for a plumbing fixture) on Maui, doing it in the same manner that any Navy order would prescribe. Pinky hunted out the best steaks the Islands had to offer, then taught us a letter game by which he never had to pay for one. He also found places in Eureka that only Paramount Studios are supposed to find (and they employ thousands of people). His stand-out words . . . "This is my private jeep, goddamit, just because it was issued to the squadron doesn't mean a damned thing."

PETERSON, Robert Willard
Born: July 20, 1921
School: Montana State College
Trained at: Jacksonville and Miami, Fla.
Previous Squadrons: VF-29, VC-95
Married
Address: Billings, Montana

PETE is from Billings, or something, Montana—it doesn't make too much difference, Montana is enough. Pete is an old time advocate of the FM-2, or of any Grumman Aircraft. "There I was on my back at three thousand feet in the Atlantic with a U-boat under me. What happened? I righted myself and the U-boat submerged. What didya expect, a fight?" Peterson is our engineering officer. This is an extremely arduous occupation which consists of periodically telling the pilots, "if the damn thing won't fly, down it and the mechs will fix it." Pete subsists on coffee and cigarettes and on strike days, just cigarettes. "If you think this is fighting, you should have been on the SANTEE. We got six whales, four certains and two probables. God, what blubber slicks!" Pete and his family rented a forest retreat during our Arcata stay and every day at the ready room we'd listen to him tell about the "big bear," or the "snake as long as a train," he had slain on his doorstep. Says he, "The best way to start the F6F is to turn the ignition switch from 'off' to 'on'."

PFEIFER, Edward
Born: October 29, 1919
School: West Philadelphia Catholic High
    School
Trained at: Pensacola and Deland, Fla.
Previous Squadron: VB-86
Address: 208 Ardmore Ave.
    Highland Park, Pa.

SMILIN ED Pfeifer, sometimes known as "Curly" is famed in a small way, for his almost perpetual frown and his Hollywood hair style—in that order. He offers the deplorable state of the world as an excuse for the scowl, but can only claim in defense of his crowning glory that any kind of hair is better than no hair at all. Our version of Laughing Boy once pruned the top of a pine tree, inadvertently to be sure, during a night bounce drill at Otis. Imagine his intense chagrin at hearing this strange noise immediately followed by a shower of pine needles in his cockpit. After minor repairs, including the removal of hunks of the tree limb and assorted pine cones from the engine, the plane was OK. The damage to our boy . . . merely the erasure of his wrinkles and five years of his life. When not airplane driving, Smiley can be found in the sack or behind a chess board. "I'm getting better; Stauffer only beats me nine out of ten times now."

PILLAR, M. Nelson
Born: November 30, 1916
School: University of Illinois
Trained at: Pensacola, Fla.
Previous Squadrons: VN 1-9D, VF-99,
    VF-100
Married
Address: 1239 Madison Park
    Chicago, Ill.

NELS spent two of his happy navy years trying to teach kay-doodlers how to fly; this taking place in Chicago. Some people wonder how his cadets learned anything unless it was in some nite spot where Nels did all his high flying. After several years of being the Windy City's leading Casanova, our Romeo finally stalled out in the slipstream of a beautiful girl from Michigan. Since then his conversation has changed from flying to Barbara. His pleasant personality when clean shaven has earned him the nickname of "little sunshine." But an amazing change takes place with the coming of that well known five o'clock shadow. It seems his mood changes for the worse with the growth of his beard, an amazing phenomenon for which neither Nels nor his buddies can sanely account. Like all great men of the sea, Pillar too has spoken. His famous words "Where in the hell is that carrier?" will long be remembered.

PLAUT, Robert E.
Born: November 7, 1920
School: U. S. Naval Academy
Address: 1522 16th Avenue, North
    Seattle, Wash.

PLUTO was one of the most easy going people we have ever known; he kept his serious side to himself and his close friends. He was a natural athlete interested in all sports and especially keen on horse racing, boxing, and basketball. This athletic ability made him an excellent fighter pilot and a good all-round flyer. Two of our more vivid memories of Atlantic City are the rough and tumble basketball games that Pluto was always in the middle of and his '36 Ford, the "Blue Beetle," which had become famous through its trips between New York and Florida . . . Pluto used to claim that he had to brush the women off it it was so attractive. Pluto was symbolic of the free, happy American youth and his untimely death gave us more drive to fight that America would be kept for people like him.

RICHMAN, George Hurt
Born: June 14, 1922
School: Wittenberg College
Trained at: Pensacola and Sanford, Fla.
Address: 1416 Delia Ave.
　Akron, Ohio

RICH, after a treble-clef, is the Laughing Boy of 86. He was the death of a hyena once when he out-laughed one in the Bronx Zoo. He was given orders to the Charger (a raft) at one time during his naval career, but from the day he reported on board the ship ran backwards . . . so the Charger sent him to us with a note of explanation pinned on his P-jacket. We gave him to Hoppy and Hoppy has been taking care of him ever since. He taught Rich the meaning of the words "Double" and "Vodka" when used together. Says Rich, "I think I'll have just one more before hitting the sack." He does, and leaves . . . a dull thud is heard off stage. From a brisk hop with Bahrom he runs to a brisk game of gin rummy to a brisk bit of exercise in the work-out room to a brisk laugh in the shower. "I'm as busy as that admiral was making out the paper work for my slow roll at two hundred feet. Hee-hee-hee-hee-hee-hee-hee."

ROTHENBERG, Allen
Born: June 16, 1919
School: George Washington University
Trained at: Pensacola, Fla.
Previous Squadrons: VF-54, VP-51, VF(N)
　110, VF-5
Address: 2710 Cortland Pl., N.W.
　Washington, D. C.

ROTH, or Condition-eleven-Roth, our ex-P-Boat pilot. The night fighter skipper, he was forever sing-ing the praises of PBY's and Washington, D. C. We could never decide whether he was hired by Con-solidated Aircraft or the Washington chamber of commerce. Holds the record for longest "taxi hop." He was "accidently" launched with a strike and ended up strafing an airfield on Japan. "They can't launch me, I'm just up here to taxi!" The only man in the squadron who would smoke A. B. Thomp-son's gift cigars. "These really aren't as bad as they smell." Roth's main ambition is to hit a winning daily double at Hialeah and retire to a life of ease. He was always available for a game of acey-ducey, gin rummy or monopoly, although we never saw him win at any of them. Forever worrying about whether his night fighters would be spotted and loaded in time, Roth wore a path between Ready

One and Air Plot. "Wait 'til we hit them with those 20 millimeters. Okey, Roth, switch to channel four."

SARGENT, Channing Claire
Born: June 7, 1924
School: Sheldahl High School
Trained at: Pensacola and Miami, Fla.
Previous Squadrons: VF-100, VT-100
Address: Ankeny, Iowa

TIGER JACK tallyhoed the Navy from Ankeny, Iowa . . . that's in the United States. He climbed from the cockpit of his Farm-all to the cockpit of the Hellcat with ease. He is convinced there is very little difference in operation and thinks that maybe the Farm-all is a little faster. With an outlook that life is real, life is earnest, Tiger Jack set out to conquer the cadet training program. However, after a few weeks in close proximity with the posture squad he decided that conquering would be the easy way out . . . what would a few mis-placed stoop-fallings ever amount to. So he majored in singing, now sings a mean tenor . . . anybody that sings like he does would have to be mean, although they claim he was a big success on the Happy Hour. He says, "Anyway, I only sing when I fly with Wolfard, we synchronize our throttles to doodlee-doo."

SCHOLL, John Edward
Born: July 20, 1922
School: Falls City High School
Trained at: Corpus Christi, Tex.
   Sanford, Fla.
Married
Address: Route No. 4
   Falls City, Nebraska

JOHN thinks that Nebraska is the center of fashion, not Paris, and that all things that grow there are miracle, life-giving products. He is in a continuous state of discussion trying to prove that he weighs less than A. B. Thompson. We don't know of anyone whom he has convinced of this fact and it is said that he won't get in a chow line until he sees A. B. in it. Stauffer says the division has to take turns towing him off the deck. Scholl won't talk about this. He always changes the subject to his favorite sport, swimming. He claims it a breach of etiquette to indulge in this exercise without taking your favorite airplane along. Extended swims are John's favorites. The time he got mad at the squadron he stayed away two weeks. We finally came upon him on a tanker surveying the landscape with a pair of field glasses, "I'm not trying to find native women on these islands," he said, "I'm looking for Nebraska."

SCHWARTZ, Theodore
Born: July, 1922
School: Rutgers
Trained at: Pensacola and Vero Beach, Fla.
Address: 1729 N. Franklin St.
    Philadelphia, Pa.

HONEY-BEAR, that great, big bundle of joy from Philadelphia, is one of the squadron's leading morale builders. His unending witticisms (most of which stink), ceaseless chatter, and reappearances in the chow line are all good for laughs. He's at his best when working on unsuspecting, innocent people. His best record for laughs to date . . . three rolling in the aisles, two holding their sides, three laughing uproarously, and twelve walking sullenly away. "Fatter-than-you" Schwartz has an extremely creative mind and has assembled a Turkish water pipe from a used catsup bottle, pipe, and red insulating wire. "It's the first step towards my own harem," says Honey-Bear, "and it will sure be a relief to have one, and not have to play gin rummy with Wolfard all the time."

SHUPTAR, Daniel
Born: December 23, 1923
School: Mt. Carmel High School
Trained at: Pensacola and Miami, Fla.
Previous Squadron: VF-100
Address: 247 S. Market St.
    Mt. Carmel, Pa.

DAN tossed away the Candy Mountain and gave himself up to the muscle-builders at pre-flight hoping they would instill the romance of the sea in his soul. What they really did instill we can't say here, but if it was romance, it was not like any we've ever seen. Dan has been known to argue a midwesterner into a frenzy over the existence of any middle-west states and then to win him back to normalcy with a friendly grin. One of Hill's boys, Dan was a little late getting in the outfit, but he has already accepted us as good arguing material and we have acc . . . well, there's no need for going into that. Professing athletic prowess he has been seen trying to prove to Whitey that you can play basketball on the side of the number one elevator and he claims that is one of the best ways to become a good family man. Takes a six instead of a seven and says, "Oh, Rothenberg, I don't have to cheat when I play monopoly with you."

SMITH, Leon Milton
Born: November 23, 1923
School: Alabama Polytechnic Inst.
Trained at: Corpus Christi, Tex.
    Melbourne, Fla.
Address: 1751 Oxmoor Road
    Birmingham, Alabama

SMITTY, with his little victory garden on his upper lip, stepped right out of a tintype of the Gay Nineties into his native Alabama. He was there long enough to pick up a drawl then one day he saw a picture of Uncle Sam with his finger pointed straight at him and saying, "I want *you,* buddy buddy." So Smitty took three steps to the general store and post office and said "Ah does." While in cadet training he fell in with the Rover boys (those guys . . . Lord give us strength) and he, with the rest of them, has been milling around up front ever since. Smitty will argue at the · drop of a Budweiser bottle, especially if it's half full. He flies in Thomas's division of four ready room chairs and can always be heard in the back of the room gunnin' his motor. "Let me see now, with that many points I am allowed to stay in the Navy ten more years."

STAUFFER, Mahlon Roy
Born: April 10, 1920
School: Kansas State University
Trained at: Pensacola, Fla.
Address: Newton, Kansas

STAUFF, they say he's the wild man of the Sun Flower State, has answered to the names of Stoof, Stough, Strafford, and Bee Bee Eyes. Built like an airplane, he has retractable legs (for bridge tables?), flaps (in the down position) under his eyes, and a hydraulic system constantly in need of a refill. He was imported from the Chateau Renault in Upper Bullreignya to help the Navy missionize Atlantic City. Upon the completion of twenty-five missions on the boardwalk he was awarded the Distinguished Trying Cross, then sent on to Otis and, more recent and well-known, Arcata to conquer new fields. The fields were impenetrable but Stauff penetrated and again was awarded . . . this time the Cruxe de Luxe. Skipping over many of his adventures we next see him in action in the Pacific gathering material for his essay "The Hub-Cap versus the Sub-Cap." An essay which we hope he will dedicate to his famous line, "Mumble . . . mumble . . . mumble . . . sack."

THOMAS, Kelt Lamar
Born: January 29, 1920
School: Jacksonville, Fla.
Previous Squadron: VB-86
Married
Address: Meridianville, Alabama

KELT, Watch-'em-go, Thomas, the Country Gentleman (share cropper) rang into the Navy with "Hello you all." He hung up the plow and kissed old Beck goodbye saying, "This is it, Beck; this is rea-a-lly it." Of course the Navy only got him because the draft board stumbled in the chase. They say Kelt was a good-looking boy back in his youth and it is true that his I. D. card (touched up) looks like a young confederate cavalry officer . . . curls and all. He wins with the pasteboards at times, but he always crams the folding stuff in his shirt pockets and says, "I know I'm not winning." And after he has lost five straight games of acey-ducey he'll say, "All right, let's play the rubber off now." He even flies a little, too, but only when he has to. He's really very good when he gets started . . . last to dive, first to the rendezvous point. He has the only four section division in the squadron. Ask him about raising frogs and making money at it. "I know I can. Just a pair of big frogs in a bitty ole pond and watch 'em produce. I know I can make all kinds of money at it."

THOMPSON, Allen B.
Born: December 14, 1921
School: Southwestern Louisiana Inst.
Trained at: Pensacola, Fla., Corpus Christi,
    Tex., Miami, Fla., Jacksonville, Fla.
Previous Squadrons: VC-21, VF-36
Address: 2118 Webster Street
    Alexandria, La.

A. B. is our undernourished boy who consumes six or seven cans of anchovies as a prelude to evening chow. A. B. can only carry a 250 pound bomb when the rest of the boys carry 500s . . . there is a limit to the F6F weight load. His division declares he's really eager. He can make three passes while they're joining up for a second. "Schedule me for another strike, Hawke, I've only got 94 this month." First in the chow line, AB only eats two desserts on the days the sun shines. A thrifty character, AB has Brown buy his cigars so he won't have to pay an extra ten per cent to the cigar mess. And speaking of those ugly smelling cigars, most of the boys want him to . . . oh, well. And the briefing would be going well until, "Well, Skipper, when we were up in Attu, yapidy-yap."

TRYCINSKI, John Francis
Born: August 25, 1924
School: Haaren High School
Trained at: Corpus Christi, Tex.
    Melbourne, Fla.
Address: 1057 Faile Street
    Bronx, N. Y. C.

SAM is the youngest of the Rover boys. In eight more years they'll let him vote. He'd always hear "May I see your I.D. card please" right before he'd get bounced out of the Frisco taverns. Occasionally he'd "soft shoe" past the bouncer or convince him his I.D. card had a typographical error. Serious-minded Sam is now studying, picking up the word on romance from some pulp literature that is being furnished him by one of his disillusioned admirers. "I think Dick Tracy will marry Gravel Gertie in the end." Coming back from Wake he backed up Hoppy's story of getting a direct hit on an AA emplacement by bursting into the ready room scream-ing, "God, Hoppy, did you even hit the island?" Sam flamed and splashed a Grace in the closing days of the war. Said Sam "Gosh. It had a thousand guns on it . . . all shooting at me . . . but I got it."

VANNATTA, Robert Henry
Born: June 3, 1923
School: Lakewood High School
    University of Mexico
Trained at: Pensacola and Vero Beach, Fla.
Previous Squadron: VF (N) 75
Address: 2200 Northland Ave.
    Lakewood, Ohio

VANNATSU, or just plain Van. The man that many proclaim will even be late for his discharge from the Navy. He does, however, develop full power if you mention the word bourbon and follow it closely with Ginger. Van holds the distinction of being able to wear submarine wings as well as "wings of Gold." He spent the biggest part of his first time out riding destroyers and Bretches Buoys. To Van all women are, as he puts it, "just good friends, you know." From the number of letters he gets from far and wide, we are beginning to believe that he read a book on friendship that we didn't. Van spends the biggest part of his time singing, "Old Man River has Fish for Supper" as he beats himself in solitaire, never cheating mind you, just prearranging the deck so that he couldn't lose. In the best tradition of The Order of the Night Fighters, he says, "We're backing the attack while we're still in the sack."

WARTON, David
Born: April 22, 1923
School: Wheaton College, Wheaton, Ill.
Trained at: Pensacola and Melbourne, Fla.
Previous Squadrons: VF-100, VF-99
Address: 3747 Fremont St.
    Chicago, Ill.

DAVE was raised in the land of the Magic Carpet, Ali Baba, and Barems harems. The latter, it seems, was firmly imprinted on his young and innocent mind when he returned to the states to get his two years of college and enlist in Naval Aviation. It is easy to understand why his mailing list reaches such tremendous proportions. The old saying "a girl in every port" isn't quite adequate for Dave, he has them inland too. Upon first meeting the tall, dark-complectioned lad, one could hardly believe that his extra-curricular activities would include such favorite Navy pastimes as babes, bottles, and ballads. His reserved manner is very deceiving, however, and after close association you realize that "Egypt" is truly "one of the boys." Dave also has his serious side. An avid reader, he has often been seen on an intellectual spree for as long, at least, as twenty minutes. Then he emerges and says, "Take me back to Egypt. How they wail when you lift that veil."

WEBBER, Ralph Stites
Born: January 5, 1924
School: University of Wisconsin
Trained at: Pensacola and Melbourne, Fla.
Address: 3623 Haven Ave., Racine, Wis.

WEB was always greatly instrumental in keeping the morale of the squadron on a high level. He was always among the leaders in helping us organize our parties and picnics, and he was usually leading us in all the squadron song fests. We remember the great enjoyment he derived from drinking the "schnapps" so popular in his ancestral Germany. Outwardly he appeared to be a very easy-going and light hearted person and, to a great extent, was just that. However, he also had his serious moods during which one could recognize the stability of his personality. His good nature and unselfishness gained for him a popularity among the other members of the squadron which few could equal. What he gave to all of us out of this generosity will be with us forever.

WHITE, Donald Edward
Born: April 18, 1924
School: Athens High School
Trained at: Pensacola and Melbourne, Fla.
Address: RFD No. 1, Cantrall, Ill.

WHITEY is our athletic officer. "Lansing and me can whip any guy in the squadron, except Dobbie." Whitey is Pacific-theatre renowned for his Earthquakes, a simple mixture of beer, whiskey, wine and residue from other people's glasses. White is morbidly informal; a simple thing like hoisting the ship's exec onto a table in the Pearl Harbor O'Club and making him chug-a-lug appeals to his sense of democracy. Whitey is from Springfield, Illinois and Springfield is damned glad he is *from* there; that Crewson routine did not go over with the local bobby-sox mothers. Whitney has meticulously schooled his wingman "Ak-ak" and is attempting to make him a hot pilot like himself. Incidentally, he refers to Harris as the Ensign . . . Whitey outranks him by three hours. "Join up, Harris, goddamit, or I won't let you read my Dick Tracy comic book."

WILSON, Milner Bradley, Jr.
Born: June 21, 1903
School: Wofford College
    Columbia University
Trained at: Quonset Point, R. I.
Previous Squadron: VT-48
Married
Address: Mayesville, South Carolina

TOUGHIE (not Tuffy) is our very likeable Administrative Officer who came to us from Torpedo 48 early in '45. "I do declare!" blurts the amiable gentleman from South Carolina every hour on the hour. The "Checkage Chief," as he is occasionally called, has had his hands full every minute of the time that he has been with us . . . full of beer bottles, highballs, or checkages. Toughie is a renegade high school principal. "I'm not going back into school work after this war. My wife and I are just going to run away from it all." How about that . . . and at his age, too. At "turn to" each day, Toughie chains Moye (yeoman) to the typewriter and away they go to the land of multi-syllables and brave adjectives. We can see him now reaching for his helmet and we can hear him exclaim, "Don't tell me that those Kamikazes are here again!" Weary at night, he is often heard saying, "With all this work they give me, I do believe they are gonna ask me to fly an airplane in my spare time! Oh, well, I'm gonna be a pilot in the next war anyway, damned if I'm not."

WOLFARD, Robert Eugene
Born: October 17, 1922
School: University of Oklahoma
Trained at: Pensacola and Vero Beach, Fla.
Address: 324 So. Santa Fe
    Norman, Okla.

WOLF is a long way from home, but you'd never know it to hear him sing . . . chirping in the gay manner of the mongoose basoon. In Atlantic City he became famous by having an apartment house for eight families closed for the duration by a narrow-minded landlord who heard him render "I'm in Love with the Slop, Oh Garbage Man" and Wolf, himself, was put out of bounds. The co-author of that smash hit "The Song Book of the Wild Hares," he preserved for posterity the south pacific flier's community sings. His greatest tribulation, however, was keeping track of a set of mated playing cards. We have all lived in dread of being routed out of the sack by the bull-horn to "report to Ready One and account for Wolfard's missing cards." As far as we know they survived the cruise, but Wolf has grown older (and they say wiser) for the ordeal. "If Schwartz hadn't been so busy eating he could have helped me, if I hadn't been so busy learning a new song."

VF OVER THIRD FLEET DURING OPERATION TINTYPE

SKETCH OF FIGURES IN MOONLIGHT SCENE
ABOARD SHIP

Pappy GRAFF, ART 1/C is one of our radiomen. You can never find him but somehow or another, his work always gets done. He's allergic to the Maui Shore Patrol and wants to get back to Philly, where he gets along with the police.

WHITE, R. S. ACRM, Whitey to his buddies, is our code boy from Indiana. He left his radio work to Graff while he took care of plane assignments and dart games during this cruise.

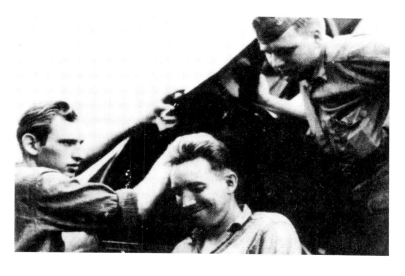

Chief CONGER looks on while two of his mechs mess up a wing. Lonnie hails from Iowa, the corn state . . . you can tell by looking at his waistline. He divides his attention between planes and cards. Needless to say, cards get most of his time.

Robert WARD, AMM 2/C is a quiet lad that spends most of his time milling around the hangar deck looking for a place to lie down. However, he does get up occassionally . . . when Conger passes by.

Don WONDER, AMM 1/C works on the flight deck picking up squawks from the returning pilots. We don't know what he did with the squawks . . . but he got 'em. He's a modest boy and swears that the horde of mail he receives is all from his mother.

Jim NOON AOM 1/C works while his boss watches . . that's the way it usually was. Jim is a hardworking ordnanceman that came to us from the bombers and wants to go from us back to Pennsylvania and bock beer.

Fred EDWARDS, ACOM, the ordnance chief and ex-telephone repairman from Oakland. Fred is an old timer with 86 and worked his way to Chief while at Maui. When he wasn't arming planes he could usually be found pressing the sack in CPO Quarters.

Eugene MOYE Y 1/C was Toughie's right hand man in all of his administrative ventures . . . including running to the island, helmet in hand, during the Kamikazee attacks. Moye did a lot of work . . . well.

Arbie WILLIAMS Y 3/C was Moye's first assistant who had only two hobbies, women and alcohol . . . like most men. Williams was as busy as hell in Eureka keeping all of his gals apart so that they couldn't get together on him.

Al KLIMA S 1/C is our Yoeman striker. Here he is gazing intently at some paper . . . don't know why, he can't read. He was the only man that Williams outrated on the ship and he really let him know it.

George HUCKINS AMM 2/C the kid with all the tattoos. George is from New England and spends half his time trying to find out when we are going home. He's a newlywed . . . maybe that's the reason.

Ed HARRIS AMM 2/C is one of the night fighter mechs. He quickly picked up the night fighter code of staying in the sack and stayed there. He is hurrying home so that the stateside babies can run their hands through that pretty hair.

Stretch PINKHAM AEM 2/C and Tinny TINNI-RELLA AEM 1/C are looking at some motor that they know absolutely nothing about. Tinny plans on retiring shortly and going to work for the Log Cabin. Stretch is getting himself in shape to wrestle his one year old son when he gets home.

Ed KLIPPERT AM 1/C is the squadron's metal-smith. He buttoned dzus buttons, made wristwatch bands, ash trays, bathtub stoppers, and other essential war supplies. Ed had a bang-up time in Eureka, both before and after Elaine.

Raymond LIGHTBODY AMM 3/C, the guy who gave the seabees a bad time in the Log Cabin. Ask him what State he's from and he'll answer Boston, and even that is better than the hangar deck.

Gordon MUMPOWER AMM 1/C is from Appalachie, Virginia and is dying to get back there and watch that cotton make with the blossoms. Being a plank owner, he says, takes a helluva long time.

Joe STEELE AMM 1/C is our leading mechanic on the hangar deck. He sees to it that the tail hooks come out of the tail . . . sometimes. Is torn between two loves, to wit: Gravel Gertie from Eureka and Sunburned Sadie from Maui.

Tom PROBERT PR 1/C is shown here assembling a parachute which may or may not open when the rip cord is pulled . . . it would be practically impossible to find him to explain the situation anyway. Says his old man is a joint Babe Ruth, Harry Truman and D. Eisenhower.

Bill ROSS Ph 1/C is the squadron's shutter snapper. He was in the V-12 program until they asked him to repeat the alphabet and he said, "Focal length 4.5." Can't understand why the photo planes are always on the flight deck for pre-dawn launches. "Damn it, they know I like to sleep late."

Nels NELSON ART 1/C, Gus ALBRIGHT ART 2/C, and Billy CRICE ARM 2/C are here ganged around that secret Navy gadget that they get out of the sack once a week to re-paint. Nelson seemed to have been involved in a "shot in the leg" episode in the vicinity of Alameds; he was probably the only survivor. Albright spends his spare time writing letters and dreaming about the time he can wear levis without the M.A.A. giving him a bad time. Crice is an eager beaver night fighter radioman who can be found under a helmet on the flight deck, if you pick up the right helmet.

Ralph HELLER AOM 2/C, Marvin GOETSCH AOM 2/C, and Woody WOODRUFF AOM 2/C three of the squadron ordnancemen snapped in the act of making perfectly good fifty calibres into perfectly lousy fifty calibres. Heller is a quiet lad who loves beer, his wife, and shore duty . . . but we don't know in what order. Goetsch, a big hearted Iowan, is an old timer who started with the Squadron in Atlantic City and who has been clearing jams, with both the wife and the guns, ever since. Woodruff is the night fighter ordnance man. He dodges work, working parties, parties, work, and Edwards. He has been known to favor dollies on the slightly plump side.

OPERATIONS SECURED

VF-86 MOVES AGAIN

LAIRS OF THE WILD HARES
Atlantic City

ALONG with the opening of the board-walk season and the issue of a new "A" book we were commissioned as Fighting Squadron 86 on June 15, 1944 on the Naval Air Station at Atlantic City, New Jersey, with Horace Tennes as skipper and Pinky Palus as exec.

We had 54 pilots, 3 ground officers, and 21 enlisted men. Training started immediately, both in F6F-3's and the Chateau Renault, and for the weary, which we always were, there was no rest.

Affaires de l'amour (some terminating in wedlock), automobile accidents, tradings with the black market, and the eternal search for a better anchovie took up most of our free time. At the squadron we trained and trained . . . and trained. A still-unfinished tennis tournament was started. Wolf made the better people of Ventnor community-sing conscious. . . . And we trained.

Jim Lansing, Og, and Rack Morton spent the month of July happily secluded in the Bolton in Harrisburg, Penn. where they were learning the intricacies of aerial photography. Ham acquired and operated an establishment called by many a "snake ranch" with the able assistance of Hoppy, the Mole, R. A., and Swede Manson. Said "ranch" was closed with the kind wishes of the F.B.I. who couldn't be convinced that A.B. could eat all that food and still be mortal.

On July 24, Lt. Robert E. Plaut and Ens. Willis G. Howie were killed in a mid-air collision while on a training flight.

In September Dobbie Dobson came in as exec and brought a new life to our Claridge Hotel parties. Same parties being the place where Clem preached the value of the married life and Whitey learned that they hadn't taught him everything in pre-flight.

Late in September we were changed from a 36 to a 54 plane outfit, with a corresponding increase in the number of pilots. Fifteen characters were given to us by Bombing 86 . . . need more be said.

Our training culminated in a spectacular night tail chase at 30,000 feet (Horace was in ecstacy) and on the sad day of October 2nd we lined up in the most irregular V aviation has ever seen and trundled our little Hellcats to Otis Field in Cape Cod, Mass.

Otis Field

We came here to work for Joe and to coordinate the fighters, bombers, and torps. In so doing we started our never ending series of group gropes.

Otis was originally the Army's and we were quartered in Army enlisted men's barracks where the heat was either inadequate or overwhelming. The closet in each room consisted of three nails, and the head resembled a public bathing place in India. The best that could be said of the food was that it was substantial. Most of us found it a great comfort to live off the base and the Coonamessett Ranch was extremely cooperative in finding us lodgings and in serving us good cocktails and food.

Bubber, Russ Myers, and Max converted an old chicken coop into a strange sort of abode and became the neighbors of Stauff, Hoppy, and Rudolf who were living a luxurious life in an artist's studio.

Grouch finally coughed up enough money to bring his wife to his side (like it says in the ceremony) and Gravel Lowrie (amazed at the situation) sent for the little girl back home and spent his honeymoon on the CVE P-Willie (like it doesn't say in the ceremony).

The inclement weather went from worse to worser. It finally got so cold that we had to learn about a new switch in the cockpit, a feat which took days for the whole squadron to accomplish.

On November 20 Ens. Andrew C. Butko was killed when he failed to pull out of a rocket dive.

We did impact work with the Army some place in New Hampshire and between hops Jack Mellin taught the boys, at pretty steep fees, a new game called "choose-it-with-a-twist."

And the fog rolled in and rolled in . . . but when it rolled out enough so they could see the Coonamessett they dragged us off and we trained and trained . . . and trained.

Across the Continent to San Diego

On December 1 we all got orders to be on the West Coast soon, so we all borrowed money from Reuben, dug out the old schedules again, visited the next of kin, and fought our way across the country as slowly as possible.

People straggled in from odd places at odd times. We lived in the Coronado Hotel and begrudgingly reported to the squadron once a day. The rest of the time we lived as fast as we could . . . someone had turned up the sand clock in a helluva hurry.

Aboard the U.S.S. Nassau

On December 9, the last stragglers hurried madly to the dock, left their rented cars with the marine guards to return (they never did and we're still paying for them), and boarded a small raft which after the trip we all fondly called the Good Ship Nausea.

The trip to Hawaii is remembered by everyone in terms of gains or losses in the continuous poker game in the bilge (where we lived). Pete bragged constantly about his great seamanship acquired while on board another raft called the Santee, but he lost all our admiration when we saw him turning just as green as Fatty Schwartz.

Conversation centered around how soon we would be in combat . . . God, weren't we green.

Maui

On the 15th of December we arrived at

Pearl Harbor, ran off the Nassau, and were loaded on some light brown, twin-engined planes and taken to the magical, sex-less island of Maui. We immediately broke out our Hellcats and started training. Whenever someone couldn't think of anything to say we started to train . . . some more.

Boredom came to live with us the next day, so we started a series of coming out parties for Maui. The social event of the season was the Christmas party held at the luxurious home of Steve, Rudolf and Stauff . . . complete with a tree trimmed with empty beer cans and Scott tissue. We took pictures of the event, but the confusion was far too much for the cameras.

On January 1, 1945 the squadron was split so that VBF (that's that strange bombing squadron always milling around in Corsairs) could be formed. Dobbie became our skipper, and Pinky once again our exec. We had 36 airplanes and 53 pilots and then they added to the confusion by thrusting three ground officers upon us. Toughie arrived in a jeep whose motor was knocking with a southern drawl. Bill Bahn was seen coming in the distance with a rocket in one hand and a bomb in the other . . . we all rushed to the O'Club to avoid him, but he followed us. Pagenstecher un-wrapped the ticker tape and claimed he was, much against his will, our new A.C.I. officer. We soon became accustomed to these people . . . and kept on training.

B.O.Q. 306 (the community playhouse . . . where we lived) was well on its way to fame . . . we rushed it to its peak between trips to Sweetie Wilson's (reputed to be Toughie's daughter). We never did solve the Mystery of the Vanishing Vehicles, but we do know that Hoppy traveled twenty miles quite often to visit his namesake Jess.

On February 10th Pagenstecher wormed his way back to the States and a person named Bob Camp came in loaded down with easels, brushes, palettes, and a frightening grin and said he would be our A.C.I. in his spare time. We said o.k. We didn't know what an A.C.I. was, anyway. But we knew he was supposed to come to squadron every once in a while . . . so we spent the next two months searching the surrounding marshes for his body. We finally found it behind a beer bottle, wedged in between a Yarp and a ravenous Polynesian.

In unchronological order we indulged in Luaus (that's Polynesian for milling around up front), movies, swimming, golf, tennis, and Molokini Rock. Brown eliminated everything but the golf and spent so much time on the links we thought he had been transferred. But he came down to the O'Club every once in a while to eat hamburgers and poi with the rest of us.

Ben Leland and Jack Morrison decided that barracks life was too uncomfortable and investigated the inside of a local bastille . . . with the help of the shore patrol . . . for wearing their flight jackets in the rain, they said. The bastille vomited them back to us . . . what could we do?

The monotonous monotony was broken up when a USO troupe (and perhaps LIFE) came to a VF-86 party. We didn't tar and feather them, but the rumors said that they went away stoned.

The next morning we found a group of boys on our doorstep. They finally admitted shyly that they were the Rover boys and were lost . . . this was the first time they had been out without their scoutmaster. So Andy took over and saw that they got to the beach everyday. By the end of our stay he had gotten most of them into the water up to their knees.

And the VBF continued to brag about their Corsair . . . they did manage to keep a few in the air . . . the rest were usually splashing around the runways.

Web Webber talked Wolf into helping him compose a book. They came up with a wild, disorganized thing called "The Song Book of the Wild Hares" or "How to Be the Life of the Party . . . If Everyone is Damned Liberal Minded."

And every time we went into Wailuku we found Russ Myers showing off his biceps in the local drug store . . . we won't even mention the fact that a young girl was jerking sodas.

And the monotonous monotony continued, relieved in the middle of February by a short shakedown on the Franklin, but we never got out of sight of Haleakala or out of range of "Sea Horse". And we trained and trained and memorized the luscious curves of Molokini.

The Tragedy of Molokini Rock
Molokini Rock is not rally a rock . . . not

rally. It is a symbolic perversion. Located in the ocean just off the island of Maui, T.H., to us it embodied the repulsiveness of leprosy, the agony of the rack, and the dread of a husband's unexpected appearance.

That Goddamned-Hawke was the direct means through The-Whip-Harlan through Dobbie through Cag through Only-The-Navy-Knows which kept us pounding the damned thing. Into its scaly body we put 21 million .50-calibres, 10,000 rockets, and 13,000 tons of bombs.

The last thing we did at night and the first thing in the morning was hit Molokini. Never a schedule appeared without its name in bold, black type. It finally got us. Holy Joe made up a song about it and we sang it for days to the tune of the "Little Brown Jug." Everyone came to the conclusion that the only reason we didn't take it was that Bill Bahn must have given us faulty armament and that the marines wouldn't cooperate.

. . . And so it still stands . . . and probably always will . . . and in its scarred old heart there will always be a soft place for Fighting 86.

Crossing the Bar

On March 1 after singing "Farewell to Maui" for 47 hours straight (we finally ran out of beer), Jim Lansing and his Bat boys, Bart, Lowrie, and Brownie, packed up the gear again. Toughie was in a complete dither, demanding a separate truck to carry his six file folders. The gear, Corps de Lansing, Toughie, Bahn, and Crampo were put aboard the Stinky Maru, a snappy inter-island scow. Ham and his serenaders came down to the pier and sang Aloha as the ship struck her ugly bow toward Pearl. The sea was heavy and Jim and Bill resorted to some very pleasant mal-de-mer medicine called Dr. Schenley's Ebony Label . . . which completely eased the turbulence.

On March 2 the pilots left for Pearl on the same brown twin-engined planes; this time they noticed a white star on the fuselage. Upon arriving at Ford Island there was the normal confusion . . . everybody wanted to go to town once more. They stayed . . . went aboard the Intrepid . . . just out from

the States after repairing her 67th torpedo hit. We were guest of Air Group 10 for transportation to the forward area and our own ship.

Aboard the Intrepid

We sailed on March 3. Air Group 10 was very hospitable . . . and saw to it that our cots were placed in the noisiest and busiest passageways . . . ensigns slept on top of lockers. Fatty Myers asked where the head was after five days at sea; he thought he might have to use it in a day or so. Grampa Datte and Andy were beaten in the pea-nuckle game each night, Kelt started his expoundation on raising frogs, and Bahn picked up 55 smackers as a guest of VBF 10 in a poker festival.

There was nothing to do but listen to Camp mumble some jumble about the Nips in his briefing and attend an occasional squadron meeting . . . if they could find you . . . the sack muster was the thing. Myers finally found the head and Jones found a ship's officer who was foolish enough to argue with him about the last election. We gathered on the bridge every time Air Group 10 flew and criticized and criticized. Everyone in 86 thought 86 was a helluva lot better. We were nearing the fleet anchorage . . . all hands were normally apprehensive.

Arrival in Ulithi and Boarding of the Wasp

On March 13, in the splendor of a cool tropical sunrise, we entered the beautiful atoll of Ulithi. We were soon routed out of the tranquility of the sack, piled with, and like, our gear in a floating hand-ball court, and sent on our way to find the Wasp . . . which was going to be our new home.

No one knew where it was so we headed in a general heads-up direction, explored the Atoll and all the ships, finally came to the battle-scarred Wasp. We were greeted with great pleasure in the following manner.

"Ahoy, Wasp."

"Ahoy, boat."

"We're 86. The new Air Group."

"Well get your goddamned gear aboard as fast as you can and get the hell out of the way."

Since a gangway would be too easy they lowered a cargo net and hoisted us aboard in groups of eight people and twenty-one boxes. We were soon forgotten but our boxes gurgled so fascinatingly that they dropped one onto the deck from a height of twenty feet. It was Dobbie's and they found out about the gurgles.

When we had stopped discussing the ape-like characteristics which Grampa Datte had displayed on the net we came to find out that E. T. Mort was missing. We didn't worry much, ensigns always turn up. He did later that afternoon and explained, we all thought it a good enough reason, that he had been so engrossed in a game of chess that he hadn't gotten the word.

And we tumbled off to start the mad scramble for rooms.

Aboard the Wasp

On March 14 we left Ulithi headed for combat at last . . . destination unknown. There was another mad scramble for rooms and everyone except Cag and his staff were dissatisfied with the assignments which were made by Cag and his staff. The room boys were really thirsty so they cut open most of our bags and took our whiskey as any thirsty man would do. We loused up the flight operations for a couple of days and strained Goodyear's tire production with many, repeat, many blowouts on landings.

Scholl went into the drink trying to scoop up a flying fish and was picked up by a minesweeper which ultimately delivered him back to us via Suez and the Black Sea. Vannatta and Taylor couldn't get together on the catapult signals and Van did two swell jack-knifes into the sea. Lowrie smeared a barrier and we were looking better every day.

We went into combat AT LAST and found Kyushu easier than Molokini. The Nips couldn't take a joke and smacked us with a bomb the second day out (they should have hit us; we were so close, we were sending in our laundry). However, we still operated. The seriousness of the war was brought much closer to all of us as we lowered many of our shipmates into the deep.

We started back to Ulithi for repairs and we wondered if we were to spend three more sexless months on some rock.

Back to Ulithi and Operating off Faleolap Island

On March 24 we arrived back at Ulithi, preceded by twelve planes which were land-based on Faleolap, part of the Ulithi chain, until we left. The rest of us stayed on the ship.

On March 25 Ensign Ralph S. Webber was reported missing in action after a flight to Yap Island, a nearby Jap garrison.

When the boys finally came back from Faleolap, they amazed us with the following stories. Hoppy and Christy set a speed record for the two mile track around the island. Cuth led the line of Ensigns who immediately began to draw jungle gear. Rich lauded the praises of the late O' club hours and Barron found a native that could talk louder than he could. Of course, Sam Trycinski just generally milled around the island.

We learned one morning that three of the squadron men were under suspicion for conspiracy to blow up the number three elevator so the ship would be sure to go back to the states. And the rumors began flying better than the Hellcats again.

The Saga of Mog Mog

Geographically speaking, Mog Mog is an island in the Ulithi Atoll of the Caroline Islands. Historically speaking, it was discovered in 1212 by Nafor the Great and rediscovered in 1213 by Horace the Horrible. In 1414 it was settled by the Arf-Arf Indians for the purpose of propagation. In 1515 it was abandoned on the belief that it made all female children under four infertile. In 1616 it was re-inhabited by a Professor UrSerNay who went there to study the synthetic rubber properties of the decayed wisdom tooth. In 1717 his descendants abandoned it in search of a fifty gallon gas coupon. The U. S. took it from a tribe of Japs with very little effort in 1944.

The name Mog Mog comes from the curious sound Navy field shoes make walking on empty beer cans.

We were sent there for a day to go through the Mog Mog ordeal, a thing greater than the one with fire and water. This was to be one of our great battle tests.

We left the WASP in a Higgins Boat (he has a big ferry system in the Pacific) and then transferred to an LCI (another kind of boat) where we had a refreshing tropical shower which completely drenched us. Finally we got into another boat (which I guess

belonged to Higgins, also) and gained the beach in another refreshing tropical shower.

We checked our knives and .38s (Grover kept a concealed weapon) with the local Shore Patrol, studied the flora and fauna for ten seconds, became bored and headed for the O' club to look at the funny people and to start the ordeal in earnest.

Explanation of the ordeal . . . its primary requisite is speed. The speed must be attained in a cycle in this order (a) run for beer, (b) talk and drink the beer, (c) sing and drink the beer, (d) pee and drink the beer, (e) fight and drink the beer . . . and then run for more beer to start the cycle again.

Fighting Eighty Six, adapting itself easily, went through the Ordeal (authorities said) with more glory than any other squadron has ever done. A new record was set in each part and a stupefying record was set for the whole.

Among the winners were Rack Morton for singing the beer, Whitey for running for and fighting the beer, Ham and AkAk for talking the beer, and Holy Joe for swimming the beer the last fifty yards to the WASP.

After completion of the trial we found that the cycle had worked. Everyone was laid

carefully into the Higgins Boat and kept off that big thing up front that they land on beaches with (called technically, That Big Thing Up Front). We proceeded south southeast and the WASP came into sight.

We were wet. We were tired. We were beered. But, we were proud. We had gained the comparative safety of the Ward room and we gave a lusty cheer for Mog Mog Island . . . we had survived the Ordeal.

Back to Pearl

The Ship Repair Officer at Ulithi took a seventh look at the hole in the WASP and muttered, "Big, isn't it?" At any rate he couldn't fix it because of some labor trouble he was having or something and we headed toward Pearl Harbor. We were now convinced that they were dusting off the mat at Maui for our return and that the Navy didn't really intend for us to have a ship anyway.

Ensign Richard Gould was lost on March 28 while making his cross leg approach to the carrier.

We started a long list of Flight Deck Parade Rehearsals. We were mustered in ranks, in the nude, and standing on our heads to see how we would look for our

entry into Pearl—the ship has been in combat for over a year.

Dilemma at Pearl Harbor or . . . Milling Around Up Front

We arrived at Pearl on the third of April. We were mustered on the deck in uniform and the WAVES sang ALOHA (of course, Smith whistled at them) as we tied up alongside Ford Island. We were told to pack up again . . . yep, you guessed it, we were going back to Maui to await the ship. Morale was at an all time low. Lansing had Bart pack up the squadron gear again and they headed for Maui in a large, brown, twin-engined plane.

Recognizing the utter fatigue of the pilots, ComAirPac decided to give them all a couple days rest at the Navy Rest Home (one week in that joint and you really need a rest). Holderman's and Ham's divisions, starring O'Bryan in his swimming trunks and the Gold Dust Twins, Clem and Bucket, already started toward the Home, via Trader Vic's, when the uproarous news came that we were going back to the states with the ship. We quickly retrieved Lansing's safari and hid in the bilges so that they couldn't change their minds about sending us home.

Amid martial music and flying a "going home pennant," we slid out of the harbor toward the states. We were at attention in Slattery's 689th Flight Deck Parade and we didn't mind it a damned bit.

Trip to the States . . . Arrival in Seattle

An albatross followed us all the way across the Pacific. We entered Puget Sound on the morning of the eleventh and the United States looked at its best. Everyone was milling about the deck. The Rover boys were eager to get home to some kind of a Boy Scout jamboree. O. E. Myers and Mets-calfe said "Navy, youse is a good boy" in unison. Jack Morrison had to go all of twenty miles to his home, and was there and had a baby before the echo of the anchor drop left the sound.

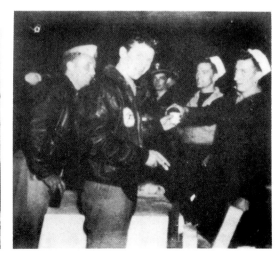

The Seattle Ferry came alongside and they slid us and our bags down a coal chute into the boat where some guy lifted you up and at the same time extracted a half buck from your jeans. Navy trucks picked us up and delivered us to Sands Point, a really classy air station, and the homecoming parties began. The Seattle staff arranged everything for the homecoming veterans (well, we were in action for two days). Some cute dollies were recruited from the U. of Wash. for the dance and we reestablished in our minds that the white woman was here to stay.

The party went well into the night. Stauff went to sleep in his blues alone. Pinky waited until everybody got stoned and then started to take up various collections . . . two dollars for laundry . . . five for whiskey . . . three to send his son to college.

Then we got those mathematical travel orders and there was a mad scramble for airline tickets. The Whip had especially good luck in obtaining a ticket, although it was not without some effort on his part. By Saturday the fourteenth, Fighting 86 had been assimilated into the U. S. . . . all except Lansing and T. R. who were going on a Yarp expedition on the West Coast.

Leave, Alameda, On to Arcata
The leave was wonderful . . . we didn't

have to write letters and we didn't have to hold our noses when we ate eggs.

We returned to Alameda by the 28th, at least most of us did. There were many trips to Frisco for many reasons . . . Grover was taking a complete course in Chinese in some Chop Suey joint . . . Lansing was joining the spook of the month club . . . Hawke was visiting maternity hospitals wondering how people had babies.

On May 1 everyone who had a car started for Arcata . . . these were the married people, who are always getting the breaks . . . and that isn't all. On May 3 the hard workers flew to Arcata in brand new F6F-5's . . . what a change. Upon arrival in Arcata there was a mad scramble for tourist cottages, rooms, the newest books on sex, and the Cinnabar.

Arcata

Arcata is a beautiful small base. The lieutenants were assigned rooms in the B.O.Q. and the ensigns slept in tents . . . the jaygees, good operators, had rooms in town. The base had a built in fog bank and therefore was ideal for an airfield. Fog . . . fog . . . fog . . . fog . . . fog . . . which when translated reads . . . sack . . . sack . . . scotch . . . sack. It was very nice, and very attractive. The Captain had a wife who liked Manhattans for breakfast, so he had 'em too. The Captain also had a daughter who almost married all of the Rover Boys, Cuth, and Gunn at the same

time. There were many parties, and we had an alternate ready room in the Tropics in nearby Arcata.

In Eureka there was the DeLuxe Club, Log Cabin, Tiny's, Double A, Walt's, Tony Baronti's and the Cinnabar. The Sinbar was just as its name implies. The married men hunted homes, discussed ration points, went to wrestling matches with their wives and played house. The single men just played house. There was a picnic, a big picnic. There were many beers, hot dogs, hamburgers and girls . . . some married and some trying. Toughie got bored and begged to be pulled around on a nearby portable fire truck, so we pulled him around. Whitey made Earthquakes, of course. By midnite we had run out of beer and we found that distilled Redwood juice was not intoxicating, so we went home.

There were many tail chases, some legitimate. We gave a big air show in connection with the Seventh War Loan and Stauff flew a record reaking seven minute hop. We celebrated the German surrender . . . we already had a party planned for that nite, so the surrender made it legal. After all of this we returned to Alameda—the Stinger was ready.

Back to Alameda and the WASP

Kaiser had done it again . . . the WASP was ready to go. While we waited . . . Frisco again, over and over . . . Swimming in the

Alameda O' club pool where Cisco Baker rippled his muscles between hot dogs and beer. Rack Morton and Wolf missed a muster. The luckies were presented with awards in a big impressive ceremony.

Westward Ho on July 13. Weeping and wailing wives on the docks. Fatigued spouses and hung-over bachelors on the fan-tail. Mist-laden San Francisco vanished under the Golden Gate. Would we really be back by '48? And the married men went below and read a book and the single men slept.

Flying began the next day, the beginning of our beautiful, eternal attacks on the SPAR. Hot JayBee was the only happy guy aboard, he could start his conversation of energy again. The rest of us were looking way ahead to when we would be coming home again.

Barber's Point

After knocking off 72 spars and using up all of the ship's scars and waterfills, we were allowed to pull into Pearl—again. The planes were flown ahead to Barber's and the overflow proceeded on foot to the tune of Wilbur's Whip. After landing at Barbers, the pilots rushed to the O' Club. There were two weeks of sunning, swimming, beering and getting healthy. We were billeted right alongside the WAVES barracks and, of course, the VBF jokers tried to pull their rank on the girls. In fact the VBF became a general nuisance all over the place. They tried to destroy the barracks that the Captain was saving to sell the natives after the war and were ultimately restricted as they should have been from the start. There was another short shakedown on the WASP off Kaena Point and we were really hot . . . we said. There was the Snack Shack where you met your best drunken friends and the Stag Club, a Navy sponsored opium den.

We all shopped for provisions to take aboard the ship and the time was drawing short. Kurfis, George and Bellinger cried because they had really become fond of Bar-

ber's. Farmer and Lautz were still optimistic and hunted right up to the last minute. The night fighters had swapped Hunter for some character named Rothenberg . . . Ratberger, or something. Barbers also gave us a new division called Hill's Hotrocks, which consisted of Hill, Lawton, Drew, Sargent and Schuptar.

There were a couple more parties and one more luau on the beach. Pinky got orders to Air Group 26 and flew to Hilo. We left Barbers on July 10th for the WASP. There was a dandy Ship's Officer—Air Group Officer Party at The Tennis Club which bid farewell to Slattery and Hello to Jumpin' Joe Clifton.

Our Second Trip Westward

We departed Pearl for the forward area on July 11th with a hope that this cruise would be more successful than the previous one. Strangely enough, everyone was aboard when the ship upped anchor. Most of us had spent a rather quiet evening at the Tennis Club the nite before. We smacked Wake

Island on the way out and arrived at Eniwetok on the nineteenth. The Air Group went ashore in a boat (Higgins, of course). It was a beautiful beach and Baker added to the local color by rippling his muscles while parading up and down the sand.

Rothenberg and his owls were out in the sun for the first time in a year . . . the room boys insisted on airing the night fighter's mattresses. The beach was the best that we had ever visited. The O' Club was nearby and served beer, sardine sandwiches, sardine sandwiches and beer. At 1600 the local Prohibition Agent hit the sack and then they broke out the Three Feathers, that rare old Kentucky Bourbon. The bar was as jammed as Macy's on dollar day. However everyone managed to get his share and then some. Higgins called for us at dusk and the blind led the blind down to the sea in ships. We steered east northeast and half the passengers swam the last fifty yards to the Wasp in complete uniform, of course. Everyone fell down the ladder into the wardroom and then

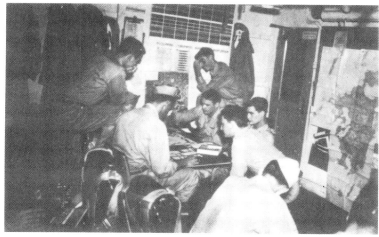

assembled, demanding food and creating a scene that only Steinbeck could describe.

We went north to join the Third Fleet the next morning, gayly bombing the spar en route. Halsey had been reported alongside the Empire and the general attitude began to be a bit more serious. One of the more memorable scenes was the passing of Iwo Jima . . . everyone was up on deck to look at the tiny island where so many gallant Americans had given their lives. Mount Suribachi seemed to stand out as a memorial to the great sacrifice that had been made there.

We went into action on July 26 and stopped on the morning of August 15, with a full deck load of planes waiting to take off. The peace negotiations continued for the next two weeks and we patrolled the empire. Somebody reported a typhoon nearby so we immediately headed into it . . . the Admiral was hot and wanted to cool off. The winds got up to around ninety knots and promptly

blew the bow off . . . one of the lady welders at Quincy had welded her lunch box in as a support beam. The Admiral said that he had flown off the No. 2 turret of the old Pennsylvania, so we too could fly from a short runway. That - Goddamned - Hawke was elected to test the catapult, and much to the dismay of his friend . . . made it.

Patrol flights were started over the Empire and everybody wanted to fly . . . there was no flak. Russ Myers, on a photo hop, was the first pilot to locate the prisoner of war camp in the Nagoya area. The camp was photographed and provisions were dropped that afternoon. It was one of the most touching and impressive scenes of the war.

We flew off the drooping bow until Aug. . . when we were relieved by the Lexington and started for Eniwetok, Pearl Harbor and —home.

C'est finis

ENIWETOK, MARSHALL ISLANDS, AUG. 5, 1945

BOMBING-FIGHTING SQUADRON

EIGHTY-SIX

SQUADRON VBF-86

Bottom Row (sitting on deck) (left to right):

Lt. R. M. Telfair, Lt. Com. A. H. Chadwick, Lt. Com. R. S. Auchincloss, Ens. T. J. Gossman, Lt. (jg) J. C. Irwin, Ens. L. B. Connell, Ens. M. E. Massey, Lt. (jg) H. L. Proctor, Lt. (jg) R. V. Raehn, Lt. F. C. Ford, Lt. (jg) G. H. Winslow, Lt. E. J. Ruane, Lt. (jg) R. L. McGrew.

Second Row (kneeling):

Ens. J. R. Dillingham, Lt. (jg) R. T. Wagner, Lt. (jg) F. L. Knight, Ens. E. R. Swan, Lt. (jg) H. R. Cheuvront, Lt. (jg) E. C. Schuler, Lt. (jg) W. G. Whisler, Lt. (jg) M. L. Flint, Ens. G. D. Cayton, Lt. E. E. Graf, Lt. (jg) R. F. Wear, Lt. (jg) W. E. Bridwell.

Third Row (sitting):

Lt. W. R. Bell, Lt. (jg) L. Wernèr, Ens. M. H. Marriott, Ens. R. E. Kennedy, Lt. (jg) J. F. Rapp, Lieut. Com. H. E. Tennes, commanding; Lt. Com. J. R. Thomson, Lt. (jg) J. E. Ivy, Ens. W. B. Hudson, Ens. L. E. Smitley, Lt. R. S. Berton, Lt. (jg) J. S. Qualley, Lt. (jg) J. T. Milnes.

Fourth Row (standing):

Lt. (jg) W. S. Stevenson, Ens. F. J. O'Malley, Lt. (jg) B. L. Fugal, Ens. R. J. Schwartz, Ens. T. W. Barnes, Ens. K. L. Turk, Ens. W. R. Bartling, Lt. (jg) T. W. Elliott, Lt. E. K. Holmberg, Lt. L. A. Edmonston, Lt. (jg) L. G. Gifford, Lt. (jg) J. W. Christy, Lt. (jg) D. W. Connell.

Top Row (standing):

Lt. (jg) L. C. Behling, Lt. (jg) W. E. Russell, Ens. B. A. Sample, Lt. (jg) W. B. Haynes, Lt. C. W. Alford, Lt. (jg) E. L. McNett, Lt. (jg) H. R. Hanson, Lt. B. Y. Weber, Lt. (jg) L. Morris, Lt. (jg) T. D. Brown. *In Cockpit:* Lt. (jg) E. D. Swinden.

LIEUTENANT COMMANDER HORACE EDWARD TENNES
COMMANDING OFFICER
FIGHTING BOMBING SQUADRON EIGHTY-SIX

LIEUTENANT COMMANDNER HORACE EDWARD TENNES, commanding officer of VBF-86, entered flight training with one of the early reserve classes at Pensacola, in 1937. Receiving his wings in 1938, he first went to sea as an aviation cadet, assigned to Fighting Five aboard the Yorktown. Transferred to Fighting Squadron Six, he spent three years on the Enterprise before returning to shore duty as an ACTG fighter tactics instructor. The next two years were spent waving paddles as a Landing Signal Officer. Early in 1944 he became the executive officer of Fighting Squadron 81, in which capacity he served until assuming command of the original fighter squadron in Air Group 86. With the formation of a fighter-bomber squadron, he was relieved of his duties in Fighting 86 to become skipper of his present squadron. Active in soaring circles, his intense interest in aviation has made him versatile as well as proficient in the leading of the squadron.

LIEUTENANT COMMANDER JAMES R. THOMSON
EXECUTIVE OFFICER
FIGHTING BOMBING SQUADRON EIGHTY-SIX

Oh! I have slipped the surly bonds of Earth
    And danced the skies on laughter-silvered wings;
Sunward I've climbed, and joined the tumbling mirth
    Of sun-split clouds, and done a hundred things
You have not dreamed of—wheeled and soared and swung
    High in the sunlit silence. Hov'ring there,
I've chased the shouting wind along, and flung
    My eager craft through footless halls of air. . . .

Up, up the long, delirious, burning blue
    I've topped the wind-swept heights with easy grace,
Where never lark, or even eagle flew—
    And, while with silent, lifting mind I've trod
The high untrespassed sanctity of space,
    Put out my hand and touched the face of God.

                               "High Flight" *by John Gillespie Magee, Jr.*

AUCHINCLOSS, Richard Salstonstall
Born: November 15, 1909
School: St. Paul's School, Concord, N. H.
    Yale University
Trained at: NAS Quonset Pt.
Previous Station: NAS Miami
Married
Address: RFD No. 1, Malvern, Pa.

With the bong-bong-bong of the general alarm we present the fleet, long-legged apparition of our beloved AUK (that rare old bird), swishing through the office and ready room with the speed of light only to find that his equally nimble conferees, Chad and Burton, have just beaten him to the catwalk. When SECURE is sounded, Auch doffs his tin chapeau, Mae West, Gas Mask, flash light, shark knife and first aid kit—to resume his talk at the mike. The aristocratic country squire from Paoli, Pennsylvania is at his best when briefing on Friendly Natives. In giving these talks, AUK frequently solicits the aid of Elliott in illustrating the high points. When the attacks cease and the orders of his Field Marshall subside from a roar to a shout, AUK retires to that wonderful sack. Lying prone, he dreams leisurely of the good days to come—testing paper bags by blowing them up and popping them, his job at the Betner Bag Co. He contemplates, probably in vain, presenting his three spirited young sons with a sister. Having absorbed a lot of salt in the Navy, he plans to run his household like a ship. There will be a "Plan of the Day," and when one of his charges err, Captain's Mast will be held. So if you visit him, don't look askance if you see young Charlie giving the house a good sweep-down fore and aft, and emptying out all spit kits.

CHADWICK, Arthur Henry
Born: July 12, 1911
School: Wesleyan Univ. and
    Univ. of Wisconsin
Trained at: NAS Quonset Pt. and
    NAS Norfolk
Previous Squadron: Hedron 9-2
Married
Address: Livingston Street, Westbury, N. Y.

ARTHUR H., alias A. "DUCHIN" Chadwick, alias "G. Q. CHADWICK." While not under contract in the Persian Room, Chad may be found entertaining the assembled throng in his brilliant manner either upon the harpsichord in the Wardroom or through the medium of the "pipes" on the Hangar Deck. We all remember how his rendition of "Minnie the Moocher" and other assorted numbers helped revive flagging spirits following our March 19 experience with the "Divine Winds" and "Mother Ocean." Suffice it to say, his versatility is so great that be it jam session or accompanying Catholic, Protestant, Jewish, Mennonite and Latter Day Saints services, he's right in there pitching. In a more serious vein, Chad's squadron activities as Administrative Officer are just as varied as his musical ones. They run the gamut from fitness reports and bunk assignments to delivery of his famous lecture on "The Carrier approach and the HAPPY-ASS Circle." Chad, perforce, has become a confirmed traveler, having absorbed the varied delights of Maui by the Sea, drunk the curative waters of Mog Mog, enjoyed the off season at One Biga Wan and sunned at lush Eniwetok. However, in spite of all this, we sense he'll not be adverse to returning to wife, young son and job. To him we give many "Haleakalas."

ALFORD, Colin Wilson
Born: April 6, 1919
School: Okla. Poly. Tech.
Ark. Poly. Tech.
Trained at: Corpus Christi
Previous Squadron: VS-68
Married
Address: Corn, Okla.

Another Indian fighting "Okie" out to add a few scalps to his belt, AL has chased the Meat-ball League from the Solomons to the shores of Nippon. With the vanquishing of the Rising Sun, he decided to gamble with his remaining time afloat in the cultivation and mustering of a facial fur piece, which has defied all urgings to blossom. Midnight poker games stir his imagination to extremes, with dreams of new and greater condiments brewed up from behind his local drug counter—"prescriptions filled with either an olive or orange peel." Our flying pharmacist revels in the joys of chasing wild geese, thereby giving him the excuse of sowing wild oats, and he's off to reap the wild wind! AL's ready smile sparkled many a dull day, though after his eighty-sixth CAP he was heard to whistle thrice before passing a quick grin at the Flight Department. This is the lad whose battle cry has long been "Smile boys, that's the style." Just before we said au revoir to our planes at Eniwetok, Al was seen furtively siphoning the contents of the water injection system to sell over the perfume bar at $10.00 per ounce.

ANDERSON, Arthur William
Born: March 3, 1924
School: Niles Central High
Trained at: Corpus Christi
Previous Squadron: VB-86
Address: 742 Oak Street
Niles, Mich.

ANDY drew more enjoyment from mixing with the crowd than anyone else in the squadron. He possessed that light-hearted nature that one associates with more carefree days, rather than with times of strife and the fighting of wars. A vivid imagination enabled him to see through to a logical conclusion the more undesirable situations of life that so often confront us all. He took to flying easily, being the first member of his flight training class to solo, and this inherent trait enabled him to quickly adapt himself to fighter planes, after spending months as a dive-bomber pilot. For him, life was vital, and he lived it to the fullest extent, giving in return a genial and affectionate personality.

BARNES, Thomas William
Born: July 29, 1924
School: Lake Worth High School
Trained at: Corpus Christi
Address: Lake Worth, Fla.

This fierce Seminole warrior has come a long way since he set out to beat his path through the smoke and flame of the Everglades to the side of his first trainer. Eager to wedge his tomahawk into the Rising Sun, the quest has led him along a strange and varied path. Roosting on the overhead satisfies his more deep-rooted yearnings, and when called down from his lofty perch, he's immediately off to the ready room to grind his ax, awaiting his turn to be catapulted into the fray. Known as the "all-around wingman," BARNEY has looked forward and upward at more division leaders than you can shake a stick at; but any way you look at it, variety is the spice of life. Swooping in and around the task force has left him well versed in the art of picking out the right carrier—"All I do is take a drift sight over the top of my left knee, grope like hell, and hope there's another plane to join up on."

BARTLING, William Arthur
Born: March 20, 1923
School: Drury College
Trained at: Corpus Christi
Married
Address: Springfield, Mo.

If there was ever anyone with an indomitable spirit it was BART. He just would not be licked at anything. Woe betide the man that bested him a contest, from dog-fighting to billiards, because Bart would show him no peace until he was thoroughly beaten. This keen, competitive nature of Bart's made him one of our best fighter pilots, and earned for him the highest respects of his squadron mates. He lived strenuously and zestfully, expecting and giving the very best in life.

BARTLING, William Robert
Born: October 3, 1924
School: Kansas City Jr. College
Trained at: Corpus Christi
Married
Address: 1037 Ella Ave.
　　Kansas City, Kan.

When the dust had settled we discovered a handsome young sunflower on the squadron stoop. This was BART, whose timely arrival bolstered the ranks of our rapidly evaporating youth, and caused an uneasy stir among our more senile members. The squadron had a new baby, an heir apparent, and VBF remained on the active list a while longer. He has committed no heinous aerial crimes worth mentioning in this erstwhile White Paper, and while not laying claim to the dubious fame of having fired the last shot of the war, he never misses the last one in the JOB. Needless to say, his mellow fellow wingmen are a bit chagrined to find that Bart's case of pineapple juice contained *just that*.

BEHLING, Leroy Clarence
Born: June 19, 1920
School: Oshkosh Business College
Trained at: Corpus Christi
Married
Address: Caroline, Wisconsin

REDDY TEDDY's jump from Wildcats to Corsairs was not nearly as sensational at his near leap while soaring over the sparkling atoll of Wake Island. Our dashing aerialist hung poised for his rocket run, when a shower of fabric and balsam brought indications of glad tidings from the hostile coast-watchers. All hands reached for their mikes to inform him of his predicament. Thereupon, Red wafted the now immemorable words over the ether—"This is Red— Behling out!" For this gem he was awarded the Gilded Green Garter. Red is perfectly content either in the lush greenery of an oasis, or the parched earth of Twenty-Nine Palms, where he parted the sands and made himself at home, earning the title of the Desert Fox. While there entrenched and content to observe the wars from a sand dune, Red's mood was rudely and prematurely disturbed by the call of the carriers and the Tokyo Air Races.

BELL, William Rooney
Born: December 6, 1920
School: NYS Maritime Academy
Trained at: Pensacola, Fla.
Previous Squadron: Inst. Sanford
Married
Address: 307 7th St.
　　Watkins Glen, N. Y.

Here is the old and new, a product of the old steam Navy combined with combat experience gained in the flying navy. DING DONG's early training in the Merchant Marine on "banana boats" and as an Ensign in the Atlantic Fleet on the USS ALCOR plying between Norfolk and Norfolk (no kidding) has given us an Engineering Officer of a steam. His big weakness was navy nurses and we knew he and his big green Oldsmobile would trap one sooner or later. It happened in Atlantic City (of Hurricane Club Fame) when we opened our arms and admitted Ruth to our growing squadron family. Ding learned the hard way that the Uniform of the Day was Oilskins—at the Hurricane Club. While at sea, Ding's tennis game has suffered, but his acey-ducey has rapidly improved to the point where he can occasionally trounce some of the younger ensigns. With his wife and protege safely tucked away in East Jordan, which is just across the River Jordan from West Jordan, Ding at the helm of his division has become the scourge of all Jap "tin cans."

BERTON, Robert Sylvester
Born: February 3, 1917
School: Univ. of Oklahoma
Trained at: Corpus Christi
Previous Squadron: Inst. Corpus Christi
Married
Address: Cushing, Okla.

"Hmmmmm? Well wat'd ya do with the last pair I gave ya?" . . . presenting Grandmaw, curator of our Supply and Demand Department. Through his hands and thence into oblivion have passed most of the Navy's vast stock of obsolete inner tubes, skipping ropes, hot water bottles and the like. It's just like Christmas to us kids when Grandmaw hauls out the cruise boxes and hollers, "Hey, fellers . . . how many want lace for their helmets?" Bert has acquired so many boxes he's decided it's far simpler to go USN than face an inventory this late in the game. Besides, he has a passion for acey ducey, and Big Ed's been telling him that this would be a good chance to learn how to play. Then there's Sally . . . she could learn to balance a fruit basket on her head while the old man is off on his Pago Pago milk run . . . and we *know* she can't do that now. But, without jest, we're glad to see the Navy get such a conscientious worker and a swell guy. He has been an integral part of our squadron from the start.

BRIDWELL, William Ernest, Jr.
Born: April 5, 1923
School: Bedford High School
Trained at: Pensacola
Address: 913 13th Street
　　　　Bedford, Ind.

BRID came to us as we started out on our third syllabus at Maui, and proceeded to amuse himself right off with a mixture of pineapple and the product of Chance-Vought. This blend proving effective, any afternoon would find him bathing his brow in the cool Pacific, seeking deliverance from his new found stimulant. Once freed from the "rock," Brid threw himself into carrier life with a vigor heretofore unknown. In his zeal to be up and away, he even taxied over the side, exclaiming—"Look, no hands." Possessing the sauciest flying suit in Bull Halsey's Air Show, a jaunty combination of ballet tights and armored vest, he was elected fashion editor of "Flat-Top Fashions," *head* magazine of the submarine service. Performing in the air races as the Exec's other half, Brid logged many a carrier take-off and landing (minus one), and his hair-raising tales of airborne blood and thunder we know will never grow dim when he's underway in the great U.S.S. Outside.

BROWN, Thomas David
Born: September 16, 1922
School: Citadel College
Trained at: Pensacola
Previous Squadron: VF-86
Married
Address: 52 Highland Ave.
　　　　Port Washington, N. Y.

Walking like he's bucking a high wind "T.D." usually arrives in the Ready-Room bemoaning the cruel fate that is about to thrust him into the air for the umpteenth time. A graduate of Sanford's Lost Pilot Institution, he's kept his log book in the archives of the air-group since the green years of 1944, and throughout our Nomadic wanderings has been involved in the hour, per hour, per hour rat race ever since. This is the lad that had the flight department by the ears for nigh onto a year and like clockwork would slip away to New York before "group gropes" on missions d'amour, till finally the issue was put over amid leaps and cheers. Flight schedules have an invigorating effect on him, shouts of, "that kind of stuff just don't go," lay lightly on the "Stump's" ears as "T.D." learns of the latest chastisement in store for him, in the airborne orgies. "Eee-nuff is Eeee-nuff!"

CABRIALS, Sylvan Anthony, Jr.
Born: July 20, 1922
School: Corpus Christi High School
Trained at: Corpus Christi
Address: 102 Adams Drive
   Corpus Christi, Tex.

BUCK joined the squadron when it formed at Kahului. That easy Texas drawl and deadly cue-stick were quickly associated with Little Buck on those long evenings around the table. He always said that you couldn't beat a man built for the game, and proved it. A fine athlete and a good flier, he never refused any request made of him, nor failed to follow through on an assigned job. His wit and dead pan innuendoes were a constant source of pleasure to us all, and his presence was vital at our gatherings. Little Buck's friendship and loyalty have been carried with us throughout our battles and we carry them onward into the future.

CAYTON, Gilbert Darrell
Born: November 21, 1921
School: Unidis High School
Trained at: Corpus Christi
Married
Address: 1501 Oak Street
   Toledo, Ohio

This towhead from Toledo has the unrivaled distinction of being the last man to dive on the target and the first one in the rendezvous circle; a feat of speed comparable only to the Chad, Auch, Burton (yeoman) race for the door when G.Q. is sounded. As secretary of the ill-famed wingman's club, his capabilities were really put to test when these lads of the fourth form held a party celebrating the cessation of hostilities—for the third time in as many days; "CAYT" had the tedious task of keeping the minutes—and did same with unparalleled proficiency. He excels on the links, and holds the record at the Modesto Country Club—a par-shattering 176 for nine entire holes. What everyone will remember most about Darrell were those death-defying screeches that came forth from his sack at Barber's Point. Two A.M. and all are sleeping well when suddenly—"Yeeeeeooooowwwww." He claims it was only a black cat.

CHEUVRONT, Harlan Ross
Born: November 5, 1921
School: Okla. Univ.
Trained at: Pensacola
Previous Squadron: Inst. Sanford
Address: 902 Douglas
    Ardmore, Okla.

The better part of "SHAKY'S" life has been spent in the air. Before joining up, he used to instruct future Army kadoodlers in the rudiments of aviation . . . He noted with keen interest the progress that they were making and immediately enlisted in the Navy. However, his previous work paid dividends for when he finished with a gunnery sleeve it closely resembled a piece of Swiss cheese. One day at Maui we all chipped in and bought a case of beer apiece, the idea of the undertaking being to have a cold tankard of the nut-brown brew always on hand. Chev had it all figured out where some of those who hadn't kicked in would try to muzzle out a few free bottles, so he went to work immediately and proceeded to knock over all of his twenty-four in one sitting. Shaky really gets the St. Vitus trot when Morris and Gifford start to demonstrate their match trick with his un-fireproofed gunnery communiques. His dope on rocket switches was the hottest we've ever seen, while it lasted. Exhibiting that Svengalli gleam he leapt to his feet crying, "It was there two minutes ago, Skipper!"

CHRISTY, Joe Witter
Born: July 15, 1922
School: Pasadena Jr. College
Trained at: Pensacola
Married
Address: 411 No. Cloverly
    Temple City, Calif.

EL CHRISTO, a character who has fast become synonomous with "sack and mattress," is our claim for laziest naval aviator west of Pensacola. Having taken the complete course of duty with the squadron, he has shuffled into more than enough cocktail lounges, till his blue eyes and burnished hair fast became landmarks. Tiring of this everlasting pace, he left the lads to haggle with the crones, and slipped away to marry a charming girl while at Atlantic City. At most any time of day, the tinkling of the telephone will bring oaths from the direction of this energetic youth's bunk, as the cry of "taxi pilots required," interrupts the never ending siesta. Minutes later, the flight deck is treated to the sight of a red thatched head, and pair of blinking eyes, emerging from the depths, as Joe greets fresh air. By these words ye shall know him—"Hell, tell 'em I'm not here!"

CONNELL, Daniel William
Born: June 24, 1922
School: Wauwatosa High School
Trained at: Pensacola
Previous Squadron: VB-86
Address: 6221 W. Lloyd
    Wauwatosa, Wis.

"No stuff (edited), you guys may think I'm kidding, but I'm tellin' you she was a damn nice girl!"—and DAN got up and slowly walked away. We saw this fugitive from Frenchman's Creek make his first successful approach, hit the barrier, and come back grinning like a Cheshire cat. Of course we *all* hated to leave the Snake Pit. Once with the Fleet, the Lick hastened to experiment with the potentialities of radio activity. The entire Pacific was his laboratory. "Hey, Christy! How do you hear me on Channel 8?—Channel 3?—ZB?—YE?? Is my antenna down far enough?—Listen to those Spider guys! Didja ever hear so much—get off the air for crieye!!—Wha-a-a-t? How many?—Hey, Joe, didya hear that? Jeez! There's a bunch 'a Gishies down here who—." And he's our Safety Equipment Officer. "Doc, I have a safe suggestion for the Asiatic Kit"—and Doc made the latest addition. Dan's future is all wrapped up in a set of "elite" golf clubs, a new car, and the National Open, so if your Chamber of Commerce is looking for a caddy master in 15 or 20 years—we suggest it consider that character chipping shots to the 19th at Wauwatosa.

CONNELL, Lafayette Berry
Born: March 4, 1922
School: Whigham High School
Trained at: Pensacola
Previous Squadron: VB-86
Address: Whigham, Ga.

L.B. won the unflagging idolatry of our LSO the day that he waited for the cut signal before diving for the deck. Few of us have ever seen this magnificent coup de grace executed on the platform for our benefit—but not old L.B., the Dilliard Delight. He's never too busy to extend this courtesy to another gentleman from Georgia. We don't like to be catty, but some of the Yankees in the J.O.B. claim that he intentionally slows up in the traffic circle just to see the LSO. Fantastic, isn't it? This up and coming cracker hails from another garden spot of the South, Grady County—"What? You-all mean you never heard O'Grady? . . . Why man . . ." And we're off . . . another gentleman fighting two wars at once. Not one of the original midwives of VBF-86, "L.B." has adapted himself graciously to it's program of blood, sweat and beers. For this he has received the Pabst Blue Ribbon with Cherry Rivet. So swing low, sweet chariot, and deliver this lad to his julep before the habid is rabid.

CREGER, Robert Charles
Born: May 8, 1924
School: Creston High School
Trained at: Corpus Christi
Married
Address: Alcena Apts.
    Creston, Iowa

As a member of Big Ed's team, BOB came to the squadron at Maui. His geniality and youthful exuberance gained him many new friends, and his athletic prowess, especially in basketball and softball, made him well known to all of us in a very short time. Bob loved adventure, and he loved a good time; whether exploring the nearby mountain, dining at the "O" Club or pitching a ball game, he was always the gayest one present and having the most fun. Forever willing to lend a hand, he was generous and thoughtful, making the most of every minute for himself and for his friends. His easy grin and good nature are unforgetable.

DILLINGHAM, James Richard
Born: October 27, 1922
School: I.S.L.A.
Trained at: Corpus Christi
Address: 1104 East High
    Colo. Springs, Colo.

J. Richard "DON JUAN" Dillingham hails from some chuckhouse in the wilds of the wild west. Next to being in the saddle of some airborne machine, his favorite spot is on the sway back of a Colorado mustang. When this gay caballero sets his sombrero there are few women who can resist his advances. Before joining us, Dick was very active in WCTU work—"We Can Tame Unicorns". Dick is notoriously noted for his party work—and that is not talking along political lines. For the better part of his stay in 86, he was standing by to either go fetch a plane for us, or to take away some decrepit old "Flying Dud". The day finally arrived when he completed his mission and from that day on, he has been stroking his chin and thinking of sin. Dick's burning ambition (after whiling away the best years of his life in the navy) is to become a desperado, and live in Cripple Creek in Colorado.

EDMONSTON, Lilburn Adkin
Born: December 26, 1916
School: Central College, Fayette, Mo.
Trained at: Corpus Christi
Previous Squadron: VF-34
Married
Address: New Franklin, Mo.

Arriving on the Maui scene with the persecuted look of a mother hen who has just seen her brood safely across Broadway at Forty Second, "BIG ED" proudly presented his combat team to the squadron. The Flight Office took an immediate interest in this novel pre-fabricated division, subjecting it to hours of observation and detailing two plane captains to assist in the log room. Big Ed just stoically sucked on his pipe and grunted to the "new boys" to move over. He was promoted to Safety Officer—in the field, you might say—when, above and way beyond the call of duty, he demonstrated that a Corsair could be safely brought to earth with the tail wheel retracted. Since then he has knocked off the personal end of it and has been plenty busy collecting Bureau Numbers and spelling our names right for BuAer. What's more,—and this ought to show the folks back in Missouri—he really knows what RUDM means. Unshackle that! Big Ed has also seen action with VF-34, but it was not until the final days of the War that a Jap tried to surround him. "Tally Ho! It's a Jill . . . no, it's a Myrt! (pause for 1400 rounds of ammo.) *Splash one Nick!*" "This is El Toro—'Nice Work' from the Bull!" . . . "Thanks from Big Ed" . . . and history is made.

ELLIOTT, Thomas William, Jr.
Born: December 30, 1921
School: Wake Forest College
Trained at: Corpus Christi
Previous Squadron: Air Group One
Address: 209 Water Street
    Edenton, N. C.

Our chief champion of the nut brown maiden, that's Tom Elliott. With the entry of North Carolina into the war, Tom abandoned the cause of the Confederacy temporarily, and proceeded to become a connoisseur on global beauty. His lectures, (purely voluntary on his part), on the finer points of finer things, left nothing to be uncovered—the usual wide-eyed ensign audience was held spellbound as his fifty power magnifying glass brought new vistas into view. Thoroughly stimulated by strikes over the Empire, this Edenton contribution to naval warfare, after bursting back into the ready-room, with flashing blue eyes, screeches, "interrogate me!" "The large hairy things I have discovered." All hands readily agree. Of rare good humor, the Edenton Chamber of Commerce has him booked for a good-will tour of the South with a quick trip through Wake Forest, to further the development of international bathing beauty contests.

FLINT, Mitchell Lewis
Born: February 27, 1923
School: Kansas City Jr. College
Trained at: Corpus Christi
Previous Squadron: VB-86
Address: 3506 Harrison
   Kansas City, Mo.

Undoubtedly VITAMIN has the reddest hair and reddest nose in the Navy. His hair has been that color since birth, but it is believed that he got his scarlet complexion from a state of embarrasment that existed through his thirteenth and fourteenth years of life—which just never went away. "Fearless", called so because of his close resemblance to one "Fearless Fosdick", hero of the youth of America, entered the Navy handicapped by an extremely impressionable nature. Although he is now on to the prop-wash and left handed monkey wrench gags, he still believes that it takes three yarps to make a yarb. With Grover acting as interpreter or medium, Flint has been trying to reach the higher-ups in the VF outfit, to really get the final word on this yarp-yarb set-up. His burning ambition is to write a revised history of aviation. He completely debunks the popular myth that the Wright Brothers were the first to fly a heavier-than-air craft. He has definite proof that Chance Vought flew an early model (the 1-D) Corsair at Kansas City, Missouri in 1901

FORD, Frederick Clifford, Jr.
Born: March 15, 1919
School: Hill School, Pottstown, Pa.
   Andover College, Andover
   Yale University
Trained at: Pensacola
Previous Squadron: Inst. Pensacola
Address: 1032 Bishop Road
   Grosse Pt., Mich.

From the ivy clad towers of an establishment in New Haven came this specimen of Detroit's best to carve a niche in the annals of the skies. After passing out hot tips to cadets on what to do in the unpredictable, Cliff gave his students the usual "incompletes", and set forth from Pensacola for the front. As master of a gull winged monster, he proceeded to rally 'round the flag while trying to keep track of Big Ed over the leading Japanese Yo-Yo factories. Passing off all these accomplishments with a chuckle, he has kept his eye peeled on the business world by selling shares in the Dud Circle (being senior member present). In the post-war world he envisions a Rocky Mountain Goat Hunting Helicopter Club for harassed business men. He calls it his "quick trip to the head with Fred" plan and expects the idea to sweep the old goats off their feet.

FUGAL, Boyd Leroy
Born: October 22, 1921
School: Utah State Agri. College
Trained at: Corpus Christi
Previous Squadron: VF-86
Married
Address: Pleasant Grove, Utah

Is it a bird, a rocket, Superman? No, it's pretty boy Boyd Fugal, known to some as the FACE. This ardent apollo is stangely addicted to that unspeakable form of recreation known as exercise. His day is not complete unless he can lift an eight hundred pound weight with one arm many times above his head. One can never forget that cross-country that he took at Vernalis. After the fourth day of RON and still no word, a special envoy had to be sent out to bring our lost wanderer back. He was found in Pleasant Grove carving model airplanes with the boys of Scout Troop #4. "We must prepare the youth of our nation." But he hestitantly came back to duty. With an eye to the future, he spends every spare minute studying a correspondence course in construction or "How to work your Erecto set". The Skip soon realized Fuge's potentialities and placed him on his wing. Together they amassed more flight time than Berton and Bell's teams combined.

GIFFORD, Lewis Guy
Born: July 16, 1920
School: Fullerton Jr. College
Trained at: Corpus Christi
Previous Squadron: VF-86
Address: 621 10th St.
　　Huntington Beach, Calif.

It's been rumored that GIFF was born with a basketball in his hand, and we've never had reason to believe otherwise. For him, correct attire for strike briefings is nothing short of sneakers and gym trunks, waiting for the all-clear that leads to the forward elevator pit and the resumption of that "little game". Task Force radio procedure was completely reorganized with the introduction of his new call system—I just pick up the mike and say, "Hey, Morry, this is 'Giff' "—it eliminates confusion! One of the chief soap box orators in "Moaners Row", located in "jaygees" heaven, three decks below the double bottoms, Lew has collected as fancy a bit of loot from the coffers of the Material Department as anyone could desire, and sports spotless flying gloves every other hop. The ability to fly fourth position with both hands tied is his proudest accomplishment and on hitting the beach was last seen chasing three automobiles in his convertible, joining up—you guessed it—in the usual spot.

GOSSMAN, Thomas Joseph
Born: November 29, 1922
School: Preston High School
Trained at: Corpus Christi
Address: Preston, Minn.

From generously filled body to rakish chapeau, GOSS gives a good interpretation of what the well fed naval aviator should look like while underway. How he keeps this display intact and safe from the thrashings of bunk-room inmates will probably go down as the eighth wonder of carrier warfare. He's earned his "B.R." in life (standing for Bull Run) for conspicuous gallantry as chief purveyor and rouster out of taxi pilots, a job that demands brawn as well as brains. It's been rumored that the Round Man has been sweating out the mail boats for the past year, hopeful, ever hopeful, of the arrival of a pair of dashing seven league boots. What this glut of footwear is to be used for remains to be seen, however, the underlying motive for this large side order seems to be a Texas Belle, whose nimble fingers tooled the monsters. Whether sitting for nine hours playing gin rummy or steering la belle corsair, Goss is sold on the idea of foamite cushions.

GRAF, Earl Emerson
Born: January 6, 1920
School: Tri-State College
    Angola, Indiana
Trained at: Jacksonville
Previous Squadron: VB-1
Married
Address: 570 Delaware
    Tonawanda, N. Y.

Besides flying section lead for Web, Chauncey's pet peeve is the rivalry that is set up in the peace-time navy between carriers of the same task group. An old bomber pilot from Air Group ONE, he suddenly had the urge to check out in a fighter. It was one of those spur of the moment things that couldn't wait until morning, so, off into the night he went—he and some buddie who had nothing better to do with his time than to go up into the inky-black with our gambling, grumbling GRAF. However, they made it back O.K. When quizzed on the subject by ComAirPac, Graf's only excuse was that it was so hazy (he or the night) that he couldn't positively identify the aircraft—he thought it was the bomber type—SB2C. Chaunce has lately been vintner ex-officio in the black death cellars of Web's Poison Pit. "Come quaff with Graf" is the signal to button down all hatches—we're darkening ship.

HANSON, Harry Rodrick
Born: May 8, 1921
School: Franklin High L. A.
Trained at: Corpus Christi
Previous Squadron: Inst. Sanford
Address: 833 South Montecito Drive
San Garbiel, Calif.

WORTHLESS to his friends and, who knows, perhaps to the rest of the world, joined the Navy Air Arm on escaping from California. A great roué (he says), when strengthened by a round of Martinis, he is never too tired for saloon table talk when something gorgeous is involved. Modestly claiming to take only a passing fancy in bridge—"I don't claim to be exactly polished"—his partners readily agree as they pay off numerous mess bills. As some brothers-in-arms are stirred by "The Halls of Montezuma", this lad was aroused by the halls of a certain Maui B.O.Q., wherein the walls will ring forever with the echoes of the "Hanson one man rebellion", as the nocturnal hours shuddered under the chortlings and taunts of—"Okay you guys, now its my turn, you'll never get me in bed!" He is reputed to be excellent when at the controls (of an aircraft), and was tapped as the skipper's section leader. His invariable comeback, "Well, Captain, I thought . . ."

HAYNES, Wayland Bradford
Born: April 29, 1917
School: Seaman High School, Topeka
Kansas State
Trained at: Pensacola
Previous Squadron: VBF-100
Married
Address: Topeka, Kansas

PAPPY set out at an early age to make à name for himself in the Navy. After eight years of endeavor he has managed to acquire the monicker of "Baldy", which isn't much like "Pappy the kid" or "Hairbreadth Haynes" or any other title which Haynes the "boot" envisioned. Nonetheless, below that forehead—alas, quite far below—lies a countenance of unperturbed innocence and a beguiling smile which paradoxically classes Baldy as a fair haired boy, and one never to know the ignominy of lurking in darkened corners at Oscar's. It is rumored that in the dank, mouldy recesses of a hip pocket, Pappy totes a likewise mouldy stabilization fund for Ensigns who fortnightly lose their baby's last pair 'a shoes. This form of usury is the wishbone of a Kansas chicken ranch, which Pappy thinks is the only place for a retired "feather merchant" (okey, Pappy, but we hope you don't try to raise them on such corn).

HOLMBERG, Edwin Knapp
Born: February 18, 1917
School: Benson Polytech., Portland, Ore.
    Oregon State College
Trained at: Corpus Christi
Previous Squadron: Vn-13, D8A
Married
Address: Canby, Oregon

This big Swede is from Oregon way. However, since joining the Navy, his prolonged tour of duty at Corpus Christi, has practically made him answer to the call of "HEY, TEXAS." His first love is for those death-defying N3N's and the AVT's that came with each new plane. About the ship, Ed is content to go the way of the crowd, doing his little bit, but by no means over-working. It was once rumored that he was seen in gym trunks headed for the flight deck and a bit of Old Sol, but this has never been confirmed. Nightly, he and Alford bitterly contest the Cribbage Championship of the South Pacific. These games would often end in fisticuffs—you wouldn't think that of two such seemingly peaceful souls, would you. "Holm" is one of the many who add the extra fifteen knots for wife and young child. He watched the Navy point system for discharging veterans, much as the panic-stricken brokers clutched at the ticker tape. Ten minutes after the news was released which entitled Ed to get out, he was waiting on the fan-tail, baggage and all. "Where in hell is the destroyer?"

HOSE, Leonard Joseph
Born: February 3, 1921
School: Northern Illinois Optometry
Trained at: Corpus Christi
Address: 669 Copley Rd.
    Akron, Ohio

DON JOSE, as he was known familiarly in the squadron, was an optometrist before taking up flying. He had a good eye for feminine pulchitrude, thick steaks and foamy beer, and a discerning ear for good music. He was keenly interested in flying and showed the same amount of zest and enthusiasm in his ground activities. He always packed his camera and took innumerable candid shots of his ship-mates. Our bon-vivant was always the life of the party, and had a knack of looking on the brighter side of things on all occasions.

HUDSON, William Bertis
Born: July 13, 1920
School: Cullman County High
Trained at: Pensacola
Address: Cullman, Alabama

HUT, muscular sergeant at arms of the enswine bunk room, is especially well known for his ability to deal out shady hands in black-jack games. This follower of the crimson tide has spread chaos through yankee strongholds with his cry of "you all hands", "rise and move",—at 3 a.m. It's been told that Hut has never stoked a furnace, but developed into an ace fire bug by creating an incident that drew out every hook and ladder in Southern California. He must have been a singing teacher before stepping into his first "yellow peril", and we'd like to know whether he's any kin to Roy Acuff. Never a victim of mal de mer, this salty stalwart merely drapes himself over the foc'sle for exercise—(for the records anyway)—softly mumbling "let's feed the flying fishes". Strike days find him ever mindful of duty, honor, and stalling speed, as with the look of ages on his face he confesses, "Watch your air speed, Web."

IRWIN, John Charles
Born: December 6, 1921
School: Hyde Park High School
Trained at: Corpus Christi
Address: 5307 Hyde Park Blvd.
    Chicago, Ill.

From the city of big deals came John Irwin, to see how the situation stacked up on the high seas. After trying his hand at just about all the winged beasts the Navy had to offer, JOHN put his fingers in the hat and came up with a Corsair. Thusly mounted, he's been winging his leisurely way through the sky-ways ever since. Never drowning on the nectar of the grape, and always good for a round at the nearest O' Club, "preferably with a cherry please", we believe that this fellow will take back to Chicago the social graces of Naval Aviators from sea to sea. Appearing one morning, the proud owner of a DeLuxe shiner and barked shins, the inner man began to seep to the surface—"Was it a blonde or just a rough sea?" Arguing with Wagner and Connell take up a good deal of his free time, the exact source of these discussions being as obscure to them as to us—the outcome usually ending up in his familiar phrase—"Time for a cup of Java; let's drink to a long and successful CAP."

IVY, James Edward
Born: November 15, 1923
School: Kenosha High School
Trained at: Pensacola
Previous Squadron: VF-86
Married
Address: 1115 64th Street
    Kenosha, Wis.

JIM comes from Kenosha, Wisconsin—sounds a lot like Kanoya or some other horrible Nipponese town. While in high school there he won his letter in hopscotch and skip-rope; he was also runner-up in a Jack Armstrong contest for the "All American Boy". Fugal beat him out. Since with us he has continually flown wing on "Grandma" Berton—that is, when you can get the old Master in the air. Getting a little weary of the monotonous flying routine that was being put to us in the Hawaiian area, "Ivory" put his plane down in the pond—it *was* a different way of doing things. He was rescued by some old sea pirates, and when he returned, he was minus everything except a very scant pair of scanties. The next five days he kept the squadron spell-bound with his tale of the deep. He has a very cute wife to whom he is teaching the game of golf. She is starting from the bottom, toting his clubs and chasing after the little white spheroid. It's a shame to waste such a pleasing smile on the Navy, but "Kiddlee-Divy" wants it that way. We say that Kenosha's loss is the Navy's gain.

KELLER, Harold Russell, Jr.
Born: November 19, 1916
School: Noble and Greenough
    Williams College
Trained at: Pensacola
Previous Squadron: VB-41 Inst. Daytona
Address: 37 Sheffield Rd.
    Newtonville, Mass.

RUSS was a conscientious, purposeful lad and was eager to do a well above average job. He not only succeeded, but managed to be cheerful and pleasant in doing his work. His team respected him in the air and on the ground, and he was well liked by all the pilots. Russ was keen on baseball and hand-ball, and after flying had secured for the day at Kahului, he would play as hard as he would work. We will all remember his favorite expressions:—he would frequently meet a *"fabulous character"* and he witnessed many *"amazing"* things. They don't come finer.

KENNEDY, Robert Edward
Born: October 14, 1921
School: San Francisco Jr. College
Trained at: Corpus Christi
Address: 530 Flood Ave.
    San Francisco, Calif.

SPIDER—Long before renowned VJ Day celebrations, the squadron was conscious of Frisco redheads. Spider O'Kennedy is not one to become obscured by the masses, nor confused with just plain Irishmen. Nay, for there is a peculiar aura about this carrot-top—a wee bit of the old country and a profusion of thirty-cent cigar smoke which his companions find both charming and devastating. He has a natural gift for enjoying life under practically any circumstances, and after one particularly relaxing evening on Falalop was discovered at dawn with head jammed through the folds of the "Fly Speck Hotel" absorbing a tropical monsoon. Being a student of psychological warfare he seldom retired from an attack without reconnoitering the surrounding area. "Damn it lad, don't tell *me* a Gisha house ain't a primary target!" He bristles with a wit and repartee that is used most effectively (like a knife) in passing out invitations to 0345 "GQ" standby or in breaking someone to the Throttle School for Jockies. But the smile—ah! that smile 'twould brighten the 'eart of old Scrouge.

KNIGHT, Freeman Lee
Born: July 12, 1920
School: Lynch High School
Trained at: Corpus Christi
Previous Squadron: VF-86
Married
Address: O'Neill, Nebraska

Freeman is another one of the cast-offs from the good ship "Charger" where he excelled at Fly One detail. Most memorable about NIGHTY is the jalopy he used to sport around Vernalis. It was the third car to ever be run off the assembly line at Detroit—any time of the day or night he could be seen piling half the town of Tracy into the rumble seat and heading off on some wild jaunt across the orange groves of sunny California. Often while in the air, he would dive away from his division at a terrific rate of speed. Upon investigation it was found that the cause of this was the Wear, who every so often would look around and give his wingman a grusome grimace—it was just too much for Freeman; his only thought was to get as far away as quickly as possible. Just previous to joining us he had the task of giving the "pool" at A.C. a clean sweep-down fore and aft. This lasted for four months. Right now "Nighty-Night" is fighting like mad to get home to his mighty nice wifey-wife. **Nighty-Night.**

MARRIOTT, Max Howard
Born: March 13, 1924
School: Oklahoma A. & M.
Trained at: Pensacola
Previous Squadron: VF-86
Married
Address: 1611 W. Noble
    Guthrie, Okla.

'I guess you know", are the familiar words that bring all hands around to hear one of Max's tales of blood and thunder. In his native state of Oklahoma, he learned many of his well-applied tactics by keeping the Indians off the "upper 40". His ability as a leader is well testified by the fact that he was elected president of the "Wingman's Club". Some say that he got this position because he is the senior ranking ensign. We fail to believe it, though. These caucuses would be called at any time of the day or night, and Max proved to have quite a good deal of agility. He had to, the way the boys would playfully throw around the dead soldiers. Then there was the time that "Mairzy-Doats" went off on that one man toot on our last night at Barber's Point. The next day this very supple form was poured out of an airplane onto the flight deck where it remained until the air officer decided it was interfering with operations and spotted it below. The last time we were home Max's gal became Mrs. Max, and our boy hasn't been the same since.

MASSEY, Maurice Eugene
Born: April 6, 1923
School: Hernando High School
Trained at: Pensacola
Address: Hernando, Miss.

During our last blessed days at Barber's Point a bit of the deep South was wished off on us in the form of LITTLE JOE Massey. He was the last person of this generation to be reared in Uncle Tom's Cabin, being under the tutelage of Simon Legree for the first thirteen years of his life. When he came to us, Telfair had to act as interpreter; no one could quite savvy that very Southern Drawl. Classes were held nightly in the ready room though, and now we can at least tell what his primary needs are. Joe says that flying wing on "Stumpy" McGrew has been one of life's most exciting, daring (and probably death-defying) ordeals that he will ever go through. Like every other human being in Navy Blue, Joe has an ambition—nine times a day he wants to sit down to a big feast of chitlins and gravy. After describing to us what chitlins are, he can have it; we'll take the much talked of mint julep.

McGREW, Richard Leon
Born: August 13, 1916
School: Westport High School
Trained at: Corpus Christi
Previous Squadron: VB-86
Address: 3536 Troost Avenue
    Kansas City, Mo.

Dubbed with many a nickname, the one that he is most commonly known by is STUMPY or, as the Mexicans have it, "El Stumpo". At the blossoming age of sixteen, when most little boys were finding out the "why" of many a new problem, he would be safely tucked away in bed trying to grow that extra two inches, to reach the minimum requirements for Naval Aviation. He is one of the most feared of men by the rest of the pilots—not necessarily because of his pugilistic ability but rather because of the things that would result when he started pushing that pencil around on the flight desk. And, oh yes—the "little black book"—that detestable, incriminating, infuriating, but oh so truthful, goddamned book. "Yes, Behling, you've got G.Q. again in the morning. It's none of my doings." He has got a gal in Stockton down to his size and liking, and will be tying the knot upon safe arrival home. It took the LSO a week to get used to seeing a plane in the groove with no pilot in it. That's nothing; it took "Dangerous Dan" a month before he ever saw the LSO.

McNETT, Edgar Lewis
Born: September 21, 1921
School: Univ. Idaho
Trained at: Pensacola
Previous Squadron: USS Charger
Address: Hill City, Idaho

From that famous resort town of Hill City, Idaho—population of twenty people, comes MAC. Before taking up the sword, he spent his time teaching the tourist trade of Sun Valley how to beat the "House" at Faro and Roulette. Since he has come to us he has taught one and all how to eke a full house out of a pair of threes. The only man to make 119 straight passes with the cubes, Ed is considered the Jim Brady of our day. He was first discovered while sending us off the "CHARGER" during qualifica-tion work at Norfolk, and was grabbed up immediately. The original intention was to utilize his previous experience by teaching the fledglings of the outfit semaphore. However, he said he could fly and was tested. Sure enough; he could do it. As soon as he passed the 300 hour mark he was given a division. Ed's sea stories of the Chesapeake rival even the Messrs. Nordoff and Hall who have hired his services to complete their latest novel "Mutiny on the Flight Deck".

MILNES, John Thomas
Born: March 6, 1920
School: Fordham Univ.
Trained at: Pensacola
Previous Squadron: VC-7
Address: 420 Oakland Ave.
Staten Island, N. Y.

Fore! With this cry of triumph our boy J.T. warns the preceding foursome of their impending danger. Willing to walk miles to pursue this favorite sport, he may be seen any afternoon ashore foraging in the boon-docks looking for his misplaced ball among the litter of discarded beer cans and gopher holes. OLD JACKSON is not a new hand. He qualified for this squadron by serving his apprenticeship aboard one of our baby flat-tops. His first combat flight in this squadron found him flying that fourth position, also called the "Zeke Decoy". He nobly performed this task and, at the end of his run, was amazed to find but a single Zero on his tail. Thanks to the speed of the Corsair he soon left El Jappo in a cloud of prop-wash. A self-termed bridge expert, he keeps track of the rubbers that he loses by plucking a bill from his pocket and a hair from his head. How long can this last?

MORRIS, Lester
Born: November 27, 1919
School: Malden High School
Trained at: Corpus Christi
Previous Squadron: VF-86
Married
Address: Bernie, Mo.

This is one of the squadron ancient mariners who came to us with tales of lovely hula-hands. Setting forth with the motto of the "show me" state trembling on his lips, OLE MORRY set forth to view the world via a Navy Recruiting Station. A cruise in the Navy is a liberal education. The connivings of a sea going career first came to life during the attack at Pearl Harbor, and ever since have gained momentum from the boardwalk to the shores of the Empire. As the CAG's right hand navigator, Morry has popped up with many a "land ho" during runs into the target—"None of this hayrake for me!" On the matter of gas consumption, this fellow knows all the answers; his bellows of "condition queen" startled the entire fleet—"Yes sir, it's good to the last drop—and I'll take a couple more wave-offs to prove it." Originator of the "Dance of the thousand temptations", Morry will be on hand to perform at any time.

OGDEN, Robert Alan
Born: December 14, 1916
School: Ohio State Univ.
Trained at: Pensacola
Previous Squadron: VF-18
Address: 2527 Ritchie Street
    Portsmouth, Ohio

R.A., or OG, as he was affectionately known to the squadron, was the spark plug of the organization. As flight officer since the Air Group was commissioned, he ran a taut ship and inspired the fear and respect of all J.O.'s. Possessor of an extremely attractive personality, it served to make him not only the most popular man in the squadron, but also one of its leaders in all activities from the tail chase to the social graces. He never hesitated to take the junior ensigns, new to the ways of Combat Flying, under his wing and give them the benefit of his wide flying experience. His inspiration remains with us.

O'MALLEY, Frank Joseph
Born: October 7, 1923
School: Ipswich High School
Trained at: Corpus Christi
Address: 53 East Street
    Ipswich, Mass.

O'MAL, a member in good standing of "The Little Men's Marching and Chowder Society", had the opinion that an F4U, if properly ground and mashed could be used as the basic ingredient for a new concoction, to be called "O'Malley's Tomali". With this in mind, he used the pulverizing qualities of the barrier and flight deck to accomplish said purpose. Having spent some time at Barber's Point, he was used to close shaves and it didn't bother him. His only remark was, and we quote, Jeezt, unquote. Having served his country well, he is anxious to get back to Ipswich and reclaim his title of "Clam Digging King". His record: Twelve clams, two leaches, a squirm, and a gris. Being familiar with the TBF, the Navy's general purpose aircraft, he will revolutionize the industry by using it to hasten the mating of the Male and Female Clams. The Motto of said industry being, "it ain't no sham if you dig that clam".

PROCTOR, Harold Lloyd
Born: October 26, 1920
School: Humboldt High School
Trained at: Corpus Christi
Previous Squadron: VF-86
Married
Address: Humboldt, Nebraska

"Powder River, let 'er buck." Nobody knows why, but every once in a while this statement is blurted forth—either as a challenge or as a suggestion to make way — the "Governor" is on the rampage again. "Goddamnit, Commander, I'm no mechanic —what the hell has the Navy got plane captains for? No need of us getting down in that bilge." So it went. However, the "GOV's" sudden flares are well balanced by his toothy grin and chuckle, chuckle, chuckle. The surprise move of the war was his start-

ling marriage. Any time of the day or night he can be heard raving about Dixie—and we don't mean the deep South. With an eye to the future, he immediately applied for laundryman's detail upon our arrival at Maui. "If forty cents a shirt seems like too much to you guys, do your own wash—", and he pocketed a mint. "Why I wouldn't fly with that guy if we were the only two people left on the earth." "Hanson, I'll give you just one half hour to get to bed, or else—." See what we mean?

QUALLEY, John Smith
Born: March 3, 1923
School: Central High, St. Paul, Minn.
Trained at: Pensacola
Previous Squadron: VF-86
Address: 237 W. Norman Ave.
    Dayton, Ohio

This is QUALL, our erstwhile candidate for "tail-end Sholley." At times, while at Atlantic City, his days seemed numbered, being on the South end of the gunnery score-board for many weeks. However, his efforts bore fruit and when it came time to go to sea the "Quall" had risen to 79th in the standing. One will never forget the day at Maui when he and Rapp were going to beat up Raehn and Steve for making their simulated attacks not quite simulated enough. Being parachute officer (thank God none of us ever had to jump) entailed the tedious task

of making sure the rubber boats were rubber and that all the little boys had "Mae Wests". He once set a record of drawing sixty Mae Wests from supply, stenciling them all, putting in CO_2 bottles, distributing them to the pilots, collecting them again, taking out the CO_2 bottles, taking off the stenciling ink and returning them to supply, all in 45 minutes time. While trying to survive the survival checkout, the cryptic remark "O-o-h-h, I—feel —awful", quoth the "Quall Ball", "never more!"

RAEHN, Raymond Vincent
Born: February 9, 1924
School: Bellevue High School
Trained at: Pensacola
Previous Squadron: VF-86
Address: 210 N. Jackson
    Bellevue, Penn.

RAEHN, as he is affectionately called by those closest to him, is the "I wanta fly" man in the squadron. Whenever business is slack, he can be seen milling around the local CASU begging for a run-in, and is one of the few men in aviation to have more flight time than his division leader. His name and fame have been wide-spread in the Pacific. Upon one occasion he attempted a new type of strafing attack and covered the flight deck of our esteemed ship with his brass empties. The penalty for this was the maximum—twenty lashes and in the stock for 48 straight hours. One other time—we kind of hate to mention this—he came in on the wrong approach bearing. Can you imagine such a thing!?! It seems that the Messrs. Halsey and McCain were hard pressed for material to put in their dispatches so, for all that morning and half the afternoon, the wires were humming with "get that pilot, what's his name—what outfit—blah—blah—take disciplinary action—blah—blah—blah." it seems that 30,000 men were at G.Q. for over a half hour just itching to shoot our proud beauty out of the sky. Ray's retort was, "Whadda ya mean IFF and approach sector?" See—he's no different than the rest.

RAPP, John Frederick
Born: January 24, 1922
School: Univ. of Newark
Trained at: Corpus Christi
Previous Squadron: VF-86
Address: 17 Agnest Street
    Belleville, N. J.

JAKE is Noo Joisey's gift to Bomfightron 86. Before blessing us with his charms, he was woiking days in a corset factory, doing modeling, he said, but he's too thin for that sort of work now. His nights were curiously not occupied by women but rather by some book larnin' at a famed school across the Hudson. It is our guess that the woman angle was very definitely worked in somewhere along the way —that's just plain old nature, and Rapp. His activities in the squadron have been varied—one that is not varied is the people he flies with. "If our team had flown together just two more hours—we still wouldn't have flown much." Pyromaniac 1/c Rapp kept the boys in a perpetual state of fret and frenzy with his antics at Maui. It all started with a small smoke bomb; went from there to setting off five-inch fire-crackers in his room-mates' ears (he'd catch them while they were sleeping) and then to tearing apart five hundred pound bombs, dumping the contents on the floor, light a match to it and split his sides laughing as the BOQ would burn to cinders. Jake's folks had to build an extension on their house—it wasn't possible to get in their present establishment all the "trophies" that he would tote home. "Have you enjoyed your stay with us, Mr. Rapp?" "Yeah, ya might say."

ROMER, Harris Raymons
Born: March 6, 1922
School: Hawley High School
Trained at: Corpus Christi
Married
Address: Hawley, Minn.

We were very unfortunate in that HARRY was with us only a short time. Yet, in that brief span he had made many friends. Throughout his Navy career he showed up very well on the athletic field; this was a carry-over from his high school days. Whenever the fellas gathered for a song-fest, Harry was in the middle of it, leading some of the less inspired. To him home life was of prime importance. However, this did not impair his sincere and ever faithful work at squadron. To those who knew him, there never was a truer friend.

RUANE, Edward Joseph
Born: February 21, 1915
School: Boston Univ.
Trained at: Corpus Christi
Previous Squadron: Inst. Pensacola
Address: 99 Taylor St.
    Needham Heights, Mass.

Look at the face and upon close scrutiny you will find that it is not the Map of Ireland, but the image of our quiet Ruane. Generally reliable, EDDIE has a reverse side to his character as was exhibited one day in sunny Calif. On this particular Sunday we find Eddie absent from our midst while he was assigned to the all important Squadron Duty for the day. The Skipper and half of his family of bird-men had moved temporarily to the desert for rocket training and he chose this particular day to call for Ruane to join him. An intense search of the base disclosed no trace of our wandering boy. Finally a call from neighboring Frisco carried a familiar voice to our ears, He had just called to inform us that he was having a little "affair" and found it quite impossible to be bothered with the depressing worries of the squadron. Early Monday morning he returned carrying his bags under his eyes, condescended to comply with the skipper's wishes and left immediately for the desert. Our Eddie has more planes to his credit than anyone in the squadron — FRIENDLY planes — and he was riding in all of them.

RUSSELL, William Everett
Born: June 16, 1922
School: Polytech, H. H.
   Fort Worth, Texas
Trained at: Corpus Christi
Previous Squadron: VB-86
Address: 1221 E. Richmond
   Fort Worth, Texas

"Fifty mils lead, goddamnit," was bellowed out from the back of the ready room for the third time in thirty seconds. It was the "Bomb" answering some idiot's query on his specialty—"How to get the most hits with the most bombs on most targets". Whether it be bombing or women, RUSS has all the dope on proper approach angle, speed of the target, trail, drift angle, and fusing. His one firm conviction—on the push-over, always keep the nose well ahead of the target. For a spell there on Maui, his title of "Bomb" had to be abandoned for the classier call of "Clock". The duties that went with the name entailed rousing all hands from the arms of Old Morph every A.M. for a week. He hails from some town in the wilds of Texas where his family raises a certain type of poultry. His post-war plans, while not yet complete, include a trip to Istanbul where he will drool in a pool of cool gool.

SAMPLE, Bonner Alan
Born: August 13, 1924
School: Fresno High School
Trained at: Corpus Christi
Address: Clovis, Calif.

Here is the original example of the Babe in Arms, that the strains of wild war music has enticed aloft into the great adventure. Coming to us as the Ensign "junior grade", his was the not too easy task of learning the eccentric habits of Madame La Corsair, mastering all the vices she possessed, and readying himself for the task force tag games at the last minute. Getting the idea in a hurry, SAMP was soon whizzing down the flight deck, lurching off into the air with the rest of the thundering herd to join in the wild stampede of deck load rendezvous. Jap airmen were warned by "Tokyo Rose's" sister, little "Nellie Nagoya", of that rosy cheeked youth who would not yield, would not turn, would carry the attack onward in a continual swirl of singing lead. Samp has probably flown more different types of hops in less time than the rest of us put together, and he's our connoisseur of G.Q. standby.

SCHULER, Elwood Charles
Born: August 30, 1923
School: Yuma High School
Trained at: Pensacola
Previous Squadron: VF-86
Married
Address: 177 No. 7th
    Yuma, Arizona

"Lemme at 'em, lemme at 'em." Immediately after Pearl Harbor, this was the "SCHULE'S" cry, so the Navy hired him and "let him at 'em". Doing it the hard way, he went in as a mech. However, Forrestal and Artemus L. Gates got wind of his powers and pushed him into flite school. About this time his delightful wife gave birth to a delightful girl that they named "Delight". After all that they didn't have much choice—did they now? Charlie is the sparkplug of the sparkplug department, forever advising Pugleasa, Ding, Mr. Vought and Mr. Corsair on how to improve this and that on the flying machine. "Can't the dumb furriner see that this quick detachable tail just won't work on a carrier based plane? Let's put the prop where the tail is, cut five feet off each wing, place the engine in the cockpit and strike the pilot and relief tube below." That saucy captain that blew in from ComAirPac disagreed. He said we should leave the relief tube where it was. Being a determined but cautious fighter pilot Charlie said, "The heart of Tokyo was as good a rendezvous point as any."

SCHWARTZ, Robert James
Born: March 22, 1921
School: Univ. of Detroit
Trained at: Corpus Christi
Address: Adrian, Mich.

"Hup all hands" is the familiar cry that greets the sleepy-heads in Boy's Town when TALL BOB is on the early morning prowl. This self-acclaimed woman-hater is the only man who can make you laugh as he "ups you a buck" and rakes in the pot. His generosity knows no parallel. However, when he says that he'll give you the shirt off his back, it is more than likely that you paid for it. The Navy was faced with its greatest problem since the raising of the "Arizona" when they tried to get Bob in a fighter. It wasn't bad in the open-cockpit type, but the hood just wouldn't close with him in the saddle. Chance-Vought, always ready to help out (????) with any group having some particular trouble, rushed one of their best men in—a certain Mr. Mazzerelli, who together with Lt. Berton, "Big Ed", and Max Marriott, went at the job with unflinching courage. Three weeks later Mazzerelli had left and Schwartz was seen flying around the heavens with his head sticking four and a half feet above the top of the canopy. In years to come, it is Bob's secret ambition to be the bat-boy for the Detroit Tigers.

SMITLEY, Leon Eugene
Born: June 27, 1922
School: Scott High School
Trained at: Corpus Christi
Address: 2238 Whitney
    Toledo, Ohio

Leon "Stuff like that there" Smitley, better known as CHUBBY is, as everyone will agree, one of the more wholesome members of the squadron. Slightly partial to the solid South for reasons of rather questionable displomacy, he is a northern man with southern principles. It's rumored the Rotary Club of South Toledo is sponsoring his liquor ration. Having once received a special citation from Sally Rand for not leaving his seat during the finale, we're sure he's also discovered the benefits of ready-room sofas. Claiming to be one of the few characters to have ever been fed a turkey dinner by a beautiful girl; this bizarre pastime has been discussed at length by leading figures on Capitol Hill—and immediately adopted for the rehabilitation of broken down junior birdmen. Navy recruiting soared with the development of this health through joy program and we're proud to possess the source of this latest bonanza.

STEPAHIN, Walter N.
Born: July 31, 1920
School: Butler Sr. High School
Trained at: Pensacola
Address: 167 Kohler Ave.
    Lyndora, Penna.

Walt, or STEP as he was familiarly called by many of us, joined the Air Group while we were at Otis. When the fighters split, he went the way of the F4U. This was only natural as he had more experience in Corsairs than any other member of the squadron. He was constantly hounded by the less-savvy pilots on the "this" and the "that" of the aircraft. While not busy around the squadron, he would be involved in some fast and heavy bull-session or out mixing it up on the ball field. Walt's enthusiasm for flying, his dependability and loyalty made him an invaluable member of the squadron.

STEVENSON, William Sanford
Born: September 24, 1921
School: Wilbraham Academy
    Middlebury College
Trained at: Corpus Christi
Previous Squadrons: VC-70, VF-18,
    VF-4, VF-86
Married
Address: 126 Forest Street
    So. Weymouth, Mass.

STEVE, as suave as New York and as refreshing as Damascotta (that's a small Indian village in Maine), has kept the squadron flying, on paper, with the most symmetrical (albeit impossible)' flight schedules the Navy has ever seen. "Yes sir, who sir, Bell sir, no sir." He bought a hundred tins of sardines, seven unmated anchovies, a Higgins boat full of martini mix; kissed little Ingrid goodbye on the fly; left his car with an unemployed garbage collector and said, "What can the Navy do to me now?" He didn't know . . . they put him in Corsairs. So he made out some even more impossible sched-ules (there were usually two Corsairs in flying con-dition) and his name was linked with the Stump's little black book . . . they were spending all their waking hours together. Getting a little old for flying now—that belt only has one more notch in it—Steve is devoting most of his time planning a new family budget called "We Two and a Dollar" or "Oh you Dice, Why can't you be Nice." In the air he is called Steve the Weave ("I don't care if you don't have an engine, keep weaving") and his radio conversation is an art, "Cobra base this is Steve, sixteen weary chicks wending their way homeward."

SWAN, Edward Renald
Born: March 13, 1924
School: Eagle Rock High School
Trained at: Corpus Christi
Address: 4946 Wawona St.
    Los Angeles, Calif.

"I don't know what to tell you." That's the phrase that ED prescribes as an endearment to charm the hearts of Southern Maidens. After conquering the belle of Jacksonville, he set out to demonstrate his effective technique against the representatives of Tojo. In the early morning darkness we next find Ed rushing up to the flight deck to man his plane for his first do-or-die session with the enemy. Some jerk of a Jap chose this particular time to make a run on the ship. Poor Ed—in an exposed place and only his plane for protection. After the shooting subsided, he was finally located in a prone position under his plane with his plotting board over his head. Since that time the Skipper has issued Squad-ron Policy No. 4783 which states that any pilot wishing to remain a part of this unit must carry his chart board with him whenever he undermans a plane.

SWINDEN, Elbert Dennis
Born: February 11, 1924
School: Austin High School
Trained at: Pensacola
Previous Squadron: VF-86
Married
Address: 3710 Munson St.
   Austin, Tex.

FATTY Swinden, our one man crowd, is one person who believes in the slogan of "food for thought." Gracing the head of the chow line at every opportunity, except when chasing bogies at 30,000 feet, his very presence throws fear into messboys as well as fellow gluttons—will there be enough to go around? When queried on his most thrilling maneuver while aloft, the "Case of the frozen guns" invariably comes up, together with all the appropriate sighs and gestures—"there I was, it was right in my sights, all big and round, I charged my guns, licked the latest chow from my lips, and all I got were camera pictures" (this last remark coming forth as a hollow croak). A charter member of the "Tail-end Charlie" Union, his arguments with Schuler are unending on who flies the worst, the best being none too good. His sojurn at playing house on Cape Cod has dampened, quoths he, the delights of flat-top life, for sea duty on dry land beats all. Rumor hath it, however, that a little matter of not enough flight deck available for lifting "stout fellas" into the air has caused the "hound" much concern.

TELFAIR, Robert Myers
Born: Sept. 13, 1920
School: Delta State Teachers College
Trained at: Pensacola
Previous Squadrons: VC-21, VF-38
Married
Address: 401 Walthall Street
   Greenwood, Miss.

Back in the days when many of us were still sporting the latest tweed and zoot chain on the campus, EL STUDDO was playing a new kind of tag in the South Pacific. He's drawn sea pay ever since. He's a specimen of the days of hand-made air medals, so don't ask him where all of his are. Stud likes nothing better than to take a few of us poor, midget-minded yankees on a southern fried journey into rebel territory. It comes in two dishes, a LaCarte: the drawled, "Did ah ever tell you 'bout the time . . ." or, when the grease gets really hot "Robert! . . . come here! . . . Puieee, puieee, puieee! . . . Don't cross your legs, ta da dee dee dum da!" Nothing less than an emergency "G.Q." can stop him. On strike days Stud hangs his badge of office, the blackout plug, around his neck. It is noteworthy that he himself has never drawn a suit for the plug. But then, you can't draw a plane for the suit these days either, so its easy to understand Stud's passion for his job as Blackout Officer. According to his wingmen, Stud is a master in the classic art of Ouija Board navigation. Through a pair of powerful binoculars he can usually be found on the outer fringe of the task group, laying out his own lost sheep circle. By some coincidence it never interfered with Air Plot's circle, and it has certainly kept the Gunnery Department on its toes!

TENNES, Horace Edward
Born: June 1, 1912
School: Loyola Academy, Loyola Univ.,
    Northwestern Univ.
Trained at: Pensacola
Previous Squadrons: VF-5, VF-6, VF-81,
    VF-86
Address: 3240 Lake Shore Drive
    Chicago, Ill.

"It's all good experience," said UNCLE ORLY about not being invited to the Hurricane Party until the day after it was over. "You folks just don't realize it." After departure from the land of opportunity to the shores of Maui, swim fins became the order of the day, and all fish from Maui to Mog Mog jammed on water injection when they saw this new acquatic apparation. Once aboard the carrier, life settled down to a happy, normal routine—"Duty Officer!!! Where's Telfair? . . . Say, Telfair, what's the dope on the new black-out plugs?" "Oh, Steve— OK, OK, OK, get McGrew then . . . What!! Well, somebody in the flight department." "Auk, get me ten charts of Honshu; cut 'em in three pieces and give me every third piece." "Yeh, yeh, yeh, yeh." "Oh, Chad, how about getting up a green book and labeling it 'It shouldn't ought to be'." "Is there anyone here who doesn't know what a Prep Charlie is? OK, OK —now get this. We'll have no more happyassing around the screen . . ." "Now Captain Switzer MEANS WHAT HE SAYS. HE'S NOT FOOLING." "Now we're all getting good money, especially my high-priced help—IF THE TAX PAYERS ONLY KNEW!!!! But I still love every hair on your head." "See you in Eagle River. This is Mr. Tony, OUT!!!"

THOMSON, James Renwick
Born: August 24, 1918
School: Lewis & Clark, Spokane Univ.,
    Wash., Naval Academy
Trained at: Pensacola
Previous Squadron: Inst. Vero Beach
Address: 724 W. 14th Ave.
    Spokane, Wash.

Bringing with him his jaunty pipe, arabic scarf and eau de salty brine, JIM pulled up at the squadron trap-door one day, let himself down in our midst and presented his on-lookers with a good-look at a product of King Neptunes School for Young Boys. From this dramatic entry it was only a quick leap to greater things, for shortly thereafter, amongst the resounding shouts of "Haleakala," he took over the reins of "exec," in which leather thongs he has been wrapped ever since. With firm hand and a singing whip, that evil, urging, whistling lash (to make ensigns weep, "jaygees" creep and lieutenants leap), J.R. has poured the heart and soul of "Rocks and Shoals" from its golden salavar out upon us. He thus keeps the fold properly annointed and in a constant seething state; his sly grin and those electrifying words, "Don't ask me, just the way it works out," serve to quell the mutinies and hagglings of the mob. This is our good natured executive officer, who's ability to hand out the always not too welcome "word" in a quiet and gentle manner has made him ever popular.

TOLLE, James Edwin
Born: September 23, 1921
School: Tech. High School
Trained at: Corpus Christi
Previous Squadron: VB-86
Address: 729 N. Emerson
    Indianapolis, Ind.

JIM, who was from Indianapolis, joined the Navy early in 1942. Flying was a continuation of his impressive athletic career. He was well known as a basketball player and one of the top-notch bike racers in the country. As a former bomber pilot, Jim tore up many bull's eyes, and his versatile skill was borne out again when he changed over to fighter planes. Big, easy going and practically tireless by nature, he could really put out when there was a job to do. In the air he was always in dress formation. Even during the most difficult maneuvers his division leader could always look around and be sure of finding him.

TURK, Karl Louis
Born: April 8, 1923
School: Cass Tech., Detroit
Trained at: Corpus Christi
Previous Squadron: VBF-98
Address: 9372 Prairie
    Detroit, Mich.

Karl, sometimes known as CRASH TURK, hails from that thriving metropolis—Detroit. At the tender age of sixteen his parents took him off the assembly lines, gave him a few days rest, and presented our prize package to Uncle Samuel to do with as he saw fit; he was put in that experimental branch known as Naval Air. With us he has found more loose rivets in Mr. Vought's airplane than our engineering crew and CASD combined. Karl was almost launched as a passenger one day when he was too intently inspecting the bilge of one mighty Corsair. However, flight quarters was delayed long enough to let the lanky gent from Detroit disembark; the pilot of the craft was greatly relieved to know that the check had been successfully completed. Our boy is one of the few who can be called for GQ standby at 0240 in the morning, and not retort with the usual slander and foul language that greets the SDO. It's a good thing the Japs quit when they did!!!

TURNBO, Richard Weldon
Born: July 4, 1921
School: Lometa High School
Trained at: Corpus Christi
Previous Squadron: VB-86
Married
Address: Lometa, Texas

"TEX" had a smile that was more than merely a smile. It was a grin that filled everyone with a feeling of happiness. When in a crowd with him, there wasn't a worry in the world. Maybe it's that there just wasn't room enough for any cares with "Tex's" continual joshing and fun-poking. His "Hey, Hoss" has become traditional. In the air, he sparked Jimmie Thomson's division, having mastered the technique of flying fighters in record time. Being a little more stable than many of his contemporaries has very definitely affected those of us who have been close to him. Many a night we were humored by "Tex" and his slow, reassuring, easy-going line of chatter.

WAGNER, Roy Thurman
Born: September 29, 1922
School: Colorado Univ.
    Colorado College
Trained at: Corpus Christi
Previous Squadron: VB-86
Married
Address: Lometa, Texas

The MAJOR—egad. With the face of a startled cherub, the soul of old Santa, and the heart and lungs of a lion, this fugitive from silence has banged our ear from the Golden Gate to the Emperor's stable. Nothing has happened to us that hasn't already happened in Colorado City, usually in the high school. The Major is our crystal ball, in fact and figure. His acey-deucey victims, rash enough to win a game and cherish dreams of glory, are gently —like a typhoon—reminded of the first twenty. Having won his letter in dive bombing while still a freshman in 86—"Berfsk, another damn bulls eye"— the Major rose swiftly to the challenge of the fighter and then, with the modest pride of work well done, retired to the sack to await jet propulsion. VJ day had a unique affect on this hero. Hearing that the boys were tossing baskets on the elevator, he cast a reassuring glance at his scrap books and leaving the sack, ascended to the field of battle. The boys claim that the game was going very well on the hangar deck as the Major strolled onto the court from the flight deck to join them. So be it. He claimed a foul *with* flight pay and went back to the sack with a sprained ankle, water bottle and K Rations. Appointed squadron shylock he has bled our stones dry—and pounds of flesh? Ample, my friend, ample.

WEAR, Richard Fairfax
Born: February 7, 1924
School: Drews
Trained at: Pensacola
Previous Squadron: VF-86
Address: 2400 Pacific Ave.
  San Francisco, Calif.

DICKIE Wear, VBF-86's reincarnation of the court jester, kept us laughing from the Chateau Renault, through life's darkest moments on Maui, to Yoka-suka Naval Air Base. He reached his peak at an early morning beer bust when he burst forth with his description of how his car would swish up and down the mountain sides, as "Arrr—ooogga" (in a voice that woke up the whole barracks) went the horn. His title, the "Phantom," came from CPT days when he sat so low in the plane, it appeared that the aircraft was pilotless. However, Horace's memo 4-44 which requires the "Phantom to sit on a pillow," has now brought him into view. At times his plane still appears to be pilotless. "They're ditching the Dumbo." His capabilities are unlimited: he acted as master of ceremonies for the Happy Hour in the wardroom, drew up the town charter for "Wear-ville" in Northern Honshu, has favorably impressed some gal's dad to the point where he will soon be married to her, has kept Christy in continual fits of either laughter or rage. Fortunately, Dick is one of us who won't have to burn a nickel for a cup of coffee. He'll be sipping it for the rest of his life. In our post-war world his words, "Carry on, Captain," will give us strength immemorable.

WEBER, Boyd York
Born: May 5, 1919
School: Westminster College,
  Fulton, Mo.
Trained at: Corpus Christi
Married
Address: Fulton, Mo.

Although he was a late-comer, WEB fitted right into our "Happy little family." While at Barber's Point, he and his four protegees, noted with enthusiasm the definite "go-gettum" attitude that our pilots exhibited while in the air. "That's the squadron that we want to get into," and nothing could stop them. The other version is that they only had three more weeks to go before being sent back home, and were more than slightly put out when their orders came in. Web, by dint of marriage, has a very sweet wife, and one-nine-hundredth interest in some obscure brewery. Boyd's present undertaking is the attempted cultivation of some fuzz just south of his nose. However, we are of the opinion that it will be a forgotten matter by the time he makes his gallant entrance into the fair city of St. Louis to rest in peace under the Anheuser Busch.

WERNER, Louis, II
Born: Oct. 14, 1922
School: Princeton Univ.
Trained at: Pensacola
Previous Squadron: VF-86
Address: 9625 Ladue Rd.
    Clayton, Mo.

LOU THE LIP—case history: Born . . . Raised, and been raising Hell ever since. Whether ogling at the Mark or glimming through the overcast, he's primed for any situation. Pearls of wisdom become ecstatic over the prospect of being drooled by this fellow, who becomes pretty ecstatic himself as he leers over the edge of his second stinger glass scheming to get out of it and into the third without splashing his Date. No one's seen him do it yet. To this day we all wonder how that small group that sat so peacefully in an Atlantic City Bistro sipping warm gin, could be the same one that later appeared in the halls of VF-86 staggering under a load of A.C. no-parking signs. Guess who distinguished himself in this campaign . . . affirmative . . . and also received the "Mouldy Fig Cluster" in lieu of the Croix de Jois, signed by old Chad himself. Just marking time in the Navy, his real ambition is to fly a Spad with the Foreign Legion. But whether it be Navy, Legion, or tweed suit, he swears and be-damns that during the next war he'll have a seat in the Ready Room, and lead his own division. Some star!

WHISLER, William Galen
Born: November 21, 1920
School: Brookville High School
Trained at: Pensacola
Previous Squadron: VB-86
Married
Address: Trotwood, Ohio

This refugee from the plumbing works has added greatly to the efficiency and well-being of the squadron. His most recent pamphlet, "The Latest Modes in Modern Commodes," has been invaluable to us, especially at such stop-overs as Mog Mog and Eniwetok. He claims that it all started with his work as a ship-fitter, and has stuck to his story so gallantly that we have to believe him. His not-too-quiet quips from the back of the ready room have put us all in fits of rather sly humor. WHIS was startled to discover, during a discussion on animal husbandry, that a mule cannot reproduce. We were startled at Whisler. However, with an open mind, he listened to our explanation of the life cycle of the mule. Two days later he was overheard telling his plane captain that a mule is born by the cross-breeding of a jackass and a sparrow. Right now he is torn between returning to the enlisted Navy or continuing his life of ease.

WINSLOW, George Haxton
Born: July 5, 1924
School: So. Hadley High School
Trained at: Corpus Christi
Address: 52 No. Main St.
   So. Hadley Falls, Mass.

DON Winslow of the Navy jumped the gun on the draft board and sported thirteen buttons before setting forth on his quest for the "wings de gold." As the hell bent skipper of an Admiral's station wagon, he burned up the back streets of Norfolk with that same glint in his eye that makes Ding Dong Bell look back and immediately surge onward. Locked in the arms of Morpheus at the slightest opportunity, his healthy pallor springs from a 5 watt battle light and the glow of bunk-room stogies— "What good does the sun do you out here?" He says they manufacture shoes in Boston that last forever, but we think he never has 'em on long enough to tell the difference. Buying drinks at the "Top of the Mark" offers more of an obstacle to this lad than keeping track of squadron "yellow sheets," but they've promised to let him in for a quickie when he makes full commander.

TRAVELOGUE OF A BENT WING

IN late Spring of 1944 when America was just beginning to get the feel of her bulging biceps, was dancing on the ropes, so to speak, and getting ready to unleash her might against the Axis, the Navy big-wigs contemplated hatching an egg known as Air Group 86. But not believing in putting all the egg in one nest, they laid several, VF, VB, VT. This combination was later scrambled. VF being a double yoke had to be separated later, one portion becoming VBF and a few pilots strained from VB to make the ingredients potent. The Navy knows how to cook and the Japs had to be spoon fed. Cmdr. Luker is a good chef.

Now the grass is green on Atlantic City's Boardwalk and beaches in the good old summer time and we will narrow this discussion to that slippery, slimy half of a double yoke which turned up in name and force as VBF-86—the wonder squadron.

The grand commissioning followed immediately, binding the veterans and more immature operational students. We intimate an improvement, the Skipper in gunnery, the students in their parties.

Those were the hectic days. Fly to New York—see the Big Dick, fly to Washington —see the girls, fly the group gropes—see the SNAFU. Gun and bomb, dogfight and bounce, day and night. Zoom the Boardwalk by air, land and see! Just try to get a cross country approved. Rumors of flights to Cleveland. Quick trips to Norfolk to charge the Charger. Out of the path of the hurricane—fly those planes to Lakehurst. Secure those fire hose parties in the barracks. Fly! Fly! We're forging a team!

One October day after the summer had its fling, the unscrupulous prices and peoples of Atlantic City were a thing of the past; Mr. Tennes and his little chicks took their flight enmasse to a new nest on Cape Cod. He was pleased. He said we were progressing—but—seven seconds were lost yesterday folding wings and junior officers couldn't swing a compass in a forty-five knot wind. My! My!

Coonamesset Inn was a haven of refuge in the evenings and many of the happiest hours were logged there. Autumn in New England fills one with awe inspiring reverence—we also had something to fill our moments. Mass attack, mass attack, get that cruiser Vicksburg. Fly to Nantucket. Fire those rockets. Ferry those planes. Go to Quonset. Learn that night vision and survival. Pack that gear. Come on now, we're making night carrier landings on that *big* Pee Willie. Hustle, the invigorating snow is falling!

Next episode is touching. Many had gone before but now it was us. Westward Ho! Alone, without even a compass to guide us we trek the thirty-five hundred miles across the plains, mountains and deserts of treacherous sand to San Diego. The rendezvous was perfect. Not a man was lost. By plane, train, dog cart and motorscooter, they came. The Skipper jumped down from his tattered schooner, lean and weary eyed. He raised a Tomcat insignia and cried, "My comrades and I claim this entire territory in the name of VBF-86. Same territory to be bounded by Canada, Mexico, Chateau Renault, and The Mark".

The chicks had no planes. Moulting, we might say, with clipped wings. They now took passage on the good (doubtful) ship Nassau to explore the far reaches of the vast Pacific with its myriad islands and peoples. After many days they shifted to air transport and landfall was finally made on the enchanting, colorful isle of Maui, where Haleakala rears its ugly head into the light blue sky. Christmas came to Maui, but how different! Natives shooting firecrackers—weather so hot the chicks dabbled in the sea.

Here we go again. Fly those Corsairs, shoot those rockets, fire those guns, grope with the groups, play Sea Horse with the fighter director, bomb and strafe Molikini Rock! Go take that Link hop, gunairstructor, navigate, shoot that pistol and skeet. No, don't ask anymore for a jeep—the ground officers already have them as per usual. "Don't drink beer and fight all night, you've gotta fly at 0300." "No, you can't fly to Honolulu; go attack Homestead."

On and on we wend our way deeper into the Pacific. The war is closer now and we are still passengers, on the big Franklin this time. All we see is the bluest water in the world, an Albatross, many schools of flying fish and hotter weather. In due course, after refueling destroyers innumerable times, we arrive at a secluded coral atoll—a secret anchorage. Here we see the huge U. S. Fleet. All the big babies lying side by side in the harbor, their bows dipping with the tide. This is the most powerful naval array the world has ever known. They are poised to strike again. Old grand-dad battle wagons and carriers whose punches really reach out. A panorama that makes one disbelieve his eyes. Here we find "our" ship, the Wasp, and go aboard. Paint is a little drab and crew is battle weary after a year of action. The preceding air group just pat their heads and point to us, saying "you got it."

Hundreds of tankers, freighters, and other ships of the train have injected new blood into the giants. Rejuvenated, they come to life at dawn and head toward Japanese real estate, far to the north. Planes now soar on patrol over the extended battle formation. This is it! We arrive, we fight the ack ack, the kamikazes, we get hit.

Back to Ulithi and combat air patrol over the anchorage. Based on Falalop—that cozy little atoll abode—sopping wet all the time. The ships laundry and galley had been knocked out and we were short of food, dirty, tired and ragged.

Back, forever back, those six thousand miles, so happily mad, so madly happy. Anchor is dropped in the cool sound near Seattle and we get a few days of lovely leave.

The first tour was fouled but the chicks

are growing spurs. They are riding Tiny Tims now and F4U-4's, aching for that second round. Eventually, our floating home weighs anchor, sporting new guns, another catapult and a new coat of paint. The replacements have been made for lost personnel and the galley and laundry function nicely. Our Fighting Lady slides easily under the Golden Gate and into the setting sun.

At times the very elements and fundamental laws of science became adverse and much time was spent searching for gremlins in our inverted gull winged monsters.

Again we visit the little yellow devils and inquire into their temples, "inspect" their ships and planes, airfields and factories, trains and ferries. We segregate them—see what makes them tick! In a small way we urge them to initiate the surrender and relieve our prisoners of war.

Now we have one more full measure of duty. The "Bull" is in Tokyo Bay, we are in the path of a raging typhoon. The "old lady" emerges with a drape shape up near the bow. Some say it was twenty-four hundred square feet of flight deck and cat walk hanging over. At any rate it may be of help in getting us back to the States. We are all hoping now to get back to that claim we staked out in a yester year. Auch and Chad brief daily now on the friendly natives and the possibilities in that clime.

Well, the war is finished, we hear, and our little trip is over. This half of a double yoke came through. They did their bit to the best of their ability. Split, spliced, grafted and torn asunder at times, they lived through and won. In spite of hurricanes, typhoons and Nipponese. Truly on land, sea and in the air they battled against the odds.

But now it is done, it is written; no one can change it; no one wants to. The Gods have had their play.

We lost some chicks. They fell to earth heroicly. They fought well, they finished their course, they kept the faith.

FAR IN THE NIGHT, EXHAUSTS GLOW,
AND PILOTS LACE THE AIR;
DEAD, YOU SAY? IT IS NOT SO,
THEY ARE OFF YOUR WINGTIP, THERE!

THE CREW

Front Row (left to right):

J. L. Pugleasa, ACMM; J. P. Goodwin, ACOM; R. A. Prisbylla, ACMM; H. S. Urbanski, ACEM.

Middle Row:

W. E. Kruse, AM 1/C; J. F. Brians, AMM 2/C; J. F. O'Brien, AOM 2/C; H. E. Dailey, Y 3/C; H. D. Stewart, PR 1/C; A. D. Gilbert, ARM 2/C.

Back Row:

J. W. Burnett, AOM 1/C; M. W. Burton, Y 1/C; H. J. Huffman, AMM 3/C; R. P. Backderf, ART 1/C; L. Canter, AMM 1/C; A. H. Wareheim, AMM 2/C; K. K. Nevar, PHOM 2/C.

Maurice W. Burton
Y 1/C

James P. Goodwin
ACOM

Raymond A. Prisbylla
ACMMH

James F. Brians
AMMC 2/C

Homer J. Huffman
AMM 3/C

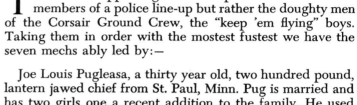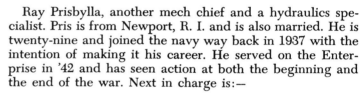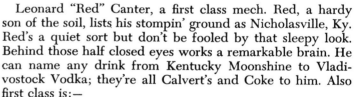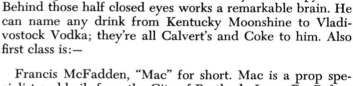

THE dubious appearing characters pictured herein are not members of a police line-up but rather the doughty men of the Corsair Ground Crew, the "keep 'em flying" boys. Taking them in order with the mostest fustest we have the seven mechs ably led by:—

Joe Louis Pugleasa, a thirty year old, two hundred pound, lantern jawed chief from St. Paul, Minn. Pug is married and has two girls one a recent addition to the family. He used to be a railroad fireman which perhaps explains the way he pours the coals to his crew. Being one of the "high points" men, Pug expects to be back to the railroad before long. With Pug is:—

Ray Prisbylla, another mech chief and a hydraulics specialist. Pris is from Newport, R. I. and is also married. He is twenty-nine and joined the navy way back in 1937 with the intention of making it his career. He served on the Enterprise in '42 and has seen action at both the beginning and the end of the war. Next in charge is:—

Leonard "Red" Canter, a first class mech. Red, a hardy son of the soil, lists his stompin' ground as Nicholasville, Ky. Red's a quiet sort but don't be fooled by that sleepy look. Behind those half closed eyes works a remarkable brain. He can name any drink from Kentucky Moonshine to Vladivostock Vodka; they're all Calvert's and Coke to him. Also first class is:—

Francis McFadden, "Mac" for short. Mac is a prop specialist and hails from the City of Brotherly Love, Pa. Before the war Mac was a machine operator but his one burning ambition is to have his own saloon. He promises all the boys jobs and free drinks if he gets it. After Mac we have:—

Alan D. Gilbert
ARM 2/C

Harry D. Stewart
PR 1/C

Leonard Canter
AMM 1/C

Harold E. Dailey
Y 3/C

Joseph L. Pugleasa
ACMM

Harry S. Urbanski
ACEM

Robert P. Backderf
ART 1/C

Konstanty K. Nevar
PhoM 2/C

John F. O'Brien
AOM 2/C

William E. Kruse
AM 1/C

Francis G. McFadden
AMMP 1/C

Avner Warheim a second class mech from Miami (the land of sunshine) Fla. Av is twenty-five, married, and the proud father of a five months old girl. He just missed her birth by five days having just returned to the states the day she was born. He was an aircraft assemblyman before coming into the navy. Another second class mech is:—

Jimmy Brians, a carburetor specialist. Jimmy comes from San Luis Obisbo, Cal., is twenty-three, married and has one boy aged three. Way back in the dim dark days beyond recall (or the navy) he worked for Bethlehem Steel building ships. He claims to have helped build everything from the Constitution to the Missouri with a little overtime thrown in on the Mayflower. Last we have:—

Joe Huffman, still third class by a strange quirk of fate (and BuPers). Joe is twenty-three and comes from St. Louis, Mo. He worked for the Missouri Kansas and Texas R.R. before enlisting in '42. Joe also fancies himself quite an actor and went in for dramatics in a big way. Although no-one will admit it to him, he is a pretty fair comedian. That takes care of the grease monkeys and now for the sling-shot mechanics or ordnance-men headed by:—

James Putney Goodwin, a chief ordnance-man from Marshalltown, Del. Putney is twenty-five, single, and a former top-notch jockey. He enlisted in the beginning of '41 also intending to make the Navy his career. He served with a scout-observation squadron aboard the U.S.S. New York for some time and has seen action in both the Atlantic and Pacific theatres of war. His two men are:—

Johnny Burnett, a first class gun-changer from Drumright, Okla. Johnny's married and has two children, a boy and a

John W. Burnett
AOM 1/C

Avner H. Wareheim
AMM 2/C

girl. He is known as the "Big John" of the ordnance crew being over six feet tall. He worked as a roughneck in the oil fields of Oklahoma. His pard and the "Little John" of the crew is:—

Johnny O'Brien, twenty-one and second class. Johnny is from Greenfield, Mass. He is the shiek of the outfit and is reputed to have left a trail of broken hearts from Massachusetts to California. His only comment on this is, "I owe it all to my fatal charm and my pocket comb." That takes care of the Ordnance Dept. and now we have the two static chasers or radiomen.

Bob Backderf, a first class radio technician at only twenty is the first of the radio gang. He comes from Pittsburgh, Pa. which explains his nickname of "Smoky." Bob is married and is another regular navy man. He enlisted on a minority cruise in 1943 his enlistment expires next August. He was with a night fighter squadron before coming to 86. With him in the Radio Dept. is:—

Alan "Gil" Gilbert, a second class aviation radioman. Gil is twenty-one, married and comes from New York City. He worked as a draftsman before enlisting in '42. He's also a self-professed artist and is always littering the place with his sketches and cartoon caricatures, some of which occasionally

prove embarrasing to their subject. Someday, someone is going to sneak up on him and do one of that receding hair line of his. Next we have the two pen pushers, the boys who keep our records straight. The first of these is:—

Maurice Burton, yeoman first class from San Jose, Cal. Burt is twenty-three and another married man. He has two children, again both girls. Burt enlisted way back in 1939 and saw duty in the Atlantic aboard a destroyer. He is another of the "44" points men and will be back in San Jose with his kids before long. The other man in the office is:—

Harold "Pop" Dailey, the old man of the outfit at thirty-two. He too is married and comes from Blacksburg, Va. Pop is yeoman third and will be the head of the yeoman department when Burt leaves for civilian life. Before coming into the navy in 1943 he tried his hand at Soil Surveying both in school and in the field. That covers the two or more man departments and now for the lone wolves. Heading that list is:—

Harry "Ski" Urbanski a chief aviation electrician with a crew of one—himself. Ski is twenty-three and lists his home as Detroit, Mich. He is single and another pre-Pearl-Harbor man having enlisted in '39. Ski is a recent addition to the chief family as he just received his hat last month. Harry has about the best rack—er—job in the outfit yet can always be found hard at work, when he can be found. Next in line is the tin-bender:—

Bill Kruse, a first class metalsmith in more ways than one. Bill is twenty-five, and like so many of the other men he is married and a father. He just received word of the birth of his daughter a short while ago. Bill is about the quietest fellow in the outfit but he manages to make noise nevertheless. He used to be a riveter for Bell Aircraft. Another rate is:—

Harry Stewart, parachute rigger first class. He has been first class longer than most fellows have been in the navy and he still has hopes of making chief. Harry is twenty-five and another career man having enlisted in 1937. His home is in Seattle, Wash. Last but not least is the photographer:—

Konstanty K. Nevar is a second class shutter-bug from Elizabeth, N. J. K.K. is the youngest man in the outfit being only nineteen yet his sea-duty extends back to a time when most of us were just starting school. He was born in Pinsk, Poland and he crossed the Atlantic back in 1926. He insists that entitles him to wear the ETO campaign ribbon.

That completes the enlisted personnel of the squadron, the men who work day and night (whether they like it or not) to keep those Corsairs in the air. Their motto as always is "we want to go home" or as they say in France, "We want to go home."

VAPOR TRAILS

OUR days in VBF-86 will best be remembered by association with places, people and events. We cannot hope to recapture every laugh, groan or tear, but towards this end we now lead you back along an old and once familiar trail. It all began among the sugar cane at . . .

Maui . . .

. . . on January 2, 1945 . . . "These men may consider themselves detached from VB and VF, with orders to the Bent Wing Squadron. All hands would do well to learn the habits of the monster as quickly as possible." Not without apprehension, some people took a look at the cockpit . . . little instrument panels signs stamped "warning?". . . . "What manner of machine is this?" Afternoon trips to the "O' Club. No mixed drinks 'till 1600. "One case of beer, please. Back to the BOQ, red dust seeping into your very soul. Keep those windows closed. Flying starts in earnest. . . . "Yes! Your division will have to bounce tomorrow . . ." "What have I gotten into now?" . . . "Who's got the bucket of ice for the beer?" The pile of beer cans reaches a zenith. Can hardly move because of the BOQ collection of debris. Steve doing his little bit to keep the flame of the perpetual party undying. For the paltry sum of 10c, you can get eggs on toast nightly in the mess hall. Everybody off to the movies. Tomorrow, gunnery at 20,000 feet, bombing in the afternoon. "When do we get our day off?" Raehn and Rapp discover the presence of deer on Molokai, and set off with machine guns. The more cosmopolitan are golfing at the Maui Country Club.

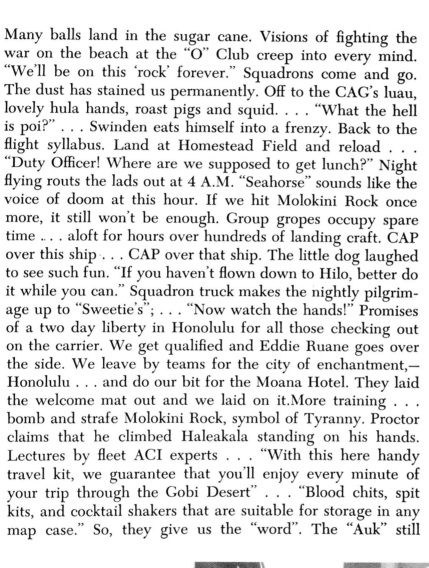

Many balls land in the sugar cane. Visions of fighting the war on the beach at the "O" Club creep into every mind. "We'll be on this 'rock' forever." Squadrons come and go. The dust has stained us permanently. Off to the CAG's luau, lovely hula hands, roast pigs and squid. . . . "What the hell is poi?" . . . Swinden eats himself into a frenzy. Back to the flight syllabus. Land at Homestead Field and reload . . . "Duty Officer! Where are we supposed to get lunch?" Night flying routs the lads out at 4 A.M. "Seahorse" sounds like the voice of doom at this hour. If we hit Molokini Rock once more, it still won't be enough. Group gropes occupy spare time . . . aloft for hours over hundreds of landing craft. CAP over this ship . . . CAP over that ship. The little dog laughed to see such fun. "If you haven't flown down to Hilo, better do it while you can." Squadron truck makes the nightly pilgrimage up to "Sweetie's"; . . . "Now watch the hands!" Promises of a two day liberty in Honolulu for all those checking out on the carrier. We get qualified and Eddie Ruane goes over the side. We leave by teams for the city of enchantment,—Honolulu . . . and do our bit for the Moana Hotel. They laid the welcome mat out and we laid on it. More training . . . bomb and strafe Molokini Rock, symbol of Tyranny. Proctor claims that he climbed Haleakala standing on his hands. Lectures by fleet ACI experts . . . "With this here handy travel kit, we guarantee that you'll enjoy every minute of your trip through the Gobi Desert" . . . "Blood chits, spit kits, and cocktail shakers that are suitable for storage in any map case." So, they give us the "word". The "Auk" still

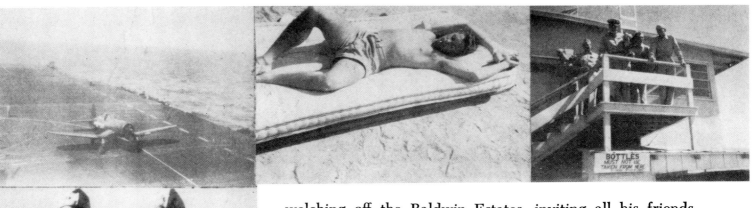

welching off the Baldwin Estates, inviting all his friends. "Get the truck and let's go to 'Fran's' for a steak,"—Hanson and Chev are off again. Waves arrive and McGrew claims a nautical edition of "Tugboat Annie". Frantic work to get through the work on the range at Molokai; then out to the "Franklin" for a little shaking down. Three days of deck-load, groping and catapulting. These Corsair replicas of the Wright Brothers' original are certainly snappy looking aircraft. Back to the beach . . . pack seabags with one shirt, eighteen sardines, all sorts of refreshments . . . and we're off to the air races. Bert ropes the Material Department gear together in a sack, lurches aboard the "Star of Maui", and is off to Pearl. The skipper requests, "Please no happyassing on the bridge." With these words ringing in our ears, we leave for the . . .

First Lap of the Air Races

March, 1945. Orders of the day read: "You have been thrown upon the mercy of the Franklin's crew. . . . Living quarters are assigned in the bilge." . . . "Prepare for a voyage of sacking out during the trip to the fleet." Between jaunts to the bridge to criticize the "Big Ben's" Air Group, some of the more eager attend Bill Cann's recognition parties. . . . "Now this is a new type . . . Three wheels and a purple tail." . . . "Yes, it also flies backward, Winslow." Lewis explains in double talk the merits of waterproof underwear. "This cot is killing me" . . . "Oh, for the sacks of Maui!" More standing in line for chow. Tour of the engineering spaces for VBF-86. . . . Down into the bowels of the ship. "Did you ever see a turbine?" Bell rises to the occasion and explains all. Thoroughly stimulated we arrive at Ulithi, make passes

at three carriers, and finally sneak aboard the Wasp. . . . "We're on our own carrier at last." Haggling over room assignments . . . Wilbur Davis is half clawed to death. "What's your file number?" . . . "Schwartz will sleep in the head." "You don't mean we start flying tomorrow!" Other flat-tops shudder . . . Eighty-Six is with the Fleet. Three days of wave-offs and we're off for Japan. The "Auk" strides forth with telescope and briefcase stuffed with horror tales of the Empire. . . . "Now nobody was forced to come out here" . . . "How are you loading your .38?" . . . "Is your evergreen showing?" Sweat, clammy hands, nervous, nervous, nervous. "Pilots man your planes!" and we're off . . . The old familiar chant, "This is Mr. Tony. Rendezvous over the Bay. Out!" Kanoya, Kure, and Ibisuki. Back to the carrier. Millions of tall tales. . . . "That lugger was blown clear out of the water." Back into the air once more. Then we get hit. "All hands keep a reverent silence on and about the deck during burial services." We sail for Ulithi. . . . Mog Mog, beer cans and Falalop. . . . CAP's, Fly Speck Hotel and Sherwood Green uniforms. "How'd those Marines get that yellow color?" R.A. has found his Isle of Paradise. Off for Pearl; more time in the sack. . . . "Careful, or you'll forget how to walk!" Chad is lashed to the piano. At last—Pearl. "Send Telfair to the rest home; he looks pale . . ." "Tell 'em we won't get back to Maui." With a shout we are off for the States. "Can't sleep any more." Seattle . . . and an Air Station out of "Town and Country". A lush party—lusher women . . . "I really didn't shoot down very many." Mestres corners the airways and we're off on leave with orders to delay, stray, and play . . . "But don't forget to report back to . . .

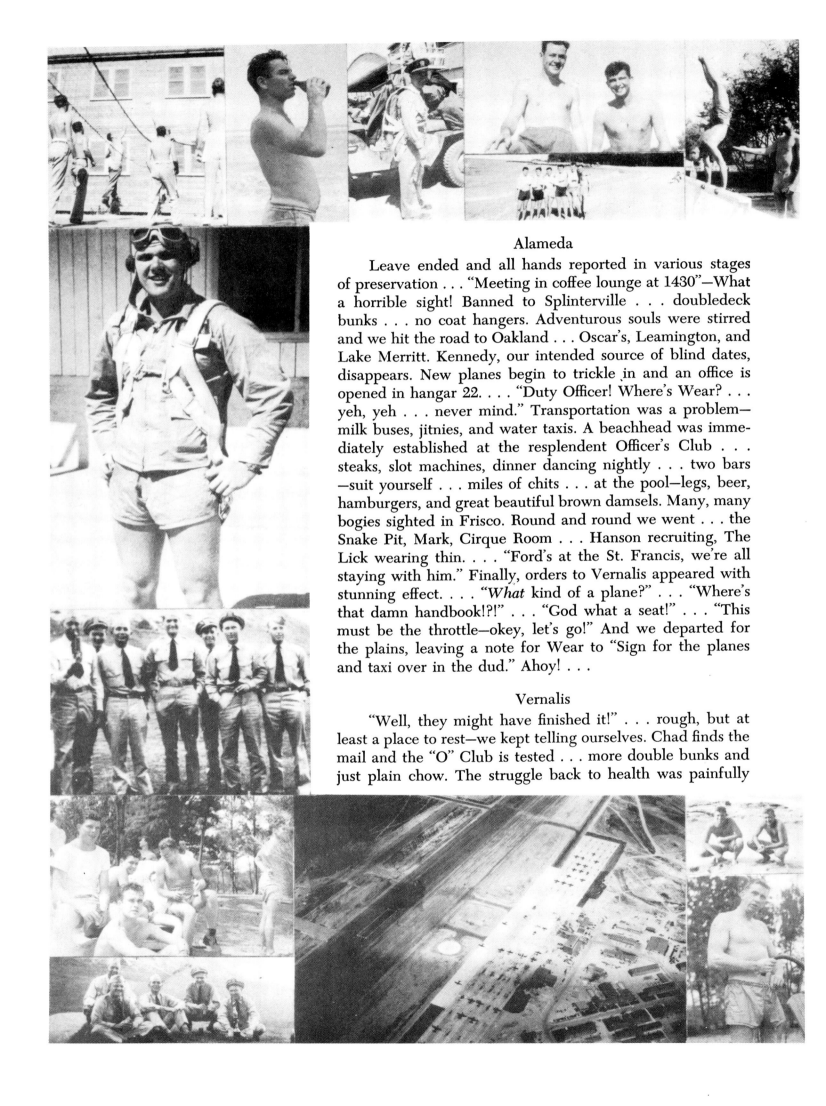

Alameda

Leave ended and all hands reported in various stages of preservation . . . "Meeting in coffee lounge at 1430"—What a horrible sight! Banned to Splinterville . . . doubledeck bunks . . . no coat hangers. Adventurous souls were stirred and we hit the road to Oakland . . . Oscar's, Leamington, and Lake Merritt. Kennedy, our intended source of blind dates, disappears. New planes begin to trickle in and an office is opened in hangar 22. . . . "Duty Officer! Where's Wear? . . . yeh, yeh . . . never mind." Transportation was a problem—milk buses, jitnies, and water taxis. A beachhead was immediately established at the resplendent Officer's Club . . . steaks, slot machines, dinner dancing nightly . . . two bars —suit yourself . . . miles of chits . . . at the pool—legs, beer, hamburgers, and great beautiful brown damsels. Many, many bogies sighted in Frisco. Round and round we went . . . the Snake Pit, Mark, Cirque Room . . . Hanson recruiting, The Lick wearing thin. . . . "Ford's at the St. Francis, we're all staying with him." Finally, orders to Vernalis appeared with stunning effect. . . . "*What* kind of a plane?" . . . "Where's that damn handbook!?!" . . . "God what a seat!" . . . "This must be the throttle—okey, let's go!" And we departed for the plains, leaving a note for Wear to "Sign for the planes and taxi over in the dud." Ahoy! . . .

Vernalis

"Well, they might have finished it!" . . . rough, but at least a place to rest—we kept telling ourselves. Chad finds the mail and the "O" Club is tested . . . more double bunks and just plain chow. The struggle back to health was painfully

begun . . . "Get out in the sun!" . . . "Play some croquet!" . . . "That look's like a tennis court—at least at one end." Leave was extended to find homes for the wives. . . . Tracy, trailers, and auto courts, or the five day hotel shift. . . . Knight liked the idea and went home to get spliced. Tally Ho! Modesto! We're off to the races again . . . the "Body" at Varney's, mob at Perk's, Wacs at the Hughson, steaks at Gould's . . . "Last bus leaves at two o'clock, the next at seven." The Auk buys a car without any gas . . . the Skipper's Blue Goose becomes a fixture. Stud hunts for a horse in Tracy, but Chad settled for the "O" Club's icebox. Flight was attempted next on a tailor made schedule . . . bombing, gropes, Bond Rally, buffeting . . . Big Ed tries out the old style tail skid . . . and the group is divided for a safari into the desert. Ding Dong becomes custodian of the cattle car and is ordered to set the Watch while we're gone. Then, adjusting our dusters we boarded a great silver boid and headed for . . .

Twenty-Nine Palms

Too much sand and a deceiving name, but more attractive than the base up North . . . "Fort Zinderneuf!" murmured Werner. We shied at the sight of Tiny Tim . . . and began to fly. Piano-wired one D's, steel mat runway, dusty lake bed, and down-wind landings. . . . "The sights need adjusting." . . . "Who figured this lead?!" . . . "Of *course* I held the pickle down!" CAG pays a visit and a few wives arrive. We're having a pretty good time . . . ball games, milk shakes, sandstorm, and naturally the bar. Rabbit hunting becomes a fad and the Skipper is seen racing across the sage in his jeep. We get "the word" before movies . . . ice-cold swimming and

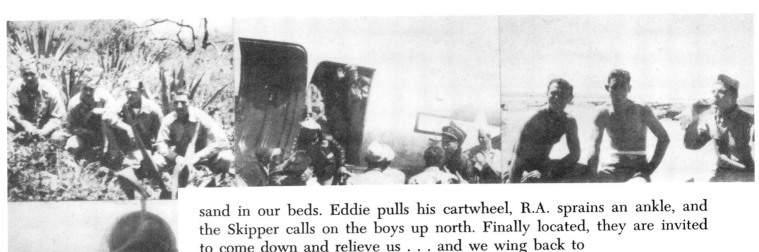

sand in our beds. Eddie pulls his cartwheel, R.A. sprains an ankle, and the Skipper calls on the boys up north. Finally located, they are invited to come down and relieve us . . . and we wing back to

Vernalis

Morry and Stump discover Stockton . . . we throw a party . . . promotions come through. Next, a bit of night flying and three way interception problems. . . . "Red one, bogie, twelve o'clock, angels eleven, closing" . . . seee WOOOSH! . . . "Goddamit Behling, let's go home!" We're not popular at BOQ so Jim sets fire to his mattress and we pack off to the greener pastures of . . .

Alameda

Back in the saddle—how we love this place! . . . each night the "last" and we're *killing* ourselves. Planes get hurried last-minute changes, inspections, and washdowns. The 8 A.M. water taxi is unusually crowded, wives have started to scatter, and our complexions are now a pale green. The Wasp arrives . . . planes are loaded, gear assembled, and bodies collected. A few wives, sweethearts, etc., come down to stare. Ghastly apparitions struggle up the gangway. "All passengers leave the ship" . . . we're moving . . . "Hey, I forgot to check out of BOQ!" . . . the Golden Gate . . . and the "apparitions" fade to the sack for . . .

The Trip Out

First day: wardroom empty, heads crowded . . . rough as hell. . . . "Gangway! here comes Cayton." What a life! Second day: too weak to move. Flying finally starts and we have many, many troubles, meetings, and lectures . . . our monster needs a veterinary. Spirits are low as we shuttle over to . . .

Barber's Point

Our planes become the problem-child of CASU 2 . . . flaps, wing locks, auto spark, camera mounts . . . and we all become assistant engineers.

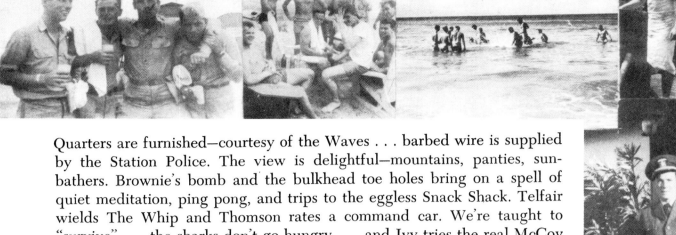

Quarters are furnished—courtesy of the Waves . . . barbed wire is supplied by the Station Police. The view is delightful—mountains, panties, sunbathers. Brownie's bomb and the bulkhead toe holes bring on a spell of quiet meditation, ping pong, and trips to the eggless Snack Shack. Telfair wields The Whip and Thomson rates a command car. We're taught to "survive" . . . the sharks don't go hungry . . . and Ivy tries the real McCoy, a few days later. The Officer's Club is good but closes too early . . . Steve boresights the Stag Club and a weave is started. There's a beach party, bowling and dampened outdoor movie. It's almost over now. The ship's party at Fort Island . . . hurried laying-in of juice supply . . . and we're off for the Wasp and . . .

Points West

A warm up game with the Wake Island Idiots is arranged—It's a walkaway . . . many hits and no errors. We sojourn for a day at Eniwetok . . . beer, sunburns and those putrid shells. Then northward past grimfaced Iwo Jima to join 38.4 and take position beside the Bull's flagship. Events which followed from Hokkaido to Kyushu, playing bulls-eye, we know are duly recorded in our minds—for the passaging years to expand and color . . . so we move on to the great moment when . . .

The War Ends

. . . suddenly . . . thanks to the Atomic Bomb, the Wasp, and Turk. We plow into a typhoon and get a facial alteration . . . patrols begin over air-lanes from Okinawa and over Japan. We stage a mass air show for the Fleet, take aboard passengers, and give away our food. Last combat air patrols are flown with the task group; no more crow-hopping off of the stubbed in bow. Refuel and shove off for Eniwetok at dusk. Hangar deck solid with sacked out "high Point" boys . . . "Movies have been cancelled for tonight." Chow lines a mile long . . . "Happy Hour" . . . watching the more eager personnel pummel each other for the glory of the V-2 division. Bridge all night, sleep all day. . . . "Have you had your cockpit picture

taken?" Latest dispatch . . . "Fly all the Corsairs ashore at Eniwetok," . . . via the catapult . . . with the ship standing dead in water. "What'll they think of next?" Underway for Pearl. Presenting Chad and the Auch who will pass on to you the fruit of their adventures in the business world. "Are you sure you don't care to go U.S.N.?" "Get in on the ground floor in this post-war aviation world." Slight assessment demanded of all hands for the Air Group "Mess", wedding gifts and Wagner's mangled bookkeeping . . . always in the red. Christy and Wear think it's fashionable to learn to play bridge. Scuttlebutt at full throttle. "Maybe we'll go to South America-Puunene-Suez-Gallipoli-Nepal-or even Boston."

We'll know soon for now we are saying Aloha to beautiful . . .

Oahu

The hatch opens, spilling out the cadaverous bodies of the squadron onto Ford Island. "Now what?" "You guessed it—Maui!" The red earth is open for business. Faint cries of "Kismet" penetrate the passageways. "A transport will be in front of the tower at 0800—take enough shirts for two weeks of the dust treatment". Even Mister Tony had a quick swig of Southern Comfort at the thought. Nothing changes here, we keep telling ourselves—They even remember us. "Pilots from the WASP will live in overturned boilers halfway up Haleakala". "You will be supplied with guides to bring you in and out every other day". Off to the beach club. "I've lost another round . . . seventeen Martini's please". No Corsairs, so it's steaks, beer, golf, and buying chit books. Several of the Monsters are located at Hilo and the braver go to retrieve same . . . Charming looking craft. "Fifty turns of the rubber band will get you back to Naska!" Corrosion catches up with Schwartz, so some go to the rest homes of Waikiki. Sportsmen pilots—at last are recognized. We live in lush greenery; "Big Ed" lives in the sack of sacks—suitable for division tactics; and "Ole Morry" spins in off the head. After Ford finished clawing at some jugs, we left, far better and far worse, to leap aboard the carrier and begin the long tedious trek to . . .

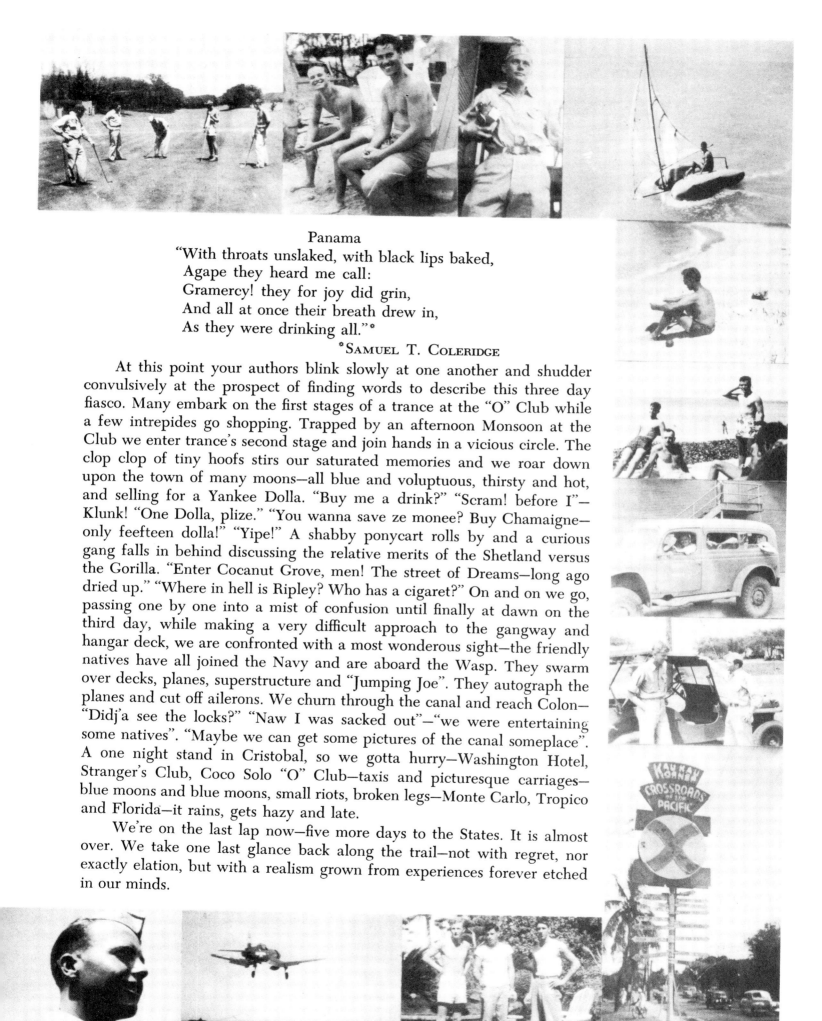

Panama

"With throats unslaked, with black lips baked,
Agape they heard me call:
Gramercy! they for joy did grin,
And all at once their breath drew in,
As they were drinking all."*

*SAMUEL T. COLERIDGE

At this point your authors blink slowly at one another and shudder convulsively at the prospect of finding words to describe this three day fiasco. Many embark on the first stages of a trance at the "O" Club while a few intrepides go shopping. Trapped by an afternoon Monsoon at the Club we enter trance's second stage and join hands in a vicious circle. The clop clop of tiny hoofs stirs our saturated memories and we roar down upon the town of many moons—all blue and voluptuous, thirsty and hot, and selling for a Yankee Dolla. "Buy me a drink?" "Scram! before I"—Klunk! "One Dolla, plize." "You wanna save ze monee? Buy Chamaigne—only feefteen dolla!" "Yipe!" A shabby ponycart rolls by and a curious gang falls in behind discussing the relative merits of the Shetland versus the Gorilla. "Enter Cocanut Grove, men! The street of Dreams—long ago dried up." "Where in hell is Ripley? Who has a cigaret?" On and on we go, passing one by one into a mist of confusion until finally at dawn on the third day, while making a very difficult approach to the gangway and hangar deck, we are confronted with a most wonderous sight—the friendly natives have all joined the Navy and are aboard the Wasp. They swarm over decks, planes, superstructure and "Jumping Joe". They autograph the planes and cut off ailerons. We churn through the canal and reach Colon—"Didj'a see the locks?" "Naw I was sacked out"—"we were entertaining some natives". "Maybe we can get some pictures of the canal someplace". A one night stand in Cristobal, so we gotta hurry—Washington Hotel, Stranger's Club, Coco Solo "O" Club—taxis and picturesque carriages—blue moons and blue moons, small riots, broken legs—Monte Carlo, Tropico and Florida—it rains, gets hazy and late.

We're on the last lap now—five more days to the States. It is almost over. We take one last glance back along the trail—not with regret, nor exactly elation, but with a realism grown from experiences forever etched in our minds.

BOMBING SQUADRON
EIGHTY-SIX

WILDWOOD

SEATED in a little tar-paper shack, NAS Wildwood, N. J., was Mr. Bush—not Captain Horatio Hornblower's Mr. Bush—but our own Mr. Bush, greeting us as we straggled to him from all corners of the nation. Naughton was the first Ensign to arrive, shortly followed 'by 46 of contemporary rank. Bush began to doubt the sanity of Com-AirLant; all these Ensigns and no Lieutenants. He was just offering McGrew as a burnt offering when his prayers were answered.

Shirley, Sewall, Ward, Kelly and Thomas reported for duty. Bagley also reported, but definitely not for duty and not for long. Johnson, who was already at the scene, finally received his orders and became a member of the squadron. Scudder, Lake and Turnbo soon became a part of us, as did Marks and Gittings. Mundy arrived to take over the duties of administration and Prentice became our ACI Officer. Rotholz popped out of a water-fillable bomb and became our gunnery specialist. We were also blessed with George Marlette, a civilian, who was Oldsmobile's finest representative for their cannon—he was our very good friend for many months. Gresham was the Curtis Representative and proved to be one of the gang.

The squadron, not yet commissioned, built up its flying time in five SB2C-1C's believed to have been donated by the Smithsonian Institute. These "Beasts" were augmented by a Wildcat; this gave us that added thrill.

By conscientiously dividing our time between the Naval Air Station and Arnold's Bar and Grill, we soon learned to recognize fellow squadron members under any condition. A new era, however, began with the Squadron Commissioning on 15 June 1944, and was the first time the present members had ever been together at one time. Even Kelly and Bagley were there. Captain Hoskins did the honors, and Bush as Senior Ranking Officer ordered us to "Post the Watch". None of us understood what the devil he was talking about. The flash bulbs ceased flashing and we were a duly-initiated, fledgling squadron. This was the first Mundy had heard or seen Captain Hoskins, but he was to chat agreeably with him again one day.

The day of commissioning was outstanding inasmuch as it ended with the Wildwood Country Club as the scene of the first of a long line of social events which were to be symbols along trails blazed by Bombing 86. As acting Skipper, Bush filled the role of host very admirably. Not only was everyone well watered, fed and entertained, but—we all got a kiss from the new brides of Myers and Metcalfe. It was the married men who tried to push through the line more than once. Bush pulled his rank and went through at least seven times. Most of us were later to learn to know the squadron wives very well and they became a big part of our squadron life. They were all good sports and no party without them would have been a success.

The squadron was to have two pilots trained at Harrisburg, Pennsylvania, for aerial photography—so Johnson and Henderson were tempted with talk of per diem, travel pay and a good time, to accept the dubious honor. Bob took his wife and his Ford and Mac took the train and off they went. Johnson developed into a fine photo pilot and Henderson developed into several other things. But they both liked Harrisburg. The talk of per diem was a hoax and both had to pay it back; an old Navy trick.

Our second squadron party was a howling success. True to old Navy fashion, Scotch and Soda ran like sea water from the briny deep and after one of Wagner's delicious party lunches and a session of "Is You Is Or Is You Ain't My Baby," the party secured to Lou Booth's where it gradually disintegrated into a mild nightmare. It was at this party that old John Naughton was bitten so deeply and maliciously by the love bug that from then on his eyes were only for one lass— his Peggy—who by the way is now Mrs. Naughton.

During this period our squadron suffered its initial loss —one that it hasn't forgotten. It was late one afternoon when we received the tragic news that John Abernethy was killed in a training flight near Georgetown, Delaware.

One morning, amid the wild rumors that our squadron had been assigned a skipper, that he was no less a second Captain Bligh and an old sea-going dog from Bombing 3— which we were to later learn was the hottest outfit in the fleet —a stately little red-headed Swede from Minnesota sauntered into the squadron offices to announce his identity as Paul R. Norby, Lt. Comdr., late of the Jacksonville Training Command and our newly-assigned C.O. It didn't take us long to learn to know our congenial skipper, who always had a minute to let you cry on his shoulder regardless of how justifiabl￀ our cause. He listened to all our woes with a smile and everyone was soon marveling at this red-head's ability to get the job done and have us like it.

The fates were with us again, for following our Skipper's arrival, came our second trade school boy, Rick Phillips, driving his dilapidated perambulator salvaged from a junk yard.

Bachelor officers of Bombing 86 were quartered in the Admiral Hotel at Cape May, N. J., a few miles from NAS Wildwood. Here many, many happy hours were spent in the Milk-Bar in the bilge (nasty word, but that's what they call it in the Navy), and in our sacks. Here also is where Harry, the East's greatest shoeshine artist, plied his trade. Each morning we were ferried to the Air Station in a contraption called a "Metro," originally built for Good-Humor vendors.

Wildwood Life—and we're not talking about the birds and bees—was a wonderful life, but it was only to seek relaxation from our military duty that made us indulge in the iniquities of a beach resort. Most of the single fellows could be found at any time—day or night, but the married guys were more conservative and had their good times at home, generally coming out only on week-ends. Parties at the Club were attended by everyone who could walk, so we got to know all the squadron wives. House parties were frequently given or thrown or whatever you do with a house party, and were fun.

One good party deserves another and another. So we had another and another. It was nice at Wildwood because a whole lot of Philadelphia girls were coming down to spend their vacations at the beach, and most of them were good sports and would go out with Navy pilots. Our parties were held at the Officer's Club and were a tribute to Wagner who did most of the arranging. It was at one of these parties that the now famous Norby System for Air-Conditioning and Circulation was developed. The Skipper discovered this when he noticed that the chunks of ice he was throwing into the electric fan had a remarkable cooling effect when they struck someone.

As the summer raced on at Wildwood, the squadron raced on, and as the squadron raced on, the parties raced on—things really moved. The automobile race between Gaffney and Shirley ended up with Shirley's winning a traffic ticket. Later Phillips and a party of eleven had a wild ride through the streets of Wildwood with the cops in pursuit on foot—some shots were heard. Several members of this same gang spent the night in Shirley's garage and suffered from exposure and mosquito bites—all this so Rick could say goodnight to someone. During the period, Rotholz used to sneak off to be gone for days—no one knew where—he retains the habit.

We flew long hours at Wildwood and we learned a lot; we had good times and interesting experiences. Our night flying and our night rendezvous were a kick in the britches. Finally we started flying pre-dawn so that we could get together when it got light. The Skipper led one night hop that eventually became a tour of the entire Eastern Seaboard—it seems he lost Point Option.

The combat experience of Shirley, Sewall, Ward and Marks augmented the Skipper's and the Exec's experience and they all proved to be worthy leaders. During the week, the Skipper made us all work and work hard at our primary job of learning to be a squadron worthy of the fleet. We learned to dive-bomb, glide-bomb, to strafe and to fire rockets; we flew at night and we flew pre-dawn; we bitched and we had fun—but gradually we began to look something like a dive bombing outfit. We had weekly drills simulating carrier take-off and rendezvous—and these separated the men from the boys. It was about 90 to 10 in favor of the boys. Soon we learned that we could do practically anything in the Beast— if we were strong enough.

We also had athletics at Wildwood.

Richards and Bartoloni found romance on the sands at Cape May, and actually spent hours holding hands with the gals on the beach. Jack married his gal but Bart dropped the ball. Jenson, Curtin, Anderson, Brown, Butko, Unger and Nubbin 'K Dubbin' were also Lotharios of the board walk.

The final blow was a real blow, a blow to be remembered —in fact it was a hurricane and it struck with all the force of a hurricane—which was exactly what it was. It ripped up the board walk and cluttered up the front of the Admiral and caused Shirleys to throw another party, and caused the officers at the Admiral to stand in the bar with their shoes and stockings off—and to drink. It caused women to run to the hotel for shelter and it caused the officers to shelter them and to console them and to give them aid and assistance, and to behave oddly, and it caused the Captain to close down the bar. Then we left Wildwood.

OTIS FIELD

After first considering Groton, Connecticut, for a short spell, ComFair Quonset changed its ever-flexible mind and sent the boys to Otis Field, Camp Edwards, Massachusetts, on October 1st for training with the other squadrons of the Air Group. Located on famed Buzzards Bay, the vultures of VB-86 soon acclimated themselves to the golden glories of historic Cape Cod, delving deep into its New England traditions, cranberries, quahog chowder, sandwich glass, scrub pine, sand and fog, with plenty of the latter.

Moody pulled one of his usual fast ones by renting fourteen houses in one day from a local yankee trader and horse-thief named Mrs. Noyes, who also ran the local garage, express agency, travel bureau etc. with a firm hand. And thereupon the marrieds entered a period of domestic life while the bachelors settled down in the homelike surroundings of the old Army barracks at Camp Edwards. Eyer, Everding Johnson, Shirley, Ward, Morris, Greeson, Gittings, Bush settled in the quaint little village of Silver Beach, nestling in the sand dunes with its trim gardens and widows walks. The Skipper salvaged a roomy house from a beaten-down pine grove, Sewall lived in solitary splendor in Pocasset, Moody had a house on a mountain crag with private lake, Prentice lived at Coonamesset Inn, and nobody ever did find out where Phillips actually lived. Lake and Marks had two houses out in the woods where it took several weeks to find them. There they

entertained the local wildlife with succulent dainties from their garbage pails until finally one night the unknown thieves sampled some of Finfield's gin (thrown out by mistake) and never reappeared.

Jealous of the domesticity of others, some enterprising Ensigns, Whisler, Bartoloni, Unger, Prince, and Brown set up a house with black sink fixtures in Silver Beach. All went well until Whisler baked some biscuits. After that the boarding house suddenly and mysteriously broke up. Some of the inmates at a later stage in their career said K rations weren't half bad. What they had in mind we don't know.

Though the delights of such quaint country inns as old Arnold's and LaMartinique were not to be had, Longfellow could not have found a better substitute for the Wayside Inn than the nearby Coonamesset Inn, where genial hostess Mrs. Harris made all feel welcome with her winning manner and warm smile of greeting. With the best of food and drink, many an evening was spent in the spinning of yarns and exchange of good comradarie at this pleasant spot.

And, Oh Yes, there was some flying once in a while, because nobody actually completely forgot what our primary mission was, if they could be torn away from their wives and sweethearts long enough and if the fog wasn't too bad. We were introduced to the delightful sport of "group gropes," which were made even more binding and interesting in the local New England fog, which at times resembled a thick split pea gruel. Nantucket, ancient home of the whaling industry, reechoed to the thunder of our rockets and gaped at Everding trying to fly without his engine turning. Brunswick, home of staid Bowdoin, likewise echoed, but to the snores of grounded birdmen sacked out on account of foul weather. Manchester taught us "close air support," which is another name for Sewall and Shirley showing off to their home townsfolk by playing a tune with their props on local picket fences. Shades of Judge Sewall, woe unto you!

And our flying circus performed even more fantastic stunts. Bill Bush tried to find out if his cockpit canopy was tougher than his own thick skull. It was. Pfeifer tried to pick pine cones with his wheels from the top of one of the few pine trees surviving the September hurricane. His efforts weren't appreciated. Bartoloni showed his contempt for the local admiral by stealing all his flags from the bridge of the Solomons Island. He had to return them. Jenson performed aerial acrobatics off the bow and was severely wetted for his troubles. Flint got tired and went for a swim 150 miles off shore. But the prize episode was donated by Desperate Dan McGrew when he bounced out of a cloud and obliterated a farmer's outhouse on the edge of a corn field and which reputedly commanded an excellent view of a local inlet. The farmer was mad, McGrew scared, but Whisler, who held down the rear seat at the time was quite taken speechless with the whole affair. He has since expressed his feelings volubly in the inimitable style peculiar to a sea-going plumber.

There were parties of course because VB-86 wouldn't be VB-86 without a stinker or two. Two group parties enlivened the duller moments, and the last one at the Skipper's house was really a hummer. Ask McGrew, Barron, Breinholt and others who chose to look for a taxi in some of the neighboring country lanes in the pouring rain.

Most of us stayed close to home on days off, but some of the more venturesome souls sought diversion in other hunting grounds. Whisler, Henderson and Jenson, Jolly Whalers all, thought the possibilities of New Bedford most enticing. Did you know that many of the scenes of "Moby Dick," Herman Melville's American classic of the whaling industry, had many of its scenes laid in this famous old seaport? What, you didn't? Well, neither did the Jolly Whalers, but that didn't stop them from having fun.

There were many interesting bits to enliven our stay at Otis. Our sterling Mascot, "Sleepy" Gresham of Curtiss-Wright, gained everlasting fame by trying and almost succeeding in burning down his hotel together with all his clothes. Then there is a certain prominent individual who bombed and strafed a target on which some local converted fishermen were working. They were reported as being extremely annoyed at the intrusion. Army Nurses' dances were considerably enlivened by the electronic maintenance department lotharios and Red Flint. In this Kuniansky shattered tradition by showing up on time. But the final drama came with the interesting excursions which took place on the U.S.S. SOLOMONS and PRINCE WILLIAM during carrier qualifications. The boys had such a thrilling time in their first taste of real Navy life on the briny deep that they just didn't want to come home to their wives, thereby adhering to an old Navy tradition. The moping, groaning, wailing and gnashing of teeth on the part of the devoted spouses was in the best traditions of the Naval Service and their courage and devotion to duty were indeed phenomenal. Finally after nine days of drinking, gambling, and carousing aboard they finished their landing, (note that landing is singular) and came home.

Of course there was the usual confusion as to when, where, how, and if there would be any leave. Finally orders were issued, the basis for checkages established and all rushed madly away by plane, bus, train, car etc. They say that when the first cork popped in the drawing room of the special train at 1701 on 1 December, 1944, as it headed slowly westward, the old inhabitants of Cape Cod churchyards quietly turned in their graves and breathed a silent prayer that all was ended.

EN ROUTE WEST

The trip was to be long-remembered by its participants. The officers Pullman became known as the U.S.S. Starkey, under the able command of Wilbur, assisted by Phillips, the senior Naval aviator present, and staffed with the steward Homer Lomax and associates, including Mr. Cream of Wheat. All went well until the second night when a broken axle caused a ten hour delay and a complete transfer of Air Group gear, a large job made more difficult by the intense cold of Bellefontaine, Ohio. Phillips and party—porters, chefs, stewards—in the meantime felt no pain. Cocktail hour was 1630 daily in the Ladies' "Head," presided over by Wilbur. Ultimately on a hot afternoon on December 6th, we arrived at our destination, San Diego. The trip will best be remembered by the pay stoppages that have been coming through ever since.

San Diego was only a short stay, but the boys were not at loss for things to do. Nightly forays were made to Tia Juana, Los Angeles, and Hollywood; life was so simple in those days.

On December 13th, we embarked aboard the Munda Bay, for one of the roughest cruises yet encountered. "Frenchy" Bouchard succumbed to the rock and roll of the sea; mal de mer to him was a mortal disease; the sight of the Hawaiian Islands however succeeded in restoring his health and faith in humanity. Our arrival was heralded by a welcome from Tokyo Rose.

MAUI

For two and a half months we basked on the sunny shores of Maui, drank its pineapple juice, absorbed tons of its red dust, and filled its skys with weary, well-worn Beasts. Our home for this period was NAS Kahului, or in the local patois, Naska. The squadron was reduced in size, at this time, from twenty-four to eighteen planes and our already closely-knit group become more closely-knit—so much so that we could almost all pile into one jeep, and, in fact, on one occasion did.

It was here on the "Rock," as the island is sometimes affectionately called, in a barn-like structure known as a Quonset Hut that the "Storm Club, Maui Annex," was born. This was the first in a successful series of Storm Clubs that have given solace, comfort, and peaceful oblivion to us in our hour of need. Under the able direction of our Assistant Gunnery Officer, Ensign (permanent) Fred Rotholz, an empty 1000 lb. bomb was set up in the Club and used as a receptacle for used beer bottles. Every week a new bomb was installed —the old ones being sent to the Fleet for use against barefooted Japanese children.

One of the most amazing phenomena that Navy pilots are apt to encounter on Maui, and encounter they will, is Sweetie Wilson. Sweetie loves the Navy, the Navy loves

Sweetie, and if you care to see the most wicked hula on the island or sing a few choruses of "I Wanted Wings," you will be welcome at any hour of the day or night at Sweetie's home. One memorable night, shortly after our arrival, the squadron moved in a body to investigate the situation. True to expectations we were royally welcomed and royally entertained by Sweetie and her amazing family, which included: Mama, Hawaiian *chanteuse* who tips the scales at a modest 300 pounds; Art, Mama's latest husband and virtuoso of the guitar; Sweetie's three Hula-performing sisters; numerous unidentifiable children of various sizes and colors.

With a slightly hilarious and most enthusiastic audience to urge her on, Sweetie gave one of her star performances. The evening, we thought, was a huge success with only a few minor difficulties encountered. Due to the unfamiliar topography of the neighborhood, Fifield fell off a small cliff. After a brief and cursory examination by Doc Gilliland, who examined the victim from a distance of twenty feet, Fifield was given an even chance to live and we all went back to the party.

Let it not be supposed, however, that our stay on Maui was all beer and skittles. We worked, we trained, and when we finished our syllabus—we went right through it again. Our primary target during this time was Molokini Rock, and let it be said a tougher adversary is hard to find. For two and a half months we attacked with relentless fury. We strafed it, sprayed it with hundreds of miniatures, scored numerous hits with water-filled bombs, and plastered it with live loads. We made dive-bombing attacks, glide-bombing attacks, and minimum-altitude runs. We sallied forth in the day, pre-dawn, and at night. But Molokini took our beating and prevailed in the end—it's hard to sink an island.

In the first of a series of farewell parties, we feted George Marlette. With Bob Johnson as the genial host in the Storm Club, the spontaneous gathering rolled along, gathered momentum, and almost broke into an uncontrolled gallop. When it was noticed that the Skipper was missing, a committee was appointed to force his attendance. He soon made his entrance, sitting in the center of a blanket which was supported by the squadron strong arm squad in the persons of Gaffney, Naughton, Paris and Golden. The Skipper's familiar midnight cry of, "Everybody Up," received its birth at Naska, and became the squadron battle cry.

Transportation was difficult enough without having to retrieve the jeep daily from the pound. We found early that four in a jeep meant four, not sixteen. The climax came not at Indianapolis, but on a mountain cliff, where co-pilot Shirley bailed out in full flight from a careening jeep, piloted by Phillips.

When it became evident that we were soon to forsake our lovely, windswept, dusty home for a drearier clime, a farewell

party was quickly whipped into shape at the beautiful Valley Isle Club. Unfortunately two of our number, Ken Marks and Duke Curtin, were forced to leave the party early in the evening, as some people are often forced to do.

Due to the never-failing efforts of that mad genius of Radar, that man with the persuasive sweet talk, Ray Kuniansky, a goodly number of females were on hand. They ranged in beauty, quality and age from lovely chaperoned high school girls to the Paia Pistol. Many a stout heart trembled and experienced hands shook before the advances of Paia Pistol, but if the word of a gentleman can be trusted, all of us escaped—honor intact. There were many well-groomed guys and gals present, but top honors go to Jense. He chose for the occasion a tie of deep pink and thereby scooped the rest of us who could produce nothing more startling than regulation black. The success of his creation was so marked that Jense wore it on every other occasion that demanded formal attire.

Never ones to pass up a good thing, we decided to have another farewell party even before the native orchestra finished playing "Aloha," at the close of the evening festivities. And have one we did—at the Valley Isle Club again, but this time we had the services of a red-hot swing combo from a local SeeBee outfit. The boys had hardly started playing when Boski Ward recognized them as fellow spirits, and soon he was on the bandstand with them, armed with a sax, pumping out his favorite brand of 1925 jazz. Frank Everding, armed with unbounding self-confidence, made his debut as a drummer—successfully too.

After exhausting the time limit on the club, the party protestingly folded, but the evening's excitement lingered and even followed some of the guests. It was after curfew; Dick Sewall was at the wheel of the carry-all with a load of Maui Citizenry, and a shore patrol jeep made its appearance. Dick made his disappearance via railroad track, cane field and golf course. Some hours later we gathered at the Storm Club and counted noses. It was discovered that we were one short. A scouting party was dispatched immediately to the scene of the night's festivities. There they discovered the recumbent form of Big Ed Nason, stretched out on the grass under the stars sleeping like a baby. Next day we bade farewell to old Maui on one hour's notice, but this quick departure did not escape the ears of Tokyo Rose.

FURTHER WEST

On March 1st, orders to leave Maui were carried out with the pilots flying to Pearl Harbor and the non-flying personnel plus gear being transported by inter-island steamer.

We reported aboard the U.S.S. Independence on March 2nd for transportation to the forward area, but due to a delay in sailing orders, the squadron enjoyed two days of liberty ashore. Only two minor operational accidents occurred and these during the night hours; namely, the Skipper lost his voice and Prentice spun in from low altitude due to vertigo acquired when Rick Phillips unexpectedly extinguished the illumination in their stateroom.

The trip to Ulithi via Eniwetok was uneventful; the routine of "sun and sack" was carried out faithfully by all hands. "Happy Hour" on the flight deck relieved the monotony and increased the desire for the "sack," tenfold. Arriving in Ulithi on the morning of March 13th, we boarded the U.S.S. Wasp during a small typhoon, via cargo nets and an LCM. By 0200 all gear and thoroughly drenched personnel were aboard.

On the morning of the 14th, we sallied forth to grapple with the enemy, never realizing that our cruise would be so brief; for on the 24th, ten days later, we staggered back into Ulithi in company with the battered Franklin and Enterprise.

HOMEWARD BOUND

While at Ulithi, we frequented the Island of Mog Mog where we consumed great quantities of grog grog, and examined with interest the bars installed in native huts, as well as other strange conveniences.

The next stop was at Pearl, where we

prepared to disembark. Mundy and his boys managed to get the gear to Puunene on Maui via air-transport before the order came to return to the ship. With much sweat, strain and blasphemy they retraced their steps and climbed wearily back aboard, just before we weighed anchor for the U.S.A., our homeward-bound pennant streaming 600 feet to the winds.

Seattle was a welcome sight in the morning of April 11th. Wine, women and song provided by understanding residents did not completely take our minds off home, to which we headed two days later.

CALIFORNIA

On the 28th of April, after a strenuous yet restful two weeks leave, we again congregated, this time at Alameda, California. Our stay there was brief, barely enough time to sample the wonders of San Francisco; nice samples they were too.

Santa Rosa, some seventy miles north of Frisco, became our next billet, it was there that we met our new "Beasts." They looked good, felt better but still remained the lumbering unpredictable "Beasts." This was to be our first real taste of Sunny California where it never rained, just a heavy dew 90% of the time. Fortunes were lost overnight in the O'club slot machines; never before have so many "one armed bandits" been assembled in one spot. Russian River became the residential section for those lucky enough to have their wives present. The frequent occasions when the Skipper, Bush, Marks and Shirley slipped up on their navigation going home cannot always be attributed to the mechanical failure of the temperamental "Blue Beetle," a 1928 Graham-Paige relic, co-owned by Shirley and the Skipper, and an object of amusement and mild ridicule to all hands.

As at Maui, two farewell parties were thrown, on successive nights and were held at Bellevue Manor, a bistro set high on the hills of Hillsburg. Cases of vertigo experienced by the carousers were undoubtedly caused by the extreme altitude prevailing.

Both were fun-loving brawls, but on the whole quite uneventful. There is some question as to how the Russian River crowd managed to find their way home and Marks is said not to have recognized his humble abode upon arrival. Finally on the 11th of June, we again shouldered our fifty tons of squadron gear and moved on, back aboard the Wasp awaiting us in San Francisco.

The ship put to sea again on the 13th, and we at once revived the familiar tradition of "Group Gropes." No matter how hard we tried nor how much we carried, we still failed to sink the target-sled.

Arrival at Pearl meant Barbers Point where we shared quarters with the Waves, separated unfortunately by a barbed-wire fence and fifty feet of no-mans land. So far as we know, nobody did any good. Here again the Storm Club came into its own, this being the Oahu Annex; it was a comparatively sedate establishment which served its purpose well during our two weeks stay.

THE LAST LAP

The Wasp sailed on July 11th for what was to be our last trip. Again "Group Gropes" were brought out and aired, interrupted by Wake Island attacks. Arriving at Eniwetok on the 19th, where we sampled briefly of the local nectar, we soon departed again for Japan and the end of the war.

The book "Shore Leave," tells you what we did on our return home. It hasn't happened at the moment of this writing—but it will.

There are several individuals who missed most of the fun, trials and tribulations of VB-86 during its lengthy history because they gave their lives in plane crashes shortly after joining our company. Those members of our organization who gave their lives for their country have a special place in our hearts. Unfortunately we do not have photographs of four of them: Ensign John Abernethy, Ensign Wendall Spaur, George T. Melleney, ARM 3/C, and Arthur W. Jenkins, ARM 3/C. Their brief biographies follow:

ABERNETHY, John—Ensign. John's death on June 29, 1944 was the first unfortunate accident to mar the squadron record shortly after its commissioning on June 15th. His plane crashed during a training hop in the late afternoon near Georgetown, Delaware. Tall, good-looking John was born in Brooklyn, New York, September 16, 1923. A graduate of Brooklyn Tech High School and Clarkson Tech, he earned his wings at Memphis and Corpus Christi. To squadron personnel, John became a symbol of the fact that some will inevitably sacrifice their lives in the performance of their duties. His untimely death deeply shocked all hands and strengthened our determination to train hard and well, so that others would not have to pay the price he did. An only son, John is survived by his parents who live in Brooklyn.

MELLENEY, George T.—ARM 3/C. George was the rear-seat gunner of Ensign Abernethy at the time of their fatal crash on June 29 near Georgetown, Delaware. He had transferred from Norfolk, Virginia, to Wildwood as an original member of the squadron upon its commissioning, following radio school at Memphis, gunnery school at Hollywood, Florida, and operational training at Jacksonville. George impressed all his fellow aircrewmen as a very pleasant good fellow, one who would have played a key part in squadron life. He is survived by his mother, Mrs. Ruth Melleney of 43 Superior Street, Providence, R. I.

SPAUR, Wendall Orvin—Ensign. Deacon was with the squadron only for a few days before he met his unfortunate death in a plane crash near the island of Lanai in Hawaii. He had come to us along with Jim Collins and Dunk Dunklee as a team from VB-100 around the end of June at Barbers Point. Wendall was a resident of Tracy, Iowa, where he was born and attended high school. A product of flight training at Corpus Christi, he had spent a brief period with VB-98 following operational training. A quiet unassuming chap, Deacon was heartily welcomed into VB-86. Intensely interested in athletics and hunting, he immediately gained the respect and affection of his fellows. Deacon is survived by his parents, Mr. and Mrs. Z. R. Spaur of Tracy, Iowa.

JENKINS, Arthur Milton—ARM 3/C. Art was born on January 21, 1924 at Clarkson, New York, and joined the squadron on June 23, 1945 at Barbers Point, four days before he met his untimely death in a plane crash in the Hawaiian Islands as rear-seat gunner for Ensign Wendall Spaur. Art had a most impressive war record. He had served aboard the U.S.S. CLEVELAND during the North African invasion in 1942 and later was with the same ship during attacks on Japanese-held islands in the Pacific during 1943. Following aircrewman school, he was with VB-100, from which he joined us. Art was a welcome addition to the crew, not only because of his experience but also because he was just a plain good fellow. His mother, Mrs. Ruth E. Jenkins, lives at 74 Spring Street, Brockport, New York.

Front Row (left to right):

    T. D. Daly, L. L. Holmes, F. "M" Rotholz, Jr., D. "E. B." Unger, G. Curtin, D. L. Dunklee, K. F. Marks, P. B. Brown, J. T. Lake, Jr., W. W. Bush, Jr., P. R. Norby, R. L. Gittings, W. G. Mundy, R. H. Sewall, R. B. Ward, W. M. Krause, R. L. Kuniansky, F. D. Everding, Jr., T. W. Hays, C. W. Coleman. . . .

2nd Row:

    C. E. Bougan, H. J. Mallia, W. G. Larsen, E. R. Daigle, W. B. Eschbach, B. C. Staba, E. O. Hazlett, M. W. Henderson, J. N. Collins, E. E. Wood, C. C. Golden, W. F. Paris, J. B. Naughton, D. B. Gaffney, D. J. Anderson, E. M. Nason, Jr., W. A. Bache, J. E. Breinholt, D. E. Prince, C. E. Neal, J. H. White, M. P. Bouchard, R. W. Baskerville, N. W. Flynn, F. S. Sabia. . . .

Back Row:

    W. H. Winkle, R. L. White, E. O'Brien, B. A. Lauzon, M. H. Ploof, A. O. Horn, J. B. Lange, W. R. Baker, C. M. Thompson, F. J. Rahilly, J. D. Forrest, A. E. Albertelli, W. F. Ray, J. G. Lightner, L. P. Strong, A. K. Reese, S. Gadjanski, O. J. Berger, Jr. . . .

Front Row (*left to right*):

D. E. Prince, D. E. B. Unger, J. D. Brown, D. B. Gaffney, W. F. Paris, J. B. Naughton, J. E. Breinholt, F. M. Rotholz, M. W. Henderson, R. Johnson.

Second Row:

L. L. Holmes, G. Curtin, T. E. Jenson, C. C. Golden, W. M. Krause, R. H. Sewall, J. G. Shirley, W. G. Mundy, R. L. Gittings, P. R. Norby, W. W. Bush, J. T. Lake, K. F. Marks, P. B. Brown, R. L. Kuniansky, F. D. Everding, R. B. Ward, E. M. Nason, C. W. Coleman.

Third Row:

R. L. White, R. L. Sayre, H. N. Taylor, M. H. Ploof, W. G. Larsen, F. J. Rahilly, S. Gadjanski, C. E. Neal, C. M. Thompson, S. C. Morris, C. W. Warchol, H. J. Mallia, A. J. Motulewicz, W. H. Winkle, B. A. Lauzon, B. C. Staba.

Back Row:

T. D. Daly, F. C. Lockett, A. O. Horn, W. F. Ray, W. R. Baker, J. G. Lightner, J. D. Forrest, E. O. Hazlett, C. E. Bougan, L. P. Strong, B. P. McGovern, F. S. Sabia, N. W. Flynn, E. R. Daigle, O. J. Berger, M. P. Bouchard.

THE  PILOTS

Pilots' Motto
"If you can't convince 'em, confuse em."

DIRECTORY OF OFFICERS

NORBY, Paul Robert	Lt. Cdr.	Naval Aviator	Commanding
***PHILLIPS, Richard William	Lt. Cdr.	Naval Aviator	Executive
BUSH, William Whiteley, Jr.	Lt. Cdr.	Naval Aviator	Executive
GITTINGS, Robert Louis	Lt. Cdr.	Naval Aviator	Flight
*PRENTICE, Sheldon Ellsworth	Lt. Cdr.	AV(S)	ACI
MUNDY, William Gardner	Lieut.	AV(S)	Administration
BROWN, Paul Bradley	Lieut.	AV(S)	ACI
LAKE, Jarrett Townsend, Jr.	Lieut.	Naval Aviator	Engineering
MARKS, Kenneth Fifield	Lieut.	Naval Aviator	Gunnery
WARD, Robert Bruce	Lieut.	Naval Aviator	Welfare
SEWALL, Richard Hartwell	Lieut.	Naval Aviator	Communications
*SHIRLEY, John Gold, Jr.	Lt.(jg)	Naval Aviator	Material
*JOHNSON, Robert	Lt.(jg)	Naval Aviator	Photography
DUNKLEE, Donald Lewis	Lt.(jg)	Naval Aviator	Asst. Gunnery
KRAUSE, William Milton	Lt.(jg)	Naval Aviator	Asst. Flight
KUNIANSKY, Raymond Louis	Lt.(jg)	AV(S)	Electronics
****BROWN, Joseph Donald	Lt.(jg)	Naval Aviator	Oxygen
EVERDING, Franklin David, Jr.	Lt.(jg)	Naval Aviator	Asst. Engineering
PARIS, Warren Francis	Lt.(jg)	Naval Aviator	Statistics
****EYER, Harold Raymond	Lt.(jg)	Naval Aviator	Logs
UNGER, Dale "E. B."	Lt.(jg)	Naval Aviator	Material
NAUGHTON, John Bernard	Lt.(jg)	Naval Aviator	Asst. Engineering
CURTIN, George	Lt.(jg)	Naval Aviator	Oxygen
NASON, Edward McCord, Jr.	Lt.(jg)	Naval Aviator	Navigation
BREINHOLT, James Elmo	Lt.(jg)	Naval Aviator	Radio Engineering
GOLDEN, Charles Carroll	Lt.(jg)	Naval Aviator	Gunnery Material
GAFFNEY, Dale Boyd	Lt.(jg)	Naval Aviator	Parachute
HENDERSON, Mac William	Lt.(jg)	Naval Aviator	Photography
**JENSON, "T. E."	Lt.(jg)	Naval Aviator	Asst. Communications
PRINCE, Dudley Edward	Lt.(jg)	Naval Aviator	Equipment
ROTHOLZ, Fred "M.", Jr.	Lt.(jg)	AV(S)	Gunnery Operations
*ABERNETHY, John	Ensign	Naval Aviator	
COLLINS, James Newell	Ensign	Naval Aviator	Log.
*SPAUR, Wendell Orvin	Ensign	Naval Aviator	
WOOD, Eugene Elmer	Ensign	Naval Aviator	
BACHE, William Austin	Ensign	Naval Aviator	
ANDERSEN, Donald James	Ensign	Naval Aviator	

*—Killed   ****Prisoner of War, Repatriated

**—Missing

***—Detached

LT. CDR. PAUL R. NORBY
SQUADRON COMMANDER
BOMBING SQUADRON
EIGHTY-SIX

NORBY, Paul Robert—Lieutenant Commander. The Skipper hails from Minnesota where he was born on May 16, 1913, in Madison. At present he makes his home in Milwaukee, Wisconsin, at 3056 North Cramer Street. True to his Nordic traditions, he married another Viking descendant, née Dorothy Erickson (Eric), whom he met while both were pursuing culture at St. Olaf College, Northfield, Minnesota. After flooding the market with Westinghouse Electric household appliances for a year with the Interstate Power Company, Albert Lea, Minnesota, he foreswore civilian life for the glamor of naval aviation. Preliminary training was at Wold-Chamberlin Field in Minneapolis before joining the wonder boys at Pensacola, where he qualified for the first $500 in June, 1938. First assignment was with VB-4 on the U.S.S. RANGER, later transferred to the U.S.S. SARATOGA as VB-3, that famous squadron whose members now hold so many important jobs throughout the fleet, including the armchair Navy. At this time he was a mere (whisper!) boot ensign. After the Sara, the Skipper spent two years instructing at Miami and Jacksonville where the Navy could best use his valuable experience. As one of those rare individuals who well knows what he is doing and does it well, his understanding and inspirational leadership have made our tour of duty in Bombing Eighty-Six a pleasure and an honor. Battle slogan—"Everybody Up!"

GADJANSKI, Samuel—ARM 1/C. Sam is the son of Mr. and Mrs. Peter Gabrich of Akron, Ohio, and was born on January 10, 1922. He graduated from Kenmore High School in 1941. He is one of the best-liked men in the squadron, having an excellent sense of humor and being noted for his loyalty and sincerity. As the "Skipper's" aircrewman and leading radioman, he has shown outstanding ability in leadership. Previous to joining Bombing 86, Ski had duty in Panama, Columbia, and Jamaica, B.W.I., with that "Sub-Busting" Squadron, Scouting Sixty.

ANDERSEN, Donald James—Ensign. A runner-up to the mighty Gaff as the Hercules of Bombing Eighty-Six, Andy is one of the trio that joined us at sea. Like Wood, he hails from the Illinois country, having been born within the corporate limits of Stager in 1924. Although he deserted the home county to attend high school at Roosevelt High, Minneapolis, (a move attributed to his parent's desire to mend his social ways), he claims Kankakee, Illinois, as his present address. Iowa City Pre-Flight started Andy on his naval career, its rugged combat training proving mere child's play for his mighty physique. After sessions at Dallas and Corpus Christi, he moved on to Bombing 98 on the West Coast, where he confesses he enjoyed his first billet beyond all expectations. His Hollywood campaigns have earned him an undying fame on the Vine Street front. Bombing Squadron 100 and 99 were stepping stones to 86. Like his teammates, Bache and Wood, Andy has profited by being put through the Phillips' mill on Saipan. Unfortunately the Potsdam terms cut short his combat tour, but his thorough training plus his easy manner with the stateside natives (female) insure a successful career. Of course the combat missions (which he missed off Japan) will be grim and the awards unpredictable, but we are counting on Andy.

ESCHBACH, Walter Bertram—ARM 3/C. Esch was born on November 19, 1924, to Mr. and Mrs. Arthur Eschbach of Ames, Iowa, where he has lived ever since. Enlisting in December, 1942, Esch was sent to Arizona for flight school. Later he decided to become a combat aircrewman. After Memphis, Purcell, and Deland, his ambitions were realized when he joined VB-98. Esch joined the squadron in August 1945, and in a short time became well-liked by all. Esch's ambition after the war is to hunt and fish in the Canadian wilds.

BACHE, William Austin—Ensign. This lad, one of the newcomers who joined us just in time to miss the fireworks, is another of our select New England group. Born in 1923 in the austere atmosphere of Providence, R. I., Billy inherits the restraint of tongue and act that marked his forefathers. With the proper stimulation, however, his melodic base voice has been known to unloose itself in non-puritanical strains which rattle the bulkheads of old Ready Five. After a tour with the Army Engineers as a surveyor, Bill decided to transfer his allegiance to the nautical service and packed up for Athens, Georgia. After Pre-Flight he continued his rigorous training program through the halls and hangars of Memphis, Pensacola, and Deland. Then came a short tour on the West Coast with Bombing 98, whence he took off for the forward areas via Bombing 100 and Bombing 99 (Rick Phillips' renowned outfit). So well has the Navy suited Bill—and vice versa—that he plans on eliminating the last letter of his USNR designation—one of our fledgling regulars. Home, however, will continue to be in old Rhode Island, where he has been seen to slip quietly into the Bacchante Room upon occasions for an evening of restrained New England fun.

BASKERVILLE, Robert William—ARM 3/C. Butch was born on July 30, 1924, the son of Mr. and Mrs. Albert W. Baskerville of Fonda, Iowa. Between the date of his enlistment on December 10, 1942, and his arrival in the squadron, he really did the rounds. Butch served with Bombing Squadron 97, 98, 99 and 100 after taking his boots at Great Lakes. One of the quieter members of the gang, he moulded himself in with the ways of the outfit, to become one of the most likeable fellas we have.

BREINHOLT, James Elmo—Lieutenant (jg). Breinie, the squadron's blonde Galahad, hails from the steppes of old Utah, and the thriving little hamlet of Venice, where he was born and has spent most of his life. On September 9, 1921, Breinie acquired membership in a family that eventually totaled five brothers and two sisters. He grew up with a fondness for the outdoors and the rugged life. He enjoys hunting and fishing above all else. His ambition to become an architect took him to Utah State College, where he spent two years. During the summers he worked for his father, a contractor, constructing houses. After leaving college, Breinie worked in the personnel department of the Remington Arms Company as an employment clerk. Breinie's flying aspirations led him into the Navy, by way of Pre-Flight school at St. Mary's College, E-base at Livermore, California and finally advanced flight training at Corpus Christi, Texas. At Deland, Florida, Breinie received his operational training, after which he joined Bombing 86 at Wildwood. As one of the squadron's original fun-loving members, he has shared aplenty in all the good times. He still maintains his unmarried status, however. His duty in the squadron is Radio Engineering Officer, a job for which he is well-fitted and one in which he has ably assisted the Communications Officer.

BAKER, William Royall—ARM 2/C. Our rebel Buddie was born February 29, 1925, in Powhatan, Va. to his proud parents, Ester and Sally Baker. He enlisted in the Navy of '43, took Bainbridge boot camp in his stride, and after the other preliminaries joined VB-86 at its commissioning in Wildwood, N. J. Bake's favorite expression is, "I'll stomp you into the deck," and his nickname is "Dimples." He is one of our non-drinking (a rare specimen in the squadron) fellows whose favorite sports are baseball, bag-punching, and weigh lifting.

BROWN, Joseph—Lieutenant (jg). Hollywood, the sleek-haired Adonis of the outfit, was born in Baltimore, Maryland on April 22, 1924, the son of Mr. and Mrs. Thomas J. Brown of 7011 Bellona Avenue. Having been born in Baltimore, gateway city to the North or South depending on which direction you are going probably accounts for the combined qualities of the suave Southern aristocrat and the smooth city-bred dillentante and Northern cosmopolite. At any rate, this graduate of Malden Catholic High School and ex-sales promotion expert for the Kellogg Sales Company of Boston (six months), certainly has something which the gals appreciate. Brownie was one of Wilbur's wonder boys at Peru E-Base, and he later won his wings at Pensacola. Since then he has acquitted himself well with VB-86. His industry has blended with the sharpness of the other members of the Material Department. In July when again attacking Kure, his plane was forced to land in enemy waters after hits by anti-aircraft fire. After a period of time spent as a POW of the Nips, and during which he charmed the local geisha girls in his own inimitable style, Brownie returned home to bigger and better things.

LOCKETT, Frederick Charles—ARM 2/C. Fred was born on June 7, 1925, to Mr. and Mrs. Charles Enock Lockett, of Ardsley, Penn. Early in 1943, Fred enlisted in the Navy and following his boot training, coupled with a successful aircrewman course, joined the gang on the squadron's commissioning day. With his grand personality and constant good words for everyone, he became one of the best-liked fellows we had. Striking against the enemy on July 28, 1945, Fred was shot down and underwent the rigors of a POW until repatriated when the Nips hollered quits.

BROWN, Paul Bradley—Lieutenant. Our ACI Officer, Paul, hails from the Middle West at large, though he is by no means isolationist. Born in Lake City, Minnesota, he attended high school in Clinton, Iowa, and at present makes his home near Detroit at 137 Elmhurst, Highland Park. An architect in civilian life, Paul received his training at Oberlin College (1933) and the University of Michigan (1936). Before joining the Navy, Paul worked for a spell with the Des Moines Register, where he gained his facile pen, and later worked with H. T. Keyes and Harley and Elkington, both architectural firms of Detroit. As a sideline he taught math and engineering at the Detroit Institute of Technology from 1937-1941. A graduate of the naval recognition school at Columbus, Ohio, and ACI school at Quonset Point, Paul immediately became a nautical sailor with VC-29 and VC-95 aboard the Santee. Later he became a dive bombing expert with VB-2 on the Hornet, which gained fame in the First Battle of the Philippine Sea. Before joining VB-86 in April 1945, Paul became well-known and almost a legend by virtue of numerous telephone calls to Santa Rosa from various points on the West Coast. It is rumored that he didn't quite get the word across in certain quarters, though since being with VB-86 he has shown great proficiency in giving the word on "target for today", even though, through no fault of his own, the target was usually later changed two minutes prior to "pilots, man your planes".

BUSH, William Whiteley, Jr.—Lieutenant Commander. Bill, or Joe, as he is known to his trade school pals, first opened his nautical eyes in Washington, D. C. on May 25 (excuse it) 25 May 1918. After graduating from Central High School in Washington, our executive officer entered the hallowed halls of the Naval Academy, Class of 1940. His wife, Charlotte, and two youngsters, Mele Lynn, and William Whiteley, III, await his return in Sacramento, California. After serving on the Cruiser Pensacola from June 1940 until October 1942 and seeing action in the Solomons, Bill gained his wings at Pensacola and Vero Beach Florida in 1943. Entrusted with the task of pre-commissioning VB-86 at Wildwood, he later served capably as Flight Officer before becoming Executive Officer in May 1945. His two main problems in VB-86 have been in trying to convert recalcitrant AV(S) officers to regular Navy ways and staying out of the submarine service. On two flights over Japan he ended up both times in the water with later temporary duty as periscope watch officer of a rescuing submarine during a short cruise along the Japanese coast. The presence of "Beelie Boosch" in the post-war Navy insures for all former shipmates in civilian life "a good deal for their money" and their best chance of knowing a future admiral.

BOUGAN, Charles Evans—ARM 1/C. Erstwhile member of the "old outfit", Duck was born July 8, 1925, in Cristobal, Canal Zone. After graduating from Balboa High School, he was employed by the Army until he enlisted in the Navy shortly after the outbreak of the war. Best swimmer in the group—he ditched twice to prove it. Duck is living for the day he can go home to his better half and the "Boss", John Charles. It's a safe bet, however, that the Mrs. will keep close tabs on Duck Butt, and make him avoid strange submarines.

COLLINS, James Newell—Ensign. Jim was born on October 23, 1923, in Corsicana, Texas but now makes his home with his parents, Mr. and Mrs. James I. Collins, in Corpus Christi. He graduated from Itasca High School and attended Texas A & M for one year. Prior to joining the Navy, Jim spent six months working as a maintenance man with the Corpus Power and Light Company. Upon entering the Navy, Jim reported to Del Monte for his Pre-Flight; thence to Hutchinson, Kansas, for elimination training and finally to Corpus Christi, where he completed his training and was commissioned an Ensign as of July 1944. Having finished his official naval schooling, Jim reported to Bombing 98, a replacement squadron at Los Alamitos, California. From here he was transferred to Bombing 100 at Barbers Point, Oahu, T. H., where we plucked him for our very own. His youth and handsome mien recommended him at the start, and the presence of vigorous young blood in the old outfit has proved to be a healthy stimulant. His favorite pastime aboard ship is sampling upper and lower sacks, and cots, in junior staterooms. After the war however, he plans to settle down deep somewhere in Texas. One other accomplishment of Jim's is that thus far he has not been contaminated by the old roués of the squadron. Stay clear, Jim!!!

HAYS, Teddie William—ARM 2/C. Ted, the son of Mr. and Mrs. Crawford Hunter, was born in 1921 and makes his home in Enterprise, Oregon. In May of '42, he was indoctrinated into the Navy, and since that time has really been around with boot camp at San Diego, radio at Texas A & M, NATTC for aviation radio and gunnery at Hollywood. Ted's first tour against the enemy was spent in hitting them in the Gilberts, Marshalls, Truk, Kwajalein, and now that he is with us he has hit Japan. Quite an all around chap!

CURTIN, George—Lieutenant (jg). Duke Curtin was born September 20, 1920, in Los Angeles, California, where he currently makes his home at 2311 LaMesa Drive, Santa Monica, with his parents Mr. and Mrs. George R. Curtin. A true son of the "Bear State", he has confined most of his activities to the sunny shores of California. After matriculating with various movie starlets at Santa Monica High School, Duke moved on to the University of Southern California. The war cut short his career there and he entered Pre-Flight at St. Mary's, followed by Corpus Christi for those bright wings he wears which have proven such a snare for the young ladies. Flying wing on the Skipper by day, and wherever fancy dictates by night, Duke is definitely saving himself for another day when he can become a California "ranchero" and cultivate the beauties of The Golden State in his hacienda high in the hills of the Coastal Range, where he doesn't have to fly to look down on the sparkling blue waters of the Pacific. Duke can well be remembered for his philosophical attitude when facing the rigors of bestirring himself in other than a leisurely fashion, his enviable war record and that famous night at the Valley Isle Club when he charmed the Army and was "too tired" to make his own way home.

MALLIA, Hubert Joseph—ARM 3/C. Another one of our New York Staters, Mal gives claim to Schenectady as his birthplace on April 6, 1925, the son of Mr. and Mrs. Joseph Mallia. Graduating from Mont Pleasant High School, he entered the Navy March 15, 1943. Having completed "Boots" at Sampson, Mal proceeded to buck his way thru aircrew training. He is an original member of the outfit and is one of the most likeable guys we know. His present feelings are, "Just show me the Mohawk Valley and I'll be happy."

DUNKLEE, Donald Lewis—Lieutenant (jg). Dunk, the prodigal son of Mr. and Mrs. Elanson D. Dunklee of Wyalusing, Pennsylvania, was born on August 18, 1922. He is one of our newlyweds, having married Frances Kester Dunklee of Long Beach, California, early in May of 1945. Dunk graduated from Wyalusing Boro High School and spent two years at Millersville State Teachers College before he was grabbed up by the Navy. Dunk took his Pre-Flight at Chapel Hill, N. C., E-Base Training at Minneapolis, and in July 1943 received his wings at Corpus Christi. After leaving Operational Training at Daytona Beach, he joined VB-1, then at Hilo, Hawaii; from here he transferred to VB-5 and remained with it for eight months aboard the U.S.S. YORKTOWN. Upon returning to the states, Dunk became an instructor and leader of a combat team, first in VSB-1 at Cecil Field, then to VB-98, CASU-7 and finally VB-100 at Barbers Point, Hawaii. In July of 1945 we picked up Dunk and his team at Barbers Point, and made him a valuable addition to our squadron. Dunk's claim to fame is in the possession of the "zootiest" piece of headgear yet seen aboard.

ALBERTELLI, Albert Edward—ARM 2/C. Al was born to Mr. and Mrs. Albert Albertelli on June 8, 1924, in Babylon, L. I. He attended Haaren High School in Manhattan and enlisted in the Navy on August 14, 1942, at Newport, Rhode Island. This tall lad saw action with VB-2 aboard the U.S.S. HORNET. Though a new member to the squadron, he is recognized as one of the gang, and is a well-liked chap. Al thinks mainly about going home to his beautiful Jo, soon to be Mrs. Albertelli.

EVERDING, Franklin David, Jr.—Lieutenant (jg). Frank was born June 24, 1921, in Baltimore, Maryland, where he intends to make his post-war home with his wife Lucille and charming daughter, Judy Lynn. At the Baltimore Polytechnic Institute, where he graduated in 1940, Frank received a thorough technical education. With a good academic record behind him, he was able to begin his career in the laboratory of the Rustless Iron and Steel Corporation in Baltimore. He worked here as a steel inspector from 1941 to 1942. Having grown up in a maritime city with sailboating as his favorite hobby, it was a very natural and right thing for Frank to go into the Navy at the outbreak of the war. He took his Pre-Flight training at the University of Iowa and then went on to E-base at Minneapolis. It was here that certain happy circumstances prevailed, and he met Lucille, the future Mrs. Everding. They were married soon after Frank received his wings at Pensacola in 1944. After operational training at Miami, Frank joined Bombing Squadron 86 at Wildwood early in June 1944. His squadron duty has been that of Landing Signal Officer and Assistant Engineering Officer. While still an Ensign, Frank was made a section leader in recognition of his flying ability and leadership. His quick good nature made him an ever-popular squadron member.

LIGHTNER, Joseph Gerald—ARM 2/C. Joe was born at Dixonville, Pa. on March 17, 1924. He is the son of Floyd and Grace Lightner of good old Pennsylvania Dutch origin. He joined the Navy April 23, 1943, and went to Great Lakes for "Boots", Memphis for radio, Yellowwater for gunnery, Cecil Field for operations, and finally joined the squadron at its commissioning. J. G.'s wife, Nonie, and son Larry live at Indiana, Pa., where he expects to live as soon as his "term" is served.

EYER, Harold Raymond, Jr.—Lieutenant (jg). Hal, affectionately known as "Porky" to the squadron, was born some 23 years ago in Long Beach, California, where his wife, Betty, and infant son, Craig, happily await his return. Hal has been listed as "missing in action", but the good news that he is prisoner of war in Japan has recently been received. After his graduation from high school in Long Beach, Hal spent two years at Long Beach Junior College studying for the legal profession. Soon after the outbreak of the war, he joined the Navy by way of St. Mary's Pre-Flight school. He went through E-Base at Pasco, Washington and received his wings at Corpus Christi in January 1944. After completing operational training at Deland, Porky joined Bombing 86 at Wildwood as Log Officer. On March 19, 1945, Hal took part in the raid on Kure Naval Base, Japan, where he was forced to ditch his plane in the Inland Sea, subsequently being taken prisoner. Everyone in the squadron will be very glad to see Hal's familiar rotund figure around again. It is believed he had a premonition that he would spend a short sojourn in Japan, for he became quite rolypoly during his stay with VB-86.

McREYNOLDS, William—ARM 3/C. Mac was born in October, 1923, to Mr. and Mrs. Hadley McReynolds of Trenton, Missouri. After graduating from high school, Mac enlisted in the Navy. Mac decided to be an aircrewman, and after training at Memphis, Yellowwater, and Daytona Beach, his ambitions were realized. He was assigned duty in VB-86, where he took over the rear-seat of Ensign Eyer's Helldiver. Shot down at Kure on March 19, Mac died of wounds during an all-night stay in the icy waters of Kure Harbor. His loss is keenly felt.

GAFFNEY, Dale Boyd—Lieutenant (jg). Gaff, the Man Mountain Dean of VB-86, thrust his ponderous frame onto the world at Tarkio (not Tokyo) Missouri on April 10, 1923. He now considers himself a true native of California, living with his wife, Florence, and Mother at 761 North Fair Oaks Avenue in Pasadena. Gaff went to the Glenwood Iowa High School, and later worked with the A & P Tea Company and Railway Express Agency before striking for naval aviator. Flight training consisted of Pre-Flight at Del Monte, California, E-Base at Hutchinson, Kansas, and flight training at Corpus Christi, Texas. Gaff has hung up a sterling record, but naval architects have caused him more trouble than the Nips. Passageways are too narrow, hatches and doors are too small, and the overhead is constantly reaching down and slapping him on the back of the neck. He has trouble squeezing himself into the cockpit of his plane, and of course his sack is much too short. In spite of this nobody has ever heard him beef (that is not too much). Because of his prowess at navigating himself around, Gaff has been in the Navigation Department and also Parachute Officer in Material. His knowledge of chutes stood him in good stead when he parachuted to safety following a mid-air collision.

O'BRIEN, Eugene—ARM 1/C. This prodigal son of Mr. and Mrs. O'Brien was born on April 27, 1924, in Queens, New York, a suburb of Brooklyn. Gene graduated from Brooklyn Tech, before joining the Navy at Newport, R. I. After having passed aircrewman's training with flying colors, he joined VB-17 aboard the U.S.S. BUNKER HILL. Gene has the dubious honor of having flown in the first Helldiver Squadron to see combat. He joined VB-86 in July '45 while at Barbers Point.

GITTINGS, Robert Louis—Lieutenant Commander. Bob was born July 19, 1916, in Grandfield, Oklahoma. At present he makes his home in Jacksonville, Fla., with his wife Ruth, small daughter Louise, and new addition, Sharon Anne. After graduation from Grandfield High School, he was awarded a B.S. degree in Mechanical Engineering by the University of Oklahoma in 1939. Shortly thereafter he entered the Navy and began flight training at Opa Locka, Florida. He went through Pensacola, and in 1940 received his wings. As one of the most experienced men in the squadron, Louis has a record that is at once impressive. His first duty was that of Primary Instructor at N.A.S. Jacksonville in 1941. He was successively Engineering Officer of VS-1D5, and Flight Officer of VS-2D5, in 1942. While serving aboard the U.S.S. CLEVELAND as Naval Aviator that same year, he saw duty both in the European and Pacific theatres. Before joining VB-86 as Flight Officer, Louis was Commanding Officer of VS-57, 1943-44. Many Flight Officers appear to be slave drivers, but Louis has been extremely fair and lenient, for which consideration every man gives him a vote of thanks. His experience and even-temper have been a great asset.

FLYNN, Nelson William—ARM 3/C. Errol is the proud son of Mr. and Mrs. Albert R. Flynn of New York, and was born on May 3, 1925. Entering the Navy July 28, 1943, and receiving Boots at Sampson, he later tried his luck at aircrew training. At this he made out very well due to his ability to learn, and willingness to fight. He entered the squadron shortly after it formed and fitted in exceptionally well. We all know Errol for what he is, a very good sport.

GOLDEN, Charles Carroll—Lieutenant (jg). G.O. was born on February 28, 1923, in Hammond, Indiana, which has been his home ever since with his Mother, Mrs. Thomas J. Golden. He graduated from the Catholic Central High School and then went out into the cruel world to earn his living with The Pullman Standard Car Mfg. Co. as an Overhead Crane Operator. As soon as the Navy beckoned and the draft board began to close in, G.O. joined up and started his Pre-Flight at Del Monte, thence to Hutchinson, Kansas for E-Base and finally on to Corpus Christi where he received his wings in February 1944. G.O. was another of the original members who put VB-86 in commission, and since that time he has been the "live-wire" of the squadron, the source of 99% of the humor. After flying the "Beast" for better than a year, he has finally realized that it is better to "fly to live" rather than "live to fly"; in other words acrobatics are out; well, almost. As Ordnance Material Officer, he has, amongst other things, maintained our bomb-sights to a point where a miss in bombing is due only to cockpit trouble. G.O. will long be remembered for his lively dissertations on the merits of green pickles and yellow olives.

DALY, Thomas Dominic—ARM 2/C. Tom boasts New York City as his place of birth, having been brought into the world on February 21, 1915. After enlisting in the Navy on April 15, 1943, and wearing his "Boots" at Sampson, he joined the boys of Eighty-Six. Always a good-natured fellow, Tom will most be remembered for his big-dealing ways of acquiring the best for us all. Now, with the war at an end, he wishes to return to Piermont, New York, where his lovely wife, Frances, is waiting for his return.

HENDERSON, Mac William—Lieutenant (jg). Mac was the final event in a series of seven girls and two boys. A boisterous, happy-go-lucky fellow, he was born December 9, 1920, in Evanston, Wyo., where he currently makes his home. As several young ladies know only too well, Mac is still a single man. He was educated at Evanston High School, graduating from there in 1938. Mac's colorful and adventurous personality has spurred him on through a variety of experiences, to his present accomplished status. This ambitious and aggressive redhead has worked, during his fabulous career, as a bill collector, hotel clerk, cowhand, construction gang laborer, and gandy dancer. Before entering the Navy, Mac was warehouse foreman in the transportation department of the Union Pacific Railroad. After beginning his naval career as a yeoman, Mac went to St. Mary's College, Calif., where he attended Pre-Flight School. He went on to E-Base training at Livermore, N.A.S. Oakland, Calif., and finally arrived at Corpus Christi, Texas, in August of 1943. He received his wings February 2, 1944. He was assigned to VB-86 and has been with the squadron since its commissioning. Mac received special photographic training at Harrisburg, Pa., and his skill at that art has made him an invaluable member of the squadron. Mac's social activities have gone far in establishing his and the squadron's reputation.

HOLMES, Lewis Lovell—ARM 3/C. Lou is the prodigal son of Mr. and Mrs. L. H. Holmes of Akron, Ohio. He was born April 14, 1925, and joined the Navy in the early part of 1943. After training as an aircrewman, he participated in the commissioning of the squadron. He is a quiet, good-natured fellow, well-liked by all. Whether he continues his studies in mechanical engineering or sets up a business of his own will be determined when he can say, "Goodbye Navy".

JENSON, "T" "E"—Lieutenant (jg). Jense, the son of Reverend and Mrs. Tilden M. Jenson, was born on September 29, 1923, in Dallas, Texas, which has been his home ever since. He graduated from Valley View High School and attended North Texas State Teachers College for two years prior to joining the Navy. Jense spent the summers of 1941 and 1942 working for the U. S. Postal Service in the capacity of money order clerk and stamp salesman. Tom joined the Navy in 1942, and being of stout heart and sound body, went to Pre-Flight at Athens, Ga., E-Base at Olathe, Kansas, and finally returned deep into Texas where he received his wings at Corpus Christi in February of 1943. Jense was in attendance at Captain Hoskins' commissioning party June 15, 1944. His ever-present humor and easy affability were always in evidence, whether at work or at play, and carried the squadron through some of its rougher moments. His easy Texas philosophy enabled him to give or take a joke equally well. As Assistant Communications Officer he was invaluable, especially in the job of helping the crewmen in the task of tuning transmitters. Jense was lost in action on July 28, 1945, while strafing an enemy tanker at Kure Naval Base, Japan. This was his fourth strike against the enemy.

SAYRE, Robert Lee—ARM 2/C. The son of Mr. and Mrs. Jesse W. Sayre, Bob was born in Sandyville, W. Va. He is reported missing in combat after participating in a strike against units of the enemy's fleet in Kure Harbor, Japan. His personality was marked by consideration and kindness to all he knew. An example of a real shipmate, Bob was outstanding in his rate as an aerial gunner and was held in high esteem among those who knew him. He was a personification of the old saying "Aircrewmen have what it takes".

JOHNSON, Robert—Lieutenant (jg). Bob was born October 4, 1918, at Showell, Md., the son of Mr. and Mrs. Robert C. Johnson now of Collingdale, Pa. He received his education at Collingdale High School and Penn State, where he graduated in 1940 with a B.S. degree in Forestry. It was here that he met Janet, whom he married in 1943 after completing flight and operational training. From 1940 to 1942 Bob worked for Scott Paper Company. His experience and training in forestry research enabled him to take the important position of Superintendent of Treated Paper. He worked in this capacity until the outbreak of the war when he enlisted as an aviation cadet. After E-Base training at Philadelphia, Bob went on to Jacksonville, Florida, and was commissioned a Naval Aviator in December 1942. In 1943-44 Bob served as a member of VB-1. Bob was the squadron's Photographic Officer and one of its outstanding officers until his death in the line of duty, July 3, 1945, in an accident. In the attack on Kure Naval Base, Japan, March 19, 1945, Bob successfully led a division through accurate and intense anti-aircraft fire and personally scored a hit on an enemy carrier. A true gentleman, Bob's friendly and amiable disposition endeared him to all his associates. His untimely death was keenly felt.

McGOVERN, Bernard Patrick—ARM 2/C. Bernie was born in Uniontown, Penn., the son of Mr. and Mrs. Patrick H. McGovern. The family soon moved to Greensburg where they still reside. He became an aerial gunner in early 1943. One of the original members of the squadron, he became known as a happy-go-lucky Irishman who always seemed to have a helping hand for the guy who needed it. Bernie was taken from us as the result of an unfortunate accident but will not readily be forgotten in the hearts of those who loved him as a son, a sweetheart or a pal.

KRAUSE, William Milton—Lieutenant (jg). Bill, familiarly called "Krunch" because of his irreverent treatment of aircraft, is a native of Portland, Oregon, where he was born some 22 years ago on June 13, 1923. Portland is his home, but he has spent much time in Chicago, and Maine, and has traveled widely in Mexico and Canada. Prior to joining the Navy, Krunch spent two years at the University of Oregon. During the summers he worked as a salesman for Standard Oil. Krunch has crowded a lot into his Navy career. He began by entering Pre-Flight School at St. Mary's College. He received his E-Base training at Pasco, Washington, and graduated September 1, 1943 from Corpus Christi. After a short time in VB-1, where he received additional training, he went to VB-100 as Material Officer. Krunch saw his first combat with VB-8, where he was assistant flight officer. Krunch joined Bombing 86 in May 1945 while the squadron was at Santa Rosa. In view of his experience he was made Assistant Flight Officer.

LAUZON, Brian Augustin—ARM 3/C. Brian, son of Mr. and Mrs. Benjamin Lauzon of Three Rivers, Mass., was born in Hartford, Conn. on December 18, 1924. His naval career began December 14, 1942, at which time he began training as an aircrewman. After winning his wings, he served in Bombing 305 which was island-based in the South Pacific. Upon entering our congregation in May, 1945, he was found to be a very likeable guy who constantly found things on the merrier side of life. His magnificent handlebar mustache is his and the squadron's pride and joy.

KUNIANSKY, Raymond Louis—Lieutenant (jg). Kune was born on February 3, 1923, in Atlanta, Ga. He attended the Boys High School at Atlanta and graduated in 1943 from Georgia Tech with a degree of B.S. in Chemical Engineering. Although his Mother, Mrs. Ann Karchmer, now resides at Springfield, Missouri, "the Kune" still fondly regards Atlanta as his true home. Since joining the Navy in 1943, Kune has attended numerous colleges and training bases before attaining his present impressive title as Electronic Maintenance Officer with the squadron. These included the Midshipmen's School at Notre Dame, Radar School at Harvard and M.I.T., and Jacksonville, Florida, where he received his aircrewman's wings. Kune came to VB-86 while the squadron was at Otis in November 1944, thus initiating his inveterate policy—"Better late than never". Since that time he has been invaluable in keeping the Radio—Radar equipment in top shape as well as keeping the aircrewmen happy—a job in itself. From the time he joined the squadron, he has been the hardest man to locate, but surprisingly enough his work is always done and done well. He has been particularly efficient in maintaining the Public Address System in Ready Five in its occasional excellent status. The Kune, in addition to his magician-like ability to stage a disappearing act, possesses an almost unbelievable line of persuasion on the telephone. His efforts in obtaining partners for squadron dances and tangling with the law as a result of his jeep driving have likewise been outstanding. Indeed Kune is quite a character.

LAKE, Jarrett Townsend, Jr.—Lieutenant. Born in Long Beach, California, in 1915, Jerry now makes his home in Los Angeles with his wife, Isabel, and two sons, Jerry III and James William. He attended Los Angeles High School, and graduated in 1939 from Los Angeles City College, majoring in Aeronautical Engineering. In 1940 Jerry began work in the Engineering Department of Lockheed Aircraft Corporation. He followed this up with a job at Douglas Aircraft in their Experimental Engineering Department where he worked on the A-20-A. As a member of the Naval Reserve, Jerry was called to active duty in 1941. After spending six months in AMM school, he was appointed an aviation cadet and received his E-base training at Long Beach, and his flight training at Corpus Christi, where he graduated early in 1942. He remained there as a primary instructor for three months, after which he went to Dallas, Texas as a primary instructor for 15 months. While at Dallas Jerry also served as Assistant A & R Officer and Test Pilot. Following this he went to operational training at Deland, Florida, and was assigned to VB-82 as Aircraft Maintenance Officer. Jerry then came to VB-86 as Engineering Officer where he has successfully flown, babied, threatened, and cajoled the "Beast" to the greater glory of the squadron.

STRONG, Leo Peter—ARM 3/C. The proud son of Mr. and Mrs. Peter Strong of Philadelphia, Leo was born December 2, 1924. Leo longs for the fragrant aroma of the Delaware River. Now that the war has ended, his only thoughts are those of going back to his home. The only gloomy light in Leo's flying career is that he wasn't in the "Old Outfit." Leo is one of the charter members of Bombing Eighty-Six. Together with Jerry, they were "Aces back to back," who participated in devastating attacks against Japan.

MARKS, Kenneth Fifield—Lieutenant. Fifield was born on May 26, 1921, in Taft, California, where he has made his home ever since. He is the son of Mr. and Mrs. H. A. Marks and is married to Inez W. Marks who hails from a hamlet in Florida known as Lulu. Ken graduated from Taft Union High School and from San Mateo Junior College in 1940. Before entering the Navy, Ken worked as a machinist for Emseo Derrick and Equipment Co. Ken took his E-Base training at Long Beach and his Flight Training at Corpus Christi, where he was commissioned in December, 1942. Fifield's billets prior to joining VB-86 are indeed impressive. Over a period of one year he was a member of four different outfits: Pilots Pool in Noumea, VB-12 aboard the Saratoga, VS-57 on New Caledonia, and finally VB-98, where he saw his first combat. Ken flew fourteen missions, of which thirteen were strikes against the Jap base of Rabaul in the Solomons Area. Ken has been a stalwart member of VB-86 since commissioning. As Gunnery Officer he has delegated authority within his department in a manner to be admired. Fifield has absolutely no respect for Bakersfield High School, Taft's hereditary rival.

BERGER, Ollie Joseph, Jr.—ARM 2/C. Ollie, the erstwhile responsibility of Mr. and Mrs. O. J. Berger, was born on April 10, 1923, at Grand Rapids, Michigan. He entered the Navy in January of '43. His desire to become an aerial gunner become more of a reality as he continued to aircrew training. Ollie later joined the squadron at commissioning, and established himself as one of the more serious-minded members of the outfit. Ollie hopes to take up the ties of matrimony someday, and have at least six children, preferably daughters.

MUNDY, William Gardner—Lieutenant. Bill "Moody" was born September 29, 1911, in Riverside, Illinois. At present his home is Plandome, New York, where he lives with his wife, Betty, and two small sons, Gardner and Edward. He was educated at The Hill School in Pottstown, Pa., and Yale University. He played on the Yale Tennis Team and always beat the Harvards whenever they became unpleasant. After graduating in 1933, Bill began a long and highly successful career in business. He first worked for the American Sugar Refining Co. in Brooklyn as a laborer. In 1934 he became traffic and warehouse clerk in Standard Brands, Inc. in New York City. Before entering the Navy, Bill held the impressive title of Assistant to Vice President in charge of sales, for Birds-Eye Snider, Inc. (Frozen foods). Bill's traveling experience is so complete that several Cook's Tour seem pale in comparison. He has traveled extensively in England, France, German, Switzerland, Hungary, Austria, Belgium and Canada, not to mention several slightly wild excursions to Bermuda. Before joining Bombing 86, Bill served as Communications and Administrative Officer in VS-36 and VS-60, both inshore patrol squadrons operating on the east coast. "Moody" has been a real power, the spark plug, the driving force in Bombing 86. With his fine intellect and affable personality, he has kept the squadron rolling efficiently and smoothly. In his capacity as Administrative Officer he has served superbly. His ever-present humor has kept morale at a high level.

NASON, Edward McCord, Jr.—Lieutenant (jg). Nas was born on August 1, 1921, at Cass Lake, Minnesota, and there he has since lived with his parents, Mr. and Mrs. E. M. Nason, Sr. He graduated from Cass Lake High School, then deserted for the War Department where he worked as a Civilian Personnel Administrator from January to December in 1942. In 1943 Nas entered the Navy, and was shunted to Chapel Hill for his pre-Flight Training, then onto Olathe, Kansas, for E-Base and finally to Corpus Christi where he was commissioned in January 1944. June saw Ed at the commissioning of the squadron, one amongst many, but a stalwart member nevertheless. His flying ability is unimpeachable and he is often known as the hottest pilot of the outfit. Rarely does Nas miss his target, be it a towed spar or an enemy ship. This one-fourth part Indian of ours holds down the job of Navigation Officer within the squadron. Nas is definitely the strong silent type when women are concerned as evidenced by his ability to sit quietly at a bar and have the women flock to his side. He is further distinguished by his swimming ability in the ocean off Japan, which he prefers to sightseeing in Nipponland.

COLEMAN, Charles Walter—ARM 3/C. Squirrel, the son of Mr. and Mrs. Risdon H. Coleman, was born on May 13, 1925. Before he could complete his schooling, the Navy beckoned, and in April, 1943 off he went to boot training at Bainbridge, Maryland, after which he breezed through aircrewmen's school, and finally joined VB-86 on the day of its commissioning. Squirrel always has a smile and a pleasant word for all hands, and has established himself as one of the best-liked fellows aboard.

NAUGHTON, John Bernard—Lieutenant (jg). John "Dinkus" Naughton, son of Mrs. Mary A. Naughton and pride of his wife Peggy and his three sisters, was born January 1, 1922, in Pueblo. Colorado. At the Pueblo Catholic High School where he graduated in 1939, this big, good-natured Irishman played an exceptionally good brand of football and rounded out his three letter status in basketball and baseball. Among his intellectual accomplishments, he edited the school paper. After turning a deaf ear to the offers of big-time college football coaches, John went to work for the Colorado Fuel and Iron Corporation. He learned the business of making steel from the ground up, and just before entering the Navy in 1942 he worked at the open hearth, doing steel analysis. John went through Pre-Flight at Del Monte, Calif. and E-Base at Hutchinson, Kansas, finishing his flight training at Pensacola. He has been with Bombing 86 since its beginning in Wildwood. It was while the squadron trained at Wildwood that John met the beauteous Peggy, who later became his wife. This romance kept us all busy for months. As Asst. Engineering Officer, John has done a thoroughly efficient job and has only been thrown once by the "Beast." That occasion was a beautiful but incomplete slow roll off the bow, not far off the coast of Japan.

WARCHOL, Chester Walter—ARM 2/C. Lou first saw the smoke of the Pittsburgh area on August 5, 1924. Since it was the custom of the time, he was sent to school, and many years later wrangled a diploma from the Union High School in Burgettstown, Pa. Lou joined the Navy April 10, 1943, and after withstanding the horrors of "Boot Camp", radio school, and aircrew training, joined the gang at commissioning. He is the most happy-go-lucky guy in the outfit, and one of the best sports we know.

PARIS, Warren Francis—Lieutenant (jg). Warren was born on May 4, 1922, in Wilmington, Delaware but now resides with his Father, Mr. Warren E. Paris, in Sharon Hill, Pa., and is strictly a Philly boy at heart. He graduated from West Philadelphia Catholic High School in 1940; then worked for two years with the E. I. DuPont Company as a draftsman, before entering the Navy. Warren started his Naval career at Chapel Hill, where he took Pre-Flight; E-Base was attained at Bunker Hill, Indiana, where he was one of Wilbur's fledglings, and in January, 1944 he received his wings at Pensacola. Upon completion of his Operational Training at Cecil Field, Warren reported to VB-86 then forming at Wildwood. In his capacity as Statistics Officer, Warren is a decided asset to the Flight Department as keeper of the ever-important figures. He is the only member who has stayed in that department from beginning to end. His two greatest accomplishments are his dancing ability, well-remembered from our Wildwood days, and his terrific gastronomic capacity. He is probably the only member of the squadron who collects K-rations to be eaten as late night snacks.

WINKLE, Walter Henry—ARM 2/C. Known to all as Baldy (for obvious reasons), Wink was born November 10, 1918, to Mr. and Mrs. Albert Winkle. His hometown is Cleveland, Ohio, where his wife and two-year old daughter await his return. Wink came into the Navy in May, 1943, and was sent through Great Lakes "Boot Camp." After a series of unfortunate accidents—Memphis, Yellowwater and Cecil Field—he joined VB-86 at commissioning. His favorite sport is brew drinking, and he can consume enormous quantities. Wink is a good gunner and a great guy.

PRENTICE, Sheldon Ellsworth—Lieutenant Commander. Sheldon, as he was usually known, was our ACI Officer from the commissioning of the squadron until he met an unfortunate death when our ship was struck by a Jap bomb while 48 miles off the coast of Shikoku, Japan, on 19 March, 1945. He is survived by his wife, the former Sheila Potter, and three fine children, Clare, Sheldon, and Sheila, of 103 East 84th Street, New York City. Few people showed more promise to the world than Sheldon. A graduate of St. Paul's School, Concord, New Hampshire, and Harvard University, he had everything to look forward to when he met his untimely end. An accomplished rated polo player, he had traveled extensively in Europe and had made a trip around the world. He was a partner of the brokerage firm of Dominick and Dominick in New York. Friendly, democratic, and genuinely interested in people, Sheldon adopted VB-86 as his own as soon as he was assigned. He is largely responsible for carrying out the splendid ground-training program made available to officers and men, and the collection of pictures and doings of the squadron which he started and organized will cause lasting pleasure to many people. As ACI Officer, he showed painstaking care in obtaining and passing out the word on combat activities. Although forced to fight the war from the deck of his ship instead of from the air, he nevertheless was in the fight, heart and soul, all the time. The world lost a good citizen and VB-86 lost a good friend when Sheldon passed on.

PHILLIPS, Richard William—Lieutenant Commander. Rick was born in 1917, a contemporary of the First World War. His official residence is in up-state New York in the city of Auburn. Rick is one of our two "Trade-school" boys, having graduated from Annapolis with the Class of 1939. Preceeding his flight training. Rick served aboard the U.S.S. QUINCY for three years as a Deck Officer. In 1942 he decided to transfer to aviation, probably feeling that the airplane was here to stay. He· was subsequently trained at Pensacola, Miami and Jacksonville, graduating late in 1942. In December 1942, he joined VB-4, based aboard the U.S.S. RANGER, which was operating in the Atlantic, part of the time with the British Home Fleet. While with this squadron, he participated mainly against German Fleet units in the fjords of Norway. Shortly after VB-86 was commissioned, Rick arrived as our Executive Officer. In May, 1945, he became Commanding Officer of VB-99, a replacement squadron based on Saipan. Rick was definitely one of the boys, a leader in all functions, particularly social. His favorite maneuver was known as the "running rendezvous" which was invariably carried out in foul weather and with little or no success. It took a good man to keep up, let alone find him on these occasions.

MORRIS, Stanley Clay—ARM 3/C. Stan was born September 12, 1922, son of Mr. and Mrs. Stanley Clyde Morris in Cumberland, Md. He enlisted in the Navy the early part of '43, joined our gang at commissioning. Blond, good-looking Stan was an immediate success because of his quick wit and sense of humor. Stan's most cherished dream was to return to his family, to Irene, the girl he loved, and to a life of settled happiness. By God's will Stan is no longer with us, but he leaves memories of a truly great guy.

(Note: Morris flew with Lt (jg) Gaffney until his death; Gadjanski was gunner for Lt. Comdr. Phillips until the latter's transfer.)

PRINCE, Dudley Edward—Lieutenant (jg). Dudley, usually affectionately known to his contemporaries as Nubbin, was born on 19 December, 1923, in Norwalk, Connecticut, a rousing Christmas present to his parents, Mr. and Mrs. Henry E. Prince, with whom he lives at 323 Main Street at the current moment when not floating around on an Essex-Class carrier. Nubbin was quite an athlete at Norwalk High School prior to going to Chapel Hill, North Carolina, for Pre-Flight, Peru, Indiana for E-Base, and finally to receive his wings of gold at Pensacola in January, 1943. Immediately prior to qualifying as a birdman, the Nub stood a tour of duty on a destroyer tender in Casco Bay, Maine, which apparently explains his saltiness. Dud first gained prominence in VB-86 by slave driving the boys into athletics at Wildwood. By keeping them in condition, he not only made the percentage figures look good for ComFair Quonset, but also made one more night possible at Arnold's or the Martinique for all hands. Since going to sea, the Nubbin can usually be found with his head in one of the big red material boxes, checking inventories for the Material Department. Few of us will forget Nubbin as one of the most loyal, conscientious, and pleasant fellows in the squadron.

SABIA, Frank Samuel—ARM 2/C. About the same time that the "Tree" was planted in Brooklyn, Frank was born to Margaret and Frank Sabia on July 10, 1919. He graduated from Textile High School, Brooklyn in 1937. In 1943 Frank joined the Navy, and upon completion of his boot training at Sampson attended radio school at Memphis, gunnery at Hollywood, and operational training at Deland. He joined VB-86, and from there on has won his way into the hearts of everyone with his cheerful singing and disposition.

ROTHOLZ, Fred "M," Jr.—Lieutenant (jg). Fred was born on September 13, 1920, in Rochester, New York, but now resides with his parents Mr. and Mrs. F. M. Rotholz in Fredericksburg, Va. He graduated from James Monroe High School and attended Virginia Polytechnic Institute for three years, one year short of his B.S. degree. Following his schooling, Fred worked for Glen L. Martin in the Production Department. Before the outbreak of hostilities with Japan, Fred volunteered for training with the RCAF and spent 5 months in training in Canada. Early in 1942 he shifted back to the USA and entered naval flight training at the Pre-Flight Base of Chapel Hill, N. C., then on to E-Base at Peru, Indiana. At E-Base Fred decided to change his designation and entered training as a Gunnery Officer at Jacksonville, then Pensacola and finally ended with a two weeks instruction tour back at Jacksonville. Fred is a pretty busy man on strike days, for as Assistant Gunnery Officer he is responsible for the loading and maintenance of all ordnance gear and that is no mean job. His unofficial capacity is scorekeeper for Kamikazies shot down as well as the base for the origination of most scuttlebutt. Fred has fought the promotion Alnavs as hard as he fought the Japs. All hands sweated JG out with him and cheered heartily when he finally made it. Where he goes or what he does on his frequent disappearances, we have never known, but he certainly can be sadder than most people when he receives no mail.

SEWALL, Richard Hartwell—Lieutenant. Deep in the land of the minutemen and sandwich glass, a son was born March 23, 1921, to Mr. and Mrs. Homer Sewall of Waltham, Mass. Dick and wife, Lonnie, are now the new and proud parents of daughter Diane, a newcomer in an old New England family. Dick attended Holderness School in New Hampshire from 1933 to 1939, when he graduated. In 1941 he graduated from Nicholas Jr. College near Boston. Before entering the Navy, Dick worked for the United Shoe Machinery Corp. in Boston. In April, 1942, Dick began training as an aviation cadet at Squantum Mass., and in December, 1942, he received his commission at Jacksonville, Fla. He shipped out to New Caledonia, where he became Operations Officer for CASU-3. In November, 1943, Dick joined VC-38 and participated in the Bougainville campaign and the all-out battles at Rabaul. This scion of New England has proved himself capable and practical in his capacity of Squadron Communications Officer. He is one of the few who understand completely the intricacies of ARA and ZBX.

THOMPSON, Charles Milton—ARM 1/C. Charlie was born August 12, 1917, to Mr. and Mrs. L. H. Thompson of Minneapolis, Minn. He entered the service in April, 1942, received boot training at Great Lakes and radio schooling at the University of Wisconsin. Prior to joining VB-86, Charlie served a tour of duty with VS-60 in Coco Solo, Panama, Columbia, and Jamaica, B.W.I. He has an exceptionally pleasing personality and proves an asset to any gathering. Charlie graduated from Central High, Minneapolis, in 1936 and before entering the service, was employed by Piper, Jaffray and Hopwood, Brokers.

SHIRLEY, John Gold, Jr.—Lieutenant (jg). John was born on November 1, 1919, in North Adams, Massachusetts, which has since been his home. An alumnus of Mt. Herman High School and Colgate University (1941), he spent eight months with Montgomery Ward in Albany, following graduation. John entered the Navy in March of 1942 at Squantum, Mass, for E-Base training, reporting thereafter to Pensacola, where he was commissioned an Ensign in December of 1942. Shortly thereafter, he joined VC-38 for his first combat tour from October, 1943 through March of 1944. From the first John was an important member of VB-86. He was killed in the line of duty while operating from his carrier, on 14 July, 1945. An extremely capable Material Officer, he was the most popular member of the squadron, and was a keystone in all its functions, whether operational or social. John is survived by his wife, the former Jean Malcolm of 31 Overlook Terrace, North Adams, Mass.

TAYLOR, Harold Newton—ARM 1/C. Harold was born in McMullin, Mo., March 5, 1922. "H.N." as he was familiarly called, left boot camp and went directly to an operational squadron. After extensive patrol duty in the Atlantic, he transferred to Bombing 86 in June, 1944. His death in the line of duty on July 14, 1945 was a heartfelt loss to us all. Harold's wife, Mildred, and son, Newton, live in Chicago. H.N. proved himself a valuable man, and was the squadron's leading first class.

UNGER, Dale "E.B."—Lieutenant (jg). The Mid-West metropolis of West Alexandria, Ohio, sent Dale Unger to VB-86, for which it receives our hearty thanks. Born on August 8, 1921, Dale graduated from West Alexandria High School in 1938 and later attended Hebron Junion College for one year before becoming involved in the maelstrom of war. Dale still calls home West Alexandria, residence of his parents, Mr. and Mrs. Ernest B. Unger. Dale spent two years as assistant manager of a delicatessen in Dayton prior to Pre-Flight at Iowa City, E-Base at Minneapolis and final graduation as a full-fledged birdman at Pensacola. Dale will long be remembered as one of the sharp operators who comprised the Material Department. First as "assistant manager" and later as "manager" he succeeded in keeping us all equipped and "almost" ready for flight. What he has in those big red boxes nobody really knows, but it is strongly felt by his squadron contemporaries that great sympathy should be shown towards the customers of that delicatessen if they were subjected to the skillful manipulation shown aboard VB-86 by the material boys. It is rumored that Dale is hot on the trail of completing his college, marrying that gal of his and settling down to the life of the gentleman that he is and always will be.

WHITE, Robert Lennox—ARM 3/C. Born September 1, 1922 in Macomb, Illinois. Bob is the errant son of Mrs. White, and now lives in Washington, D. C. Having graduated from High School, Bob joined the Navy in June of 1942 and entered Flight Training, later enrolling in the Aircrewman's School. Flying in the rear seat was not a new experience to Bob, as it was for most of us, for he soloed long before he rode in the rear seat of the SBD. It was indeed a break when Bob joined the squadron.

WARD, Robert Bruce—Lieutenant. Boski Ward was born on March 4, 1917, in Baltimore, Maryland, where he currently makes his home with his wife, Mary Elizabeth, and small daughter Jean. He graduated from Duke University in 1939 and spent two years at Johns Hopkins. A well-traveled man, Boski has investigated the high spots of Cuba, Jamaica, Honduras, and France. Before joining the Navy, he worked for Glenn Martin in Baltimore as an inspector on the final wing assembly lines. After receiving flight training at Pensacola, Boski joined the Pilots Pool at ComFair, Noumea, where he barely made his four hours monthly until August, 1943, when he joined VB-12 on the Saratoga. There followed in sequence a tour with VS-57 in inshore patrol and four months with VB-98, prior to joining VB-86. Boski took part in the Bombing of Jap ground installations and shipping in the Solomons Area. As Welfare and Recreation Officer, he has proved himself an able accountant, and dispenser of beer and "burgers" on beach parties. In the securing of ice for the "Storm Club," he has been indispensable. On the lighter side, Boski is an accomplished musician. When not in the sack, he may be heard performing ably on the clarinet in his cabin.

FORREST, John Donald—ARM 3/C. Jack is the pride and joy of Mr. and Mrs. Julian I. Forrest, having been born on February 20, 1943 in Baltimore, Maryland. As one of the original members of the outfit, Jack was outstanding for his participating in all of the squadron athletics. Previous to joining the boys he started his Navy career on February 4, 1943, and spent quite sometime at Jacksonville, Florida, where he took "Boots" and aircrewman training. Jack's ambition is to return to civilian life and scout around amid the hustle of skirts.

WOOD, Eugene Elmer—Ensign. A member of the combat team that joined us as we were recuperating from Kamikaze jitters, Woodie has taken well his quiet and unassuming place in the squadron. Born in the intellectual atmosphere of Champaign, Illinois, in 1920, he soon moved even deeper into the corn country and took up residence in Waterloo, Iowa. Here he attended East Waterloo High, and then sallied forth into the business world to work in the tool-making department of Consolidated Aircraft during his pre-war years of 1941 and '42. The Navy was not to be denied a good man, however, and Woodie left the tall corn of Iowa for the tall tree country of California, submitting his natural abilities to the polishing-off process at St. Marys. Further training at Norman and Corpus Christi prepared him for his assignment to VB-98 in October, 1944 and VB-100, Barbers Point, the following May. He accredits most of his present skill, however, (as a Naval Aviator, and otherwise) to the period of intensive training with Ricks' Rough Riders (VB-99) on Saipan. There came the final indoctrination in the rigors of fearless flying and staunch bar-work which mark a true Naval Aviator. Quiet and unassuming on the surface, Woodie is said to incorporate, in his alter ego, this rough training of Ricks'.

WHITE, Joe Hunter—ARM 3/C. Joe was born July 31, 1925, son of Mr. and Mrs. Bob White of Wellington, Texas. Little Joe started roping steers about the same time he started school. The call of the draft board was stronger than the call of the prairie, so Joe enlisted in November of '43, and was sent to San Diego for "Boot Camp." After going through the horrors that make good gunners, Joe joined the squadron in August of '45. In his short stay with us Joe has become well-liked by all.

THE  CREW

CREW'S MOTTO

"Do unto others before they can do it to you."

ALBERTELLI, Albert Edward	ARM2c	Aircrewman
BAKER, William Royall	ARM2c	Aircrewman
BASKERVILLE, Robert William	ARM3c	Aircrewman
BERGER, Ollie Joseph, Jr.	ARM2c	Aircrewman
BOUCHARD, Marcel Paul	PR1c	Parachute Rigger
BOUGAN, Charles Evans	ARM1c	Aircrewman
COLEMAN, Charles Walter	ARM3c	Aircrewman
DAIGLE, Ernest Reed	AMM1c	Machinist Mate
DALY, Thomas Dominic	ARM2c	Aircrewman
ESCHBACH, Robert Bertram	ARM3c	Aircrewman
FLYNN, Nelson William	ARM3c	Aircrewman
FORREST, John Donald	ARM3c	Aircrewman
GADJANSKI, Samuel	ARM1c	Aircrewman
HAYS, Teddie William	ARM2c	Aircrewman
HAZLETT, Ernest Ottis	ACOM	Chief Ordinanceman
HOLMES, Lewis Lovell	ARM3c	Aircrewman
HORN, Arthur Oliver	AMM2c	Machinist Mate
*JENKINS, Arthur Milton	ARM3c	Aircrewman
LANGE, Johnie "B."	S1c	Yeoman Striker
LARSEN, William Gilbert	ART1c	Radar Technician
LAUZON, Brian Augustin	ARM3c	Aircrewman
LIGHTNER, Joseph Gerald	ARM2c	Aircrewman
****LOCKETT, Frederick Charles	ARM2c	Aircrewman
MALLIA, Hubert Joseph	ARM3c	Aircrewman
*McGOVERN, Bernard Patrick	ARM2c	Aircrewman
*McREYNOLDS, William	ARM3c	Aircrewman
*MELLENEY, George Thomas	ARM3c	Aircrewman
*MORRIS, Stanley Clay	ARM3c	Aircrewman
NEAL, Calvin Eli	ACMM	Chief Machinist Mate
O'BRIEN, Eugene	ARM1c	Aircrewman
PLOOF, Merrill Homer	AMMP2c	Propellor Specialist
RAHILLY, Foch James	Y1c	Yeoman
RAY, William Fleming	AMMH1c	Hydraulic Specialist
REESE, Allan Kennedy	AEM1c	Electrician's Mate
SABIA, Frank Samuel	ARM2c	Aircrewman
**SAYRE, Robert Lee	ARM2c	Aircrewman
STABA, Benjamin Charles	AM1c	Metalsmith
STRONG, Leo Peter	ARM3c	Aircrewman
*TAYLOR, Harold Newton	ARM1c	Aircrewman
THOMPSON, Charles Milton	ARM1c	Aircrewman
WARCHOL, Chester Walter	ARM2c	Aircrewman
WHITE, Joe Hunter	ARM3c	Aircrewman
WHITE, Robert Lennox	ARM3c	Aircrewman
WINKLE, Walter Henry	ARM2c	Aircrewman

*—Killed

**—Missing

****—Prisoner of War, Repatriated

NEAL, Calvin Eli—ACMM. On November 23, 1917, Mr. and Mrs. J. T. Neal of Davidson, Tennessee, became the proud parents of Calvin. After finishing grade school, Neal attended Cumberland County High School in Crossville, Tenn. Neal joined the Navy in 1936 and has attended several schools, among them, AMM School at Norfolk, Aviation Instrument School in Philadelphia, and the Sperry Gyroscope School in Brooklyn. Neal became a member of Bombing 86 at the time of its commissioning, June 15, 1944. Ever since joining the squadron, Neal has been our leading chief, a veritable God-Father to all hands.

HAZLETT, Ernest Ottis—ACOM. Ernie, our "Gunner", was born in Millnersville, Ohio, on May 18, 1918, and graduated from Springfield Township High School, Summit County, Ohio. A 20 year Navy man, Ernie went to Boot Camp at Great Lakes, followed by Receiving Station, Norfolk, Va. and in turn Hedron 5, NAS, Scouting 60 and finally Bombing 86. Prior to entering service, Ernie was employed by General Motors Truck and Coach Division, Pontiac, Michigan. Ernie's better half is Edith Alice. They have two sons, Lynn Robert, and Christopher Lowell.

BOUCHARD, Marcel Paul—PR 1/C. Frenchy, son of Mr. and Mrs. Joseph Bouchard, was born in 1912 in Woonsocket, Rhode Island. The financial expert of the squadron, he had a roaring upholstery industry in a 9 x 12 back-yard garage in Providence, Rhode Island. Frenchy is a fiend in the water, but not on it. His susceptibility to mal de mer has made life aboard carrier somewhat unpleasant for him on more than one occasion. He constantly longs for the good earth and his wife. In spite of all hazards, however, he has performed his duty well. Frenchy's wife, Anna, awaits "the old man of the crew" at their home in Providence.

DAIGLE, Ernest Reed—AMM 1/C. Ernie increased the population of Louisiana by one in 1923. Daigle went to Church Point High School and by an Act of Congress graduated in 1941. In June of '41 Daigle entered the service and was stationed in Norfolk. He had to stay there longer than any living man should have to stay there. He finally received a break and was sent to Wildwood, and VB-86. While he was there, he met some slick chick from Philly, but that's all the dope we have because Daigle isn't talking.

HORN, Arthur Oliver—AMM 2/C. Al was born June 24, 1924, in Lincoln, Nebraska, the only son of Mr. and Mrs. George Horn. He attended Lincoln High School and joined the regular Navy in June of 1941, going through boot training at Great Lakes, then to the Canal Zone, and finally to Bombing 86. He holds the unchallenged record in the squadron for having the most gals. Al says that he will never settle down, but we all believe that he will meet the right one someday, and then—goodbye Navy!

LANGE, Johnie "B"—S 1/c. Johnie was born on July 6, 1926, in Bettie, Texas. His present home is at Gilmer, Texas, where he lives with his father, U. B. Lange. A long-legged son of the Texas plains, Johnie finds this a good asset in covering his average 20 miles around the ship each day doing office messenger work. His main ambition is to return to the great open spaces and resume the roping of real live Texas Steers (girls) instead of office door knobs and desk lamps. Johnie was welcomed to VB-86 from CASU 6 after boot camp at San Diego. He enlisted 25 July 1944.

LARSEN, William Gilbert—ART 1/C. Mr. and Mrs. Peter C. O. Larsen on February 5, 1915, were the proud parents of a child. They sent their boy William to Union Free High School and Moore's Business College where he finished in 1935. Larsen claims Cedar Rapids, Iowa, as his home, but Cedar Rapids has as yet not verified the fact. Larsen entered the Navy on January 16, 1942, whereupon they decided to make him a Radar Technician, a job at which he surpasses. He holds many records in our outfit, the main one concerning his ability never to be seen without a radome.

PLOOF, Merrill Homer—AMMP 2/C. Mr. and Mrs. H. J. Ploof had the shock of their lives in 1918 when little Merrill Homer was born. Ploof immediately ran out to check on his 100 acres of scattered timber; then ran back to the house and diapers as fast as any Dutchman ever ran. He graduated from Highgate High School in 1935. Merrill also attended P & W School and worked at Pearl Harbor for two years. He came to the States to marry a wonderful girl named Frances French, also from Vermont. After a short honeymoon, Ploof joined the Navy and Bombing 86.

RAHILLY, Foch James—Y 1/C. Mike was born on November 11, 1918, the son of Mr. and Mrs. John H. Rahilly of St. Paul, Minnesota. He graduated from Cretin Military School in 1936 with high honors. Mike married his childhood sweetheart, Jean. They now have a daughter, Barbara Jean. He joined the Navy February 14, 1942. Boot training was at Great Lakes; then duty followed at Indianapolis, Columbus, Philadelphia, Wildwood and finally VB-86. Mike is the hardest-working man in the outfit; his efficiency and ability is an inspiration to all hands, and his pleasant manner is a decided squadron asset.

RAY, William Fleming—AMMH 1/C. Pete was born in Corsicana, Texas in 1916. He graduated from Powell High School in 1935, just before he lit the fuse to burn the school down. In 1936 Pete married a beautiful girl named Harriet Brown. Everything went smoothly until 1943 when Pete joined the Navy, but things improved a great deal when he became a proud father of a boy named Mike. After Pete spent many months in the Atlantic on the U.S.S. CARD he came to VB-86 and had a fling at the Japs in the Pacific.

REESE, Allan Kennedy—AEM 1/C. Al was born in Cleveland, Ohio, on November 5, 1920, the only son of Mr. and Mrs. Jennings Reese. He is married to Margaret Williams and is the proud father of two children, Nancy and Jr. They make their home in Erie, Pennsylvania. Prior to entering the service, Allan was employed by the Erie Resistor Company. Al is a very serious-minded chap, but his seriousness is directed towards arriving at the front of the chow lines at meal time. Allan will never forget the incident at Maui when his billfold was forwarded to him via guard mail.

STABA, Benjamin Charles—AM 1/C. Born on December 13, 1919 to the proud Mr. and Mrs. John Staba, Benjie was very fortunate in that his sister, a school teacher, gave him his early education. Later he attended Bacon Academy in Colchester, Conn. Benjie entered upon his Naval career in May 1942. He went to "Boot Camp" at Newport, R. I., served aboard the Princeton, and finally joined Bombing 86. In addition to serving as squadron kom-sha artist and carpenter, he has also worked on aircraft. In April of '45 Benjie married Eva Fecenko, definitely a "10 point asset."

"LAND OF LIBERTY"

BACK in the days when the squadron was in its swaddling clothes, it underwent a period of training at Wildwood "By the Sea" New Jersey. Although this training is what enabled the squadron to chalk up its record aboard the Wasp, the social life of the enlisted personnel is by far the best-remembered phase of that era, both by the crewmen and by the blitzed civilians. Using the Biltmore Hotel as a base of operations, all the boys old enough to imbibe, and those who looked old enough to imbibe, roamed far and wide in search of feminine companionship. One radio technician named Larsen claims he never intentionally plays cut-throat; however, there have been many complaints that the ladies soon lose interest in their escorts after Larsen makes an appearance. The boys have all agreed that Larsen's a threat to any romance and now admit him to stag parties only. This roaming of course included all but the respectable married men who were forced to use night flying as an excuse to go out on the town.

Weekends saw mass migrations to such fair cities as "Leo the Lip" Strong's beloved Philadelphia and Frank "Sinatra" Sabia's famed Brooklyn—the town that claims T. Daly's Bronx, New York for a suburb. All the fellows who remained behind on the home front—Wildwood—were on hand to greet the lovely charmers as they stepped down from train and bus to relax after their week of toil in the big city. As soon as the first city belles arrived, such sterling characters as "He-man" Moore, "Lou" Warchol, "Mal" Mallia, "Stan" Morris, "Duck" Bougan, and all other comers who had the price of the initial beer, were seen squiring this pulchritude around town. Greatest of all squadron gigilos was one Jim Ballew, who could not only talk the most hard-hearted of females out of a beer but also contrive to keep the change.

Although the outfit was composed mainly of great (?) lovers, it had other famous and intellectual personalities in its ranks. First and foremost of these was one "Injun Joe" Rathburn, whose favorite pastimes were swing-drumming and necking on tombstones. Lou Warchol, when he wasn't escorting some fair maiden about town, spent his time swimming in the Scoota-boat pool at the amusement concession. His first words upon being fished out by irate attendants were, and we quote—"She dared me". Foremost in the traveling set were A. O. Horn and "Ray" Lightbody who owned an unstreamlined but highly successful heap known to all and sundry as the "Mayflower". It was at Wildwood that "Hydraulics" Miller expounded his theory that "laundries should be abolished". When kidded about tattle-tale grey in his uniform, he contended that an aged white uniform was a sure sign that its owner was a very salty character. "Ugh"

Prugh became well known for his enlightening discourses on Theology. Vocalists were Jim Crain and Bill McReynolds, who after partaking of the sudsy stuff, gave forth with sentimental ditties, usually slightly off key, at the Surf Club. E. C. Rocker based his claim to fame on the fact that he operated the first tavern that opened its doors within the confines of dear ol' Barracks "B". First man to lose his freedom was Joe Lightner, who took the fatal step soon after the squadron was commissioned. R. L. White lost his heart while in Wildwood but so far remains footloose and fancy-free.

The "Philadelphia Flash", better known as "Buddy" Zipin and "Fearless Freddie" Lockett both claimed to be checked out on all of Wildwood's night life, but when put to the test it was found that "Safari" Chimene could smell a beer two blocks farther than either of them. Several gay blades could be seen every night giving the girls a treat at the Starlight Ballroom. Amongst those dance hall lothorios could be seen such notable jitterbugs as "Sandyville" Sayre, "Lard" King, "Gremlin" Berger, "Spearsie" Spears, and M.P. "Waltz King" Bouchard. Jake "The Fake" Forrest, Jim "Knobby" Compson, Norm "Red" Bunnell, T. J. Bruce, Ernie "Gordo" Hazlett, Bill "Super Gordo" Larsen, Jim "One Gun" Noon, C. E. "Hawkey Doodle" Neal and "Mike" Rahilly, could be seen almost any night hobnobbing with the civilian population at some of the better nighteries of the town.

Some unlucky souls whose ball and chains were with them at Wildwood missed out on the wonderful liberties their more fortunate buddies enjoyed. Some of these lost souls were 'Baldy" Winkle, "Texas" Ray, "Dutchman" Ploof, "Al" Reese, and H. N. "Nuisance" Taylor—Tough, fellas! Prides of the bobby socks brigade were "Squirrel" Coleman, Nel "Errol" Flynn and Lou "The Lover" Holmes, the boys who made all the juveniles wish they could be delinquent. Squadron enigma was "Lil Abner" Baker, who remained true to his Charlie even while surrounded by a bevy of bathing beauties.

After a truly wonderful summer, we entrained for Otis Field, Camp Edwards, Mass. to undergo more advanced training—and more liberty. Otis was one of those bases where liberty, although good, was discouraged by the seventy-eleven mile trek to the nearest gate. Despite the fact that the base was so hard to get off, a good time was had by all at Bougan's "Topside" Bar and Casino, a congenial, if illegal, establishment that catered to the thirst and gambling spirit of the squadron. Ray, Ploof, Reese, Neal, Winkle and Rahilly all brought their families to Cape Cod. "Mike" Rahilly, squadron yeoman, was perhaps one of the luckiest in procuring lodging. He rented a comfortable two-story house in North Falmouth. By the time his wife Jean and daughter Barbara Jean arrived, Mike had the house all squared away, evidencing the usual efficiency he has consistently shown while working with the squadron. Incidentally, if we are to believe Daly, Sabia, Gadjanski, "Lemon" Larsen, or Thompson, Mike's wife really prepares a wicked Thanksgiving dinner. Just a hint in case you are ever in St. Paul over the holidays!

Saturday morning at Otis Field was always exciting. At the Skipper's OK, all authorized hands would take off on liberty. New York or Philly-bound, the boys would either take in a football game or see one of the numerous New York Broadway productions. That blue streak leaving the base on weekends was not Superman as many people thought, but Ben Staba heading for Providence and a certain little someone. Week days at Otis were never dull. "Bob" Sayre and "McGlouk" McGovern, leading members of our squadron baseball team, were also active in the daily hikes around the countryside. McReynolds, the Bing Crosby of the outfit, could be heard every evening harmonizing with "Whitey", Sayre and "Stan" Morris. The others sometimes wished this quartet was on the radio—so they could turn 'em off! When the boys did stray off the reservation, the surrounding towns of Hyannis, Falmouth, Buzzards Bay and New Bedford felt the impact of their presence. Roller skating was popular both because of the exercise and social contacts it afforded. At Otis, Mallia introduced a new and novel way to go swimming. He stated that "ditching" is child's play and really very invigorating. Gadjanski, Coleman, and Warchol were so impressed that they followed his example out Pacific way. Bougan so thoroughly enjoyed this form of exercise that he went thru the ditching procedure twice.

Roller skating demons seen most at Hyannis were "Lard" King, "Wheels" Sayre, "Whizzer" McReynolds, "Collision" Spears, "Whistle-stop" Moore, and "Zip" Zipin, while "Demon" Rathburn, "Speedy Squirrel" Coleman, "Flop" Flynn, "Maestro" Morris, "Up Again, Down Again" Mallia, "Wishful" Warchol, "Listing" Lockett and "Hopeful" Holmes held forth at New Bedford.

On days off, Otis saw an even greater exodus of crewmen than did Wildwood, as such cities as Boston, New York and Philadelphia were only short distances away. Sabia and Daly were still making New York on their time off, while Lockett, R. L. White, E. R. Daigle and "Buddy" Zipin zoomed to Phillie and Mallia showed "Lou" Warchol and "Injun" Rathburn the sights of his home town on several occasions. "Home Front" Bougan, being a mere matter of 3000 miles from home, teamed up with "Ollie" Horn and "Red" Lightbody to keep up the morale of the Falmouth telephone operators and also keep Howard Johnson's little establishment out of debt.

And now, dear reader, having conducted you on a rather complete tour of East Coast Liberty we shall take you out west to San Diego, where, after exploring the surrounding

countryside, we embarked for parts unknown. Arriving at our destination in the romantic (?) Hawaiian Islands, we were deposited on a rock that masqueraded under the name of Maui. The social center of this fair island was a thriving metropolis called Wailuku in which one could go to the movies, go to the movies, or—go to the movies. Night life was nil and consisted of a dance (if you cared to go) in the U.S.O. The Hawaiian girls loved the jitterbugs, so naturally "Frank" Sabia, and "Bob" Sayre stole the spot lite on that score. Most of the boys spent their leisure time promenading up and down the main street eyeing the girls now and then, but that was all. Numerous picture postcards and souveniers of the island were purchased and "Dilbert" Darr seemed to have the biggest selection of risque pictures. Should you by chance encounter him sometime ask to see his collection. They're good for a few blushes. As liberty came around only once a week, the gathering place of the boys was the beer garden—a lovely place even though it stayed open one hour and a half daily.

In order to get the red Maui dust out of our throats, the squadron threw two beer parties. The first one was conducted as a beer party should be, while the second, and more successful one, was a little freer. There were several athletic events in which most of the boys participated, while their less athletic buddies reposed under the palms and savored the cool foamy brew. Rahilly, Gadjanski, and Forrest did an excellent job of organizing this party. Naval Air Station, Kahului was built up by Seabees and proved to be a well-equipped station as far as athletics was concerned. Several trips were taken around the island. One was a precarious truck trip over to Hana, Maui. The road was a zigzag affair built along the side of a mountain. On one side of the road was a mountain wall towering up; and on the other, a sheer drop, hundreds of feet to the ocean below. It made one dizzy to look down. Chief Neal did a good job of chauffeuring on the trip. It was so late when we finally reached the native village that we were obliged to turn around and head for home, but not, however, before we had purchased some Hawaiian sherbert and a stock of bananas and a jar of peanut butter. Enroute back to the station, we ate combination peanut butter and banana sandwiches. We recovered from this several days later.

Charlie Thompson was fortunate enough to have his sister, Phoebe, living in Honolulu, T. H. She had moved there when she married her husband, Tom Shillock, and was an inhabitant of the island of Oahu when the attack on nearby Pearl Harbor came, December 7, 1941. Charlie planned to visit them Xmas but the trip was delayed. About a week later he and his pilot, Lieutenant Dick Sewall and Lieutenant John Shirley with Mike Rahilly, flew over in two Helldivers, pre-

sumably on official business and spent Saturday and part of Sunday at the Shillock home. A goodly supply of the liquid stuff was evident, so the party turned out to be a roaring success.

Highlight of our stay in Hawaii was the two day stay at the Royal Hawaiian Hotel. There we lived the life of Riley, sleeping in thirty-five dollar rooms, swimming at Waikiki, sightseeing in Honolulu and just loafing in general. Soon after our return from the Royal Hawaiian to NASKA, we received word we were shipping out.

* * *

There will be a short pause while we kick hell out of those little yellow nips—and vice versa.

Upon returning to the states all hands were offered a sixteen day leave. No one refused it. Like all leaves it was all too short and in no time at all the boys were congregating at Berry's in Oakland. While Oakland was not a bad town by any standards, our stay there was used as a rest period for several reasons —all financial.

Once paid, our period of enforced rest was over and once again the boys were enjoying the sights of town, this time Santa Rosa. Ah, Santa Rosa, land of milk and Honeys! At Santa Rosa the skating fiends once more were in their glory, with "Flop" Flynn again showing them how it was done. Highlight of our stay there was that first night, when one of the local citizens made the mistake of asking H. N. Taylor if we'd seen any action. "ACTION!!!" he screamed, as he tore out his hair, "Have we seen action! Let me tell you — — — !" Almost any night you could see "Baldy" Winkle, R. L. White, T. J. Bruce and "Lil Abner" Baker shooting pool at J. J.'s pool hall. Later in the evening you could find practically the entire squadron at Lena's or the Paris Inn, the two best eateries in town. The more venturesome souls went to work for the Red Top and Yellow Cab companies and vied with each other to see who could tear off the most fenders. "Sack Time" Bouchard lent his talents to the local upholsterer —a very profitable spare time job. On weekends "Al" Reese and R. L. Sayre could be seen making tracks for San Francisco, with Sammy "Berkeley" Gadjanski right behind them, headed for that San Francisco suburb.

All those who thought San Francisco was too far headed for Guerneville—a lovely town. It had everything — scenery, climate and no Shore Patrol. It was a wonderful little resort town on the Russian River that boasted several good dance halls and plenty of recreation. Among the semi-permanent inhabitants of Guerneville were Jake "Glass Door" Forrest, Brian "Cowboy" Lauzon, A. O. "Let's Walk" Horn and "Homeward Bound" Bougan, who could be seen at Guernewood park night or day. "Gordo" Larsen went up to Guerneville once and swore never again— he had to walk fifteen miles home. Lou "Lover" Holmes, one of the luckiest boys, was serenaded each night by his little June bug—cowboy songs. He says "She sure sang right purty."

Like all good things our stay in Santa Rosa soon came to an end and once more we sailed. After leaving the states we received several new squadron members. They are a good bunch of boys who would have been welcome on all of our earlier escapades. The new fellows are E. O'Brien, "Al" Albertelli, Teddy Hays, Joe White, "Esch" Eschbach and "Butch" Baskerville. Johnnie Lange, our yeoman striker, came to the squadron just before we left Alameda. He says he likes sea duty Silly Boy!

Once more we sailed across the shining deep sea water to keep an appointment with those yellow — — — — —.

Life aboard a carrier is made as interesting as possible. We have certain privileges that exceed ship's company privileges and consequently sometimes are known as the "Glamour Boys of the Fleet". Our work consists mostly of flying and making sure that our guns, radio, oxygen, and other equipment are in perfect working order. Each crewman has his own assigned plane to take care of. When we are not flying and all the work is done, our spare time is our own. It is usually spent in the crewmen's ready room writing letters, listening to the juke box, playing cards or just laying around in the soft upholstered reclining chairs. To tickle the palate on hot nights, Sammy Gadjanski proved to be very proficient in procuring ice cream for the crew and Tom Daly did an excellent job of getting Tex Weatherford, the movie operator, to show movies when possible.

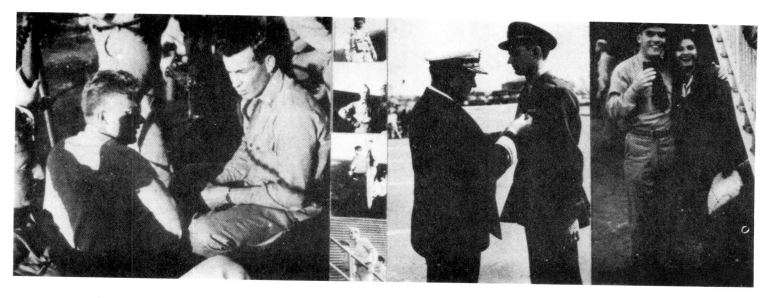

We'd like to take this opportunity to thank the several storekeepers that made our life aboard the Wasp a little more pleasant than usual—A great bunch of fellows, Thank you—we appreciate your kindness.

While at sea a favorite pastime was wishing. All hands wished first and foremost to go home but they had other wishes too. "Baldy" Winkle wished he had some of the hair on "Fred" Lockett's chest to put on his sparsely settled knob. "Duck Butt" Bougan, wishing he had some assistance while spieling off about "the old outfit", but never got to it. "Tex" Ray wished that old man Curtiss had drunk that hydraulic fluid instead of putting it in the "beast". Holmes, Coleman, Daly and Flynn wished they weren't so high on Law's black-list when working parties were read off. Leo "The Lip" Strong was always wishing he had someone to talk to on those long, lonesome hops, while Frank "Propaganda" Sabia wished that one-quarter of the rumors he started would come true. "Lil Abner" Baker wishing for homing-grits and hog jaw while eating that stuff on a shingle. All hands wished they had ten arms every time the squadron moved its gear. "Teddie" Hays wished the squadron had more hillbilly records to remind him of home. "Tom" Daly longed for more of those days he spent at Santa Rosa with his bride. "Bob" White wished his salty talk wouldn't flow forth with so much ease and "O'Bie" O'Brien wished the Wasp had gedunk service such as he got on the Bunker Hill. "Sport" Bouchard always wished the lee rail wasn't so far away in heavy weather. Last but not least, all hands earnestly wished that the ship would turn around and go home!

While off the Jap coast the war ended and once more we "sweated out" America—Land of Liberty!

LT. W.G. MUNDY

* * * * *

Well, there's your story. It wrote itself. No great thought or high ideals contained here . . . just the little thoughts of great guys who made the big thoughts operable. Never for-get the pain and suffering some guys under-went to make possible whatever snickers or chortles the previous lines brought forth. The men who created those little thoughts can never forget.

LT. COMMANDER LAWRENCE F. STEFFENHAGEN

TORPEDO SQUADRON
EIGHTY-SIX

NOW HEAR THIS . . .

THESE narrated pages are about war's waiting. The conflicts have been too readily extolled through a multitude of publications. There were a lot more heartbreaks, labors, and labors lost than these writings denote. But like any sensible group we pretended to forget them and made our retrospections along the least depressing lines.

When a group of men, composed of different temperaments, with varied principles, all coming from different ways of life, are bent determinedly to a common task, and, in order to achieve this job, must live in almost continual flesh contact with one another, then synthetic pleasures and masquerades of enjoyment must be developed. This story touches the highlights of those pleasures and depicts the masquerades we created and invented from whatever materials were available at the time. And so the curtain rose. . . .

19 JUNE, '44 . . . In the post-war memorial construction era, the owner of the Jolly Whaler in the New Bedford Hotel would be justified in installing a little plaque over the street door, announcing: The Incubation Place of Torpedo Squadron Eighty Six. Oh yes! There was also a nearby airport which was made available to us on weekdays. New Bedford was a town with a life raft plant and a screw factory. After a three day survey of the town's possibilities, the bachelors bought cars, the married men arrived equipped, and the Skipper had a wordly crimson Buick. This extended everyone's radius of action to Lincoln Park and the local country club, each a play ground in its own right. Then came the July AlNav, creating six new lieutenants, Blu, DeLoof, Pattok, Harshbarger, Hackett, and Bennett. The only one who felt the added collar weight was Blu, but the Ensigns helped him carry it. Young came aboard with his amiable disposition. The squadron grew into long pants. Ochab learned to drive the jeep . . . didn't he, WILBUR?

AUGUST, '44 . . . How can we define Hyannis . . . simple . . . women . . . women . . . women. The Coffee House doubled as a harem with every man a sultan. The Skipper won a bet from Easley. That was the sneak preview of the Eighty Six Special. Everyone set up housekeeping as a beachcomber. There were plenty of combs in the beach to prove it, too. Badgerow went home to have a baby. Foerster, Cox and Gafner sought greater luxury and rented an auto court. Charlie Case went back to cheap gas. Euler took refuge while his mother-in-law was visiting New Bedford. Filler's wife came to town; she was nobody's fool. Brown tore his pants. Everyone was flying two hops a day, dropping concrete blocks and torpedoes, with minelaying exercises at night. Charlie Lund still wouldn't talk. Poe lost his shoes but gained experience. Cross countries to New York and back became the fashion.

SEPT. '44 . . . Back to New Bedford. Torpedo Eighty-Six was getting hot. Everyone was learning their jobs, taking interest, enjoying their work, playing; doing everything as an insoluble unit. Carrier qualifications in the Atlantic delivered many sermons. Filler brought back a beaker of salt on his tail hook.

Scott and Badgerow played leapfrog with a barrier, and lost. Foerster continued to groundloop, but with improved technique. Pattok got worried about his loss of hair, etc., and started taking vitamins. Lund met a girl by the name of Marie. Fondren started dating a readhead. Louiso was going steady. Everyone was getting rosy, when a hurricane hit New England, and VT-86 attended an eastern convention of Naval Aviators at Weymouth Blimp Base.

OCTOBER '44 . . . We met the rest of the air group at a bachelor's "Siberia," Otis Field, Camp Edwards, still in Massachusetts. Starvation and thirst were beginning to tell, so CAG threw a party. The bachelors drank while the married men danced. Bennett gave the Skipper a birthday party . . . Every husband had a little cottage tucked away in some lost village where he hoarded his wife. Bowden rented a castle on an island. John Bent made Lieutenant Commander and started living at Coonamessett Inn. Everyone tried to live there after he submitted his ACA-1 report about the bar and dining room. Pre-dawn hops became the rage. Missing them created a rage, too. In Lewistown, Me., Lund lost his shirt, but won by a decision. The Brass took our ship away from us—strikes or something civilian. The squadron got an insignia. Fondren, Foerster and Gafner changed their pay accounts to support wives. We spent our last New England hurricane on a baby flattop. Everyone wished to God that Kaiser had spent just three more days in building that jeep.

27 NOVEMBER, '44 . . . Packed up the equipment, packed up the crew, packed up the wives. Sell the cars, express the trunks, and take care of the Squadron, Dane. Off went the fairhaired wonders. San Diego, here we come.

5 DECEMBER, '44 . . . San Diego...There's been a book and a movie put out on it. Why should we spoil them both by telling the truth? Artists have to live too. Turmoil...everything was a bedlam of

hush-hush and rush-rush. Confusion was the order of the day. The bar on the top of the El Cortez Hotel became a bachelor's rallying point. Badgerow took a suite at the Coronado Hotel. Case got a wire and started having sympathetic morning sickness. Easley started taking pictures like mad. At that point everyone was a little mad . . . it helped. Mexico welcomed everyone, and of course his pocketbook. Anything could be bought for a substantial sum. Dane went to Los Angeles with Wilbur, seeking the more educational attractions. Well, someone had to maintain our scholastic standing with the Armed Force's Institute.

9 DECEMBER, '44 . . . We sailed. Everyone started using their codes. A little bucket called the Nassau segregated us according to blood type and put us in cages down in the chain locker. Hospitality was the keynote, but they couldn't carry a tune. Poker games began. We lost. Pattok connived a Kangaroo Court. Louiso, Gafner, DeLoof, and Blu got haircuts. Louiso, Poe, Martin, Ochab, and Case lost the starboard half of their mustaches. Scotty stopped reading 'Call House Madam'.

15 DECEMBER, '44 . . . Docking at Pearl to the dulcet strains of Aloha, we were whisked to Kahului, Maui, by plane and set up school once again. Everyone met Sweetie Wilson the first week ashore; Badge even got a picture. On Christmas Eve, the crew and officers had a little get-together, and the native USO gave us a hula show with too much hula and too little show. The skipper was given a hat and lei by popular vote. Christmas and New Years came in that order. Blu resolved to stop walking on carpets. Cox lost a race by a roadside fence to VF. GAG threw a luau. Everyone was correctly impressed when the pig was taken out of the pit. Nolan had a farewell party at the Wailuku Hotel, and left for the States. Sweetie's became off bounds. LeMoyne began repeating himself in his sleep talking. Harsh became a father; of course a boy,

Gary Wayne. Blu okayed Staker's dispensing hatch and let him send it to the Bureau. Filler started sleeping nights, and Andy got out of hack. Everyone took a vacation on Hawaii, the Big Island, and learned the Hilo Hop, saw the Volcano, and admired the Nisei girls at the Naniloa Hotel. Scotch could be had at the Hilo O Club, so the more discriminating absorbed for the leaner days in the near future. Case bought cowboy boots from the profits from his laundry service. We had a party at the Maui Grand Hotel. Everyone went wild over the punch—grape and pineapple juice, turpentine, and whiskey . . . but good. Bent, Euler and Bowden were still trying to complete a double play. Dawn, day, and night flying exercises were stressed. Molokini Rock was beginning to crack along with the pilots. Time was drawing short, so the Skipper gave away his orchids.

4 MARCH, '45 . . . The Independence gave us a lift to Ulithi Atoll, with a fueling stop at Eniwetok. Two more ounces of saltpeter were necessarily added to our diet. Foc'sl sunbathing became the order of the day. The ship treated us like admirals, giving us chow that made New Orleans' famed Antoine's a hash and hurry joint. Charlie Case continued to call everyone a dull tool, extending his expostulating area to include the wardroom.

13 MARCH, '45 . . . Ships . . . Ships . . . Ships . . . By the time we arrived, there were more damn ships in Ulithi than Tokyo Rose ever dreamed of. It was the most completely controlled confusion that ever existed. With standard operating procedure, the-powers-that-were waited until two in the morning to transfer us to the Wasp in a porpoising LCI. The short trip was uneventful; Burk and Martin had taken pills to prevent any gastric disasters. "Welcome aboard, and angle to the starboard, Boys." The Captain had greeted us. We headed for the Nips later that morning. Everyone started briefing for the first strike. Young scheduled a little anti-sub work so we could be sure of some outdoor life. The next few days were grim, so we can skip them here. Too bad we couldn't have skipped them there.

24 MARCH, '45 . . . Back to Ulithi and everyone was surveying like mad. Somewhere off Ulithi, Fido Base, our ship, launched all aircraft for the parking lot at Falalop. What if they wouldn't fly; they floated didn't they? Everyone wandered around in his private thunderhead for two or three hours. CAG burned up his radio. Finally the navigator told us where we *really* were.

The Falalop Naval Air Station was a large swath cut in the trees into the prevailing wind. On adjacent Mog Mog Island was the local monument to Naval Aviation: A pile of empty beer cans so high, oxygen was required at the top. A rule at Mog Mog was: If you drink, you swim. Scotty swam many times. Cox started censoring mail. Washrooms began looking like laundries. Andy, LeMoyne and Staker started giving cocktail parties.

3 APRIL, '45 . . . Back to Pearl to await

another ship. The combat weary went to rest homes. Those few days of combat certainly developed a lot of neurotics when that opportunity was announced. The rest started on the familiar trail to Maui; we drew Puunene this time. This was the other side of the island, but the volcanic dust was no less penetrating. Then a reprieve . . . Bremerton bound. When Burk, Brown, Ochab, and Martin returned from Chris Holmes they were more than just combat weary. This war wasn't being fought in the front lines alone.

11 APRIL, '45 . . . All the way into Bremerton, we stacked ammunition on the hangar deck. That ship was really loaded. A rumor started going around that, instead of docking, we were going to storm Seattle. The rumor was accurate. A ferry boat came alongside while we were still anchored in the Sound. With bags and stray gear dangling, we hurriedly piled aboard, and headed for Seattle. Here was the Fatherland, and these were the fathers. Everybody squirmed in his seat and commented on the beauty of the word Home when used in the present tense. Everyone was excited as we docked in Seattle, and stampeded to the waiting buses. Competing bus drivers careened us to Sand Point, the country club of the Northwest. White women . . . College women . . . Girls. All hail the returning heroes. What a homecoming party we had. Introductions came with the drinks. Lipstick came with the dinner; it was half the meal. By the time we got to the pièce de rèsistance, they were old sweethearts. CAG put on his blouse, and everybody else bought one. We departed by air for a look at the old Main Street.

28 APRIL, '45 . . . One by one the weary warriors reported to Alameda after fourteen days of glorious dissipation. Hangover by hangover, we all got back for some more simulated attacks and group gropes. On May 1st, we started moving in stages from the wiles of Frisco to the wilds of the Redwoods. The married officers drove up with their wives. The gay young blades arrived by air three days later to start operating. Everyone submitted the proper deceptions to the local ration board. The air station at Arcata was built conveniently in the center of a stationary weather front. It was the kind of place at which any sensible aviator would dream of being stationed as an operations officer . . . then forgotten by the Bureau. Throughout, the motif of a wilderness adaptation of big city vices persisted. Instead of spending an evening on the davenport of some overheated apartment, the bachelors just grabbed a blanket and headed for the Mad River. It was so much healthier for these impulsive lads to enjoy themselves in fresh country air. For the inveterate roué who needed his ration of smoke fogged bars, Eureka had made the necessary provisions. The Cinnabar, the accent falling on the first syllable, and the Log Cabin were filled nightly. Several times during the stay, panic overcame us. When the fog lifted long enough for taxi practice. We did take time off from the rack and rail to go down to Monterey and drop fish. Steinbeck has given Monterey more publicity than it deserves. But the town bears mention because its dew point kept us weathered out of our northern retreat. Our sympathetic brethren improved our good humor by sending us a telegram, remarking how much they missed us. Their sun was shining.

The excluded Rover Boys finally got back to Arcata, their wives, and such. Nick Verano came aboard. Between bubble baths, he demonstrated small field procedures. Fondren became a father. Foerster was obviously expecting. Radar Simpson reported to the squadron to ferret out all the more cloistered coveys. The Skipper dined with the President of Humboldt College. The more meager braid continued to enjoy the student body. Gafner defeated his wife in a water fight. Gay was piped aboard with 14 photograph albums. A tremendous appetite, with John Shonk in tow, came into the squadron. Then came word that the Wasp was ready to prowl once more. We departed for Alameda to await the Stinger.

6 JUNE, '45 . . . Alameda was another intense period of packing and partying. Two planes had tow gear installed . . . dammit. The temperature of the squadron was running about 105°. Everyone was either barring or billing. Again came the intense cramming of a lot of living into a few days. Some nearby admiral stepped down from his LMD, (Large Mahogany Desk.) He gave our heroes their pretty bits of cloth. On June 13th, we sailed under the Bridges. The skyline slowly slid below the horizon in its best travelogue form. The path to Hawaii was filled with such boulders as group gropes, homesickness, and integrity watches for Nolan. Everybody got lonelier and lonelier as Point Option got closer and closer to The Rock.

19 JUNE, '45 . . . We flew into Barber's Point. Everyone learned to fly with droppable gas tanks. The O Club was the only logical contraceptive for complete boredom. An additional attraction was the Snack Shack, a hangover house after the club closed. We lived in Waves' barracks, causing many unorthodox procedures. Jones, Johnson, and Hall rebuilt our complement, and dumped the Civil War right in our laps. Down to the sea again, the lonely sea and the Wasp, for four days of oceanic homework. We returned to another mass promotion, six less ensigns to kick around. Ochab missed by a day but got the consolation of Bull Ensign. Foerster's wife beat the sailing time by scant hours.

11 JULY, 45 . . . Westward we went with a warm-up strike on Wake Island. From Wake we dropped down to Eniwetok . . . Eniwetok . . . a crustacean mass completely devoid of cultivation. Swimming and beer parties were arranged for all hands. The ship got oiled and reeled out to join the fleet. Halsey heard we were coming, but it didn't seem to change his plans in any way. We passed Iwo Jima close aboard the starboard side. In the dim dusk it looked like an immense, hard-pencilled exclamation point, laid sidewise on an undulant blue carpet.

26 JULY, '45 . . . We joined Task Force 38. Briefing sessions once more started. We struck and briefed. The Force swaggered up and down the coast of Japan. Five and one-half weeks without Uncle Sugar Mail . . . that wasn't funny. Grimness called again. An almost imperceptible trickle of peace rumors slowly ebbed its way out to the Fleet. The rivulets grew. An uncontrollable torrent of speculation overcame us. Everyone wanted to believe it, but as hard as they tried they couldn't. Was it a false rumor? A ruse? No one knew. No one dared hope. The morning press became the priority acquisiton each day. Peace came. Life became less burdensome. People told old jokes and laughed themselves delirious over them. Exuberant horseplay and backslapping came into their own. Young scheduled himself for G.Q. The Stinger became a flagship. Then a typhoon converted us to a jeep carrier. Pilots burned incense, hoping the next wave would wrap the flight deck around the island. The admiral struck his flag. The Skipper TBF'ed him to a less fortunate carrier with a flight deck.

Flathatting over Japan was a leery sensation for all. The greatest concern was for prisoners of war. Everyone went out of their way for those gutty guys. We dropped everything from Old Grand Dad to medical equipment. Everyone was awestruck over the rusty residue that was once Nagoya.

2 SEPTEMBER, '45 . . . Bound for Pearl once again to get a little plastic surgery on the flight deck. The Wasp became a transport . . . The hangar deck was cleared for passengers. An eastbound ticket cost 44 points.

THE success of any organization is dependent upon its leader and his traits . . . his ability, his experience, and his personality. With any of these requisites lacking the desired degree of perfection will never be attained. Hence, from the day that Lieutenant Commander Lawrence F. Steffenhagen, our Skipper, received orders from Washington, sending him from the beauties of Philadelphia to the rigors of New Bedford and its Jolly Whaler, Torpedo Squadron Eighty-Six was sure of becoming a well-knit, versatile, hard-hitting outfit.

His arrival crystallized two facts in the minds of all hands — they were happy to be aboard, and happy to work their hardest for a man like the Skipper. With this attentiveness for a foundation, the Skipper took the combat experience of the few, the flying experience of others and coupled with his own salt, talent, and leadership, produced a combat team that has proved itself by fire. Always present was his determination, and his exemplary judgment. He demanded those in his command to meet high standards; he, himself, always met higher standards.

Indoctrinated to naval aviation as a cadet at Pensacola in the "old days" of '37, the Skipper spent his aerial infancy in old Torpedo Two, one of the navy's first torpedo squadrons. Being the old days when a boot ensign was supposed to learn how to do everything, he absorbed the carrier procedure, squadron organization, and fleet operation, which he so freely passed on to all of his pilots. During these days he also developed an off-duty ability for ferreting out the best liberty spots at all of the ports where the old U.S.S. Lexington dropped her hook. From December 7, 1941, when the Lex was at sea until she was mortally wounded during the Battle of Coral Sea, the Skipper's experience came tempered by the fires of combat. During that time he earned the Navy Cross and the Distinguished Flying Cross.

In those weary, dark days of '42, when the Navy was recuperating strength, he displayed his genial generosity by teaching the army boys at New Caledonia how to drop torpedoes. Finally recalled to the States, he was assigned to the Naval Aircraft Factory in Philadelphia where he served as a test pilot for a multitude of new aircraft.

To complete the picture, ask anyone in the squadron about his personality. He was equally at ease having dinner with the married officers or sharing a friendly beer with the bachelors and their companions at the Jolly Whaler. More than anyone else, he understood the need of release and relaxation, of pleasure mixed properly with work. His red Buick convertible was often seen in New Bedford, enroute to Providence's Biltmore, near the Coffee Shop at Hyannis, or in Buzzards Bay. In fact it served as such conclusive proof of his whereabouts that the Skipper seriously considered the advisability of toning it down with a little paint. Although his social life was active, any serious interest in the opposite sex was limited to Philadelphia.

At San Diego or Pearl Harbor, at Maui or Eniwetok, from New Bedford to Ulithi Atoll, the Skipper liked his boys and was proud of them. They in turn were proud of their Skipper and welcomed his company anytime, anywhere, anyplace.

There is more that could be written — more of the details that would only confirm the facts. Perhaps the tremendous respect and devotion that everyone held for the Skipper can best be expressed in the following statement: There was not an officer or a man in the crew who would not have followed their Skipper through Hell. And they did!

Charles Clucas, ARM 1/C   Laddie E. Novak, AOM 1/C

Thomas F. Andrews, just "F" understand—no middle name, hailed from Decatur, Indiana, and was a good Hoosier through and through. Andy was popular with everyone that knew him. As Educational Officer he accepted the collateral duty of father confessor to many of the crewmen. His qualifications for understanding the problems of the heart and comforting the crew during any epidemic of hangovers was never questioned, for Andy could flex his elbows with champs and walk erect when they were stumbling. On all party occasions, and Andy applied the word party in its loosest sense, from New Bedford in June of '44, to Seattle in May of '45, wherever the squadron hung its hat, he was right next to the rail with the best of them. One other diversion he enjoyed was reading, and his tastes ran the gamut from comic books to Aristotle. This intellectual character's pet aversions were a smooth cheek and a Vitalis workout. Andy won our admiration and our hearts with his great fortitude, strong determination and complete optimism. While at Mare Island Naval Hospital, Vallejo, Calif., in December, 1945, Andy transferred into the multi-engine class by marrying a navy nurse of contemporary rank, who worked in the maternity ward, of all places. Andy refused to divulge under what circumstances he met his wife, Eunice.

Ens. THOMAS F. ANDREWS

Lt. HARRY L. BADGEROW
George E. Bostrom, ARM 2/C
Norman R. Aberle, AMM 2/C

HOT BADGE we called him, and in the air and on the ground he lived up to his name. The only pilot in the history of Naval Aviation to be presented with an autographed photograph of Sweetie Wilson, the belle of Maui, T. H. Also famous for his encounter with the island shore patrol, to whom he said, "Here you stand and argue, while in a week I'm gonna strafe the streets of Tokyo." Before joining the squadron Badge was an instructor at primary bases in Jacksonville, Florida, and Olathe, Kansas. It was while instructing at Olathe that he met and married Kansas City's beautiful Barbara Buell. She awaits him there now with their charming daughter, Dana, who, incidentally, is the image of the old man. Blackie's good nature, ready humor, and smiling eyes often helped the squadron members through some trying moments. His college ambition to be a big time vaudeville star was often reflected in his sudden outbursts of fast patter. He also held down a position on the squadron baseball team, playing third base. Badge's knack for making and holding friends has insured him a well remembered spot in the squadron.

With a two month start in teaching a few of the tiny tots of Maine how to string beads and stack blocks, Richard Bennett saw his escape on a billboard advertising the thrill and glamour of Naval Aviation. Before he pulled his head out of the clouds, the Navy had his name on the dotted line. And before he could pull his head out of the Navy, his wife, Janette, had his name on another dotted line. Before reporting to 86, BENNY had many noteworthy experiences in the South Pacific area and at all reunions his many early buddies felt it their loyal obligation to recount his exploits in Sidney, in Rabaul, in Bouganville, and in all the other spots he had visited. It was while operating in this part of the South Pacific that he earned the title of "Bridge Buster." He seemed to have a mania for anything that looked like a connecting link. Upon joining the outfit at Quonset Point, R. I., Benny became Navigation Officer but was soon promoted, becoming the Big Gun in the Flight Department. These duties he handled like a veteran and the Flight Department was soon a smooth running organization. After he had kept his appropriate nickname a secret for many months, fate finally dealt Benny a cruel blow. It was by the beer cans at Mog Mog that one of his old buddies let the cat out of the bag with the greeting, "Why, WEASEL, where in the hell have you been hanging out?" The thought of early rising brought forth a look of scorn, produced by simultaneously raising one eye brow and lowering the other —a look which undoubtedly would have caused the Japs to capitulate sooner had Benny arrived at an earlier date. But where was Benny? Who knows? Darn that navigation anyway!

Lt. RICHARD BENNETT
Elton L. Myers, AOM 1/C
Charles W. Foster, ARM 2/C

"How'd it go . . . What'd you see . . . When'd you attack . . . What'd you hit?" Those were just a few of the questions PLEASURE BENT asked in his post-strike grillings of returning pilots. John Bent was one A.C.I. who stood aces high. Everyone liked him because he liked everyone. But John didn't go around winning affection alone. He also earned the respect of every man because he knew his job, and a helpful bit about everyone else's, too. John exercised the wonderful ability of knowing how to make pilots laugh and how to hold their interest during dry briefings. Behind every successful man, there is a woman. As we learned at Hyannis, Massachusetts, John was no exception to this rule. It was there that the squadron met his charming wife, Mary, and their two sons, Johnnie and Stevie. An amusing situation developed when the squadron members tried to repay the Bent open door policy by giving his wife little thank-you gifts bearing the assertive label, "For use by government personnel only." So insistent were some officers that for a while John was afraid Mary was going to have to join the Waves just to accept the presents. The Throttle Benders would have had a much weaker infield had not John been there as a pivot man at shortstop. Even CAG recognized his baseball ability and tried to steal him for his team in the Air Group Tournament at Maui.. To say that John used psychology wisely would be correct but insufficient, for his psychology was ingrained in his personality. It was an integral part of a guy like John Bent.

Lt. Comdr. JOHN P. BENT

"And that shadow next to my bomb bursts is the Haruna!" With a complacent smile and a ready glare for the dubious, Bob Blu put his prize picture back in its tooled leather folder. Again it was all ready for mailing when the National Archives sent for it. MEDALS Blu of Danville, Illinois, wore his ribbons proudly; he contended that it really wasn't "mooching" to collect a few drinks from the awed civilian gentry. He argued that a man's welcome during wartime was increased by the square of the number of ribbons he wore. Bob joined the squadron when it was formed at Quonset, R. I., and headed the Engineering Department. In all the time that he was with us Ben, as he was sometimes called, persisted in his belief that he was Lawrence Tibbett's greatest threat. No one encouraged either this belief or his singing, but this baritone needed only the trickling encouragement of a warm shower to bellow forth the Toreador Song from Carmen, while Bizet spun in his grave. Bob was Admiral King's perfect example; he could recite the AlNavs for the past two years at the slightest provocation. He and Dane were often heard practicing duets; but, alack and alas, they didn't harmonize well. Blu always went crescendo when Dane wanted pianissimo. Bob was unique in that he was never known to have *THE* Woman. No one ever caught him moaning over a picture or pouring out his soul in an epistle of passion. But Bob did have a passion. He readily disclosed his weakness to be enemy locomotives; and whenever he flew over Japan, he scouted the country-side looking for one to push over on and start chipping away with his fifties. Of course, it wasn't his fault that the first one he found was chugging safely along two weeks after the "cease fire" order came out.

Lt. ROBERT E. BLU
Robert A. Massey, ARM 2/C
Walter L. Egler, AMM 2/C

Lt. (j.g.) ROBERT O. BOWDEN
Roy B. Hunter, ARM 2/C
Edward T. Canty, AMM 2/C

"Well, I don't know about that. You have to show me." That's right, you guessed it, another pilot from Missouri. How that state kept a man out of Naval Aviation to become President, this squadron never could understand. Before the Navy began planning his itineraries, BOBO's greatest traveling was done between his hometown of Eldon and the Bagnell Dam, twelve miles to the south. In his civilian days he must have been very adept with the fairer sex, for he married a sweet hometown gal, just four days after winning his wings. When we left Alameda in June of '45, Bobo began having the strains and pains of coming fatherhood. How he managed to pass his physicals and still maintain four tapeworms, no one ever discovered. The sheer enjoyment he derived from just eating was hard to understand, hardest of all for his wife, for she was still struggling with the family Bible, a cook book. A light meal to this gourmand consisted of six courses with second helpings. No matter how many of the Throttle Benders lost money on their mess bills, Bobo more than compensated the loss. Bowden has the questionable honor of being the only member in the squadron to trump his own ace and bawl his partner out for it. "But," he explained, "It didn't matter. We had tricks to burn." Basketball and baseball games found Bobo on the field or court ever ready to do or die for old Torpedo Eighty-Six. The dry mid-western humor that he injected into the day by day workings of the squadron, coupled with his pleasant personality, made Bobo a popular and well-liked man in our family.

Lt. (j.g.) ROLLIN G. BROWN
Jack C. Nelson, AOM 3/C
John W. Anderson, ARM 3/C

Rollin G. Brown—called "Rollin" by his mother, "Brownie" by most, "Brown-dog" by some, "Glamour-boy" by a few, and "The Missouri Mule" by one. Being a firm believer in flying machines, BROWNIE never faltered in his stride towards receiving his Navy Wings of Gold. After graduating from Corpus, he spent two months in operational training at Fort Lauderdale, Fla., prior to joining the squadron at New Bedford. Known for his impeccable uniforms, his mirror-like shines, Brownie's reputation as the neatest member of the squadron was marred only on that fateful night in Hyannis, when, after leaving the B.O.Q. in spotless whites, he returned with a none too clean uniform and, alas, a rent in the most compromising part of his trousers. The details of that night have remained top secret with Brownie. The world will never know the workings of some of its most distinguished men. Our Glamour-boy had left a weeping heart wherever he deigned to bestow his Judas kiss—until, one night at the De Luxe Club in Eureka he met his Waterloo. After completely intoxicating his victim with charms and glamour never before revealed, his newly acquired date reeled back from her ecstatic mood, rose to her feet, uttered an apologetic, "My Mudder broke her leg," and left the establishment. Our stunned Romeo gasped in a strained whisper, "Dropped, like a hot potato." No, the world will never know the workings of some of its most distinguished men.

"This war isn't being fought to make the world safe for democracy. 'Nosiree', this war is being fought to make both democracy and the world safe for Texas." SPEEDY Burk was a lanky, lean cowboy whose eyes seemed to sparkle everytime the strains of 'The Eyes of Texas' came to his ears. He took the thorny path to Quonset and VT 86, coming to us after a long tour as an instructor at Corpus. His beliefs about the rest of the States were those of all Texans who thought that the Panhandle was something akin to paradise. Jimmy's great love of competition, both on the athletic field and on the checker board, made it hard for him to lose any game. And he seldom did lose, trimming everyone he challenged in chess, checkers, acey-ducey, or any other game. If you could play it, then Jimmy played it too, only better. He had a lovely wife and daughter, Mary and Patty. Burk was a dancing fool, and it is a safe bet that more than one pair of shoes were worn out on the dance floor. Parties were his meat and he could always be depended on to supply enough life and wit to bring a laugh or two. Jim loved to be out with the boys. His greatest single investment was a '36 Oldsmobile which was still running and without brakes the last time we saw it. He explained this state of disrepair by saying that if there were brakes he would always know he could stop; whereas, now he had something to prevent monotony on long trips.

Lt. JAMES E. BURK

If Norman Rockwell had asked for a model of the average New Englander, we would have pressed the nomination of Charlie THE RASP Case. Charlie was a conservative New Englander from Worcester, Mass., and that is pronounced Wooster, you know. He was conservative in everything but his flying and in that he was a misplaced fighter pilot. And he probably still thinks the TBF can do an eight point slow roll. Charlie went to war before the U. S.; he crossed the border and joined the RCAF. He was well along in his training when our Brass made it possible for him to come back and join the Navy. He graduated from Pensacola and stayed on as instructor in basic training. He was railroaded into TBF's, and after operational training at Lauderdale, he came to the Throttle Benders. Charlie soon established himself as one of the most accurate bombers in the squadron. His pet was a blue Oldsmobile which he always kept locked whenever he left it. He was seldom around for any of our stateside escapades; instead, he would head home to Worcester and his wife June. "You dull tool", could often be heard from Charlie's lips, berating his partner for trumping an ace or making some other error. This was especially embarrassing one night on the Independence in a quiet Wardroom. Also to be remembered was his impersonation of a seal at Hilo, when he went around slapping his sides with his hands, singing, "Wheeeee— I'm a seal." June of '45 saw Charlie as a father to a son which was named after the old man. It is safe to say that it will be a better New England if the youngster conforms to Charlie's pattern, for he was a guy you couldn't help liking.

Lt. (j.g.) CHARLES H. CASE

Lt. (j.g.) JOHN D. COX
Richard K. Bellinger, AOM 2/C
Burnell H. Rapp, ARM 3/C

If Halsey had ever asked for a volunteer to make a message drop on Hirohito's Palace, this fly-happy Louisianan would have been the first one to speak. No one loved to fly more than COXY; he was ready for any kind of hop in anything from a Piper Cub to a C-54. Whenever an extra plane was added to a strike, Johnny was right at the head of the line, a line consisting of one person. No one else wanted to fly that badly. Anything from ferrying to flathatting, he was there to volunteer for it, just as long as it involved an airplane. Johnny's most intense campaigning was done trying to convince his contemporary pilots that it was perfectly feasible to spill their flaps immediately after takeoff. He won very few constituents but certainly created quite a sensation in the squadron. And, of course, Johnny had a girl. Marian by name, though the amount of mail ordinarily received from her didn't serve as very convincing testimony to this fact. He was forever writing her, alternating lyrical letters of soft surrender with provocative proclamations of righteous rebellion. The Navy was responsible for transporting this pilot from the unexciting rice paddies of Welsh, La., right into the turmoil and temptations of exciting cities. By no means slow to catch on, Johnny was quick to cull the best from every new experience, of which there were many. Strafing was his primary obsession and anything from a junk to a battleship was sure to get a taste of his fire. If the harbor was especially full the small boats had to wait their turn because the bigger they were the higher a priority Johnny gave them.

Lt. Comdr. WILLIAM H. DANE III

The one thing BILL wanted to do was go to sea. Hence, when orders came through to report to VT 86, he was ecstatically happy. He filled his car with the 29 bags and boxes required to carry his properties, among which were the rare cordials, the fine liquors, and the savory hors d'oeuvres that any epicurean would consider a necessity. Ah, yes! Bill was off to adventure. Being the first administrative officer to report to the squadron, he was busy from the start, and also from the start he had a loyalty to the squadron that nothing could shake. The office became a beehive of activity with yeoman Brill being stung a hundred times while Bill buzzed. The Great Dane (arf, arf) quickly fitted into the social life of the squadron. Almost nightly he was off with one or more of the officers prowling the hot spots and gathering gossip. He became the official arranger. Whether it was a beer party for all hands at New Bedford, a Luau at Maui, a dance at the Oyster Harbor Club, a swimming party at Eniwetok or a beer cooler at BOQ—he arranged it and often footed more than his share of the expense. Bill energetically scratched while his chicks ate. He also provided a much needed tonic for the squadron, somebody to gripe to and at—the resulting arguments and discussions provided many a laugh that eased the strains of flying. He was always involved in some amusing situation, whether it was driving his car over stumps (oh dear!) or wondering about the ecstasies of a bubble bath. Through all this, Bill got his adventure. He accomplished this without changing either himself or his way of life. There is no question but that in future years, the major will have many martinis with many members of the squadron in many different places.

Lt. MELVIN R. DeLOOF
Rollen L. Berquist, ARM 3/C
Thomas H. Enright, AOM 2/C

Mel DeLoof, the original flying dutchman of the Throttle Benders, hasn't yet lived down his operational training nickname of PUMPER—and he maintains to this day that its evolution had no connection with his throttle arm. When the Kalamazoo Draft Board caught up with him way back in 1941, he was forced to postpone his dreams of singing first tenor with Fred Waring and get into something quick — anything just so it wasn't the "Walking Army." Life proved to be very good to him, and he even managed to divorce himself from the rigors of war for 18 months with a timely tour of duty as a primary instructor—at Glenview, of all places! During this protracted country club vacation, he was successful in acquiring a better half. It is unanimously agreed that the merger was greatly to his advantage even though it forced him to account to Marge every time he claimed to have had the night flying duty. Included among his accomplishments since joining the Throttle Benders are a month's vacation at the photographic school at Harrisburg, Pennsylvania—with wife of course, an amazing run of luck at Gin Rummy, and the uncanny ability to develop a hydraulic leak in 312 at the most propitious moments!

Bird Dog, as senior duty officer of the squadron, was continually worrying about the "All Pilots Board". So desperately hard did he try to have the boys digest Dane's drippings, he was 'tard' most of the time. For this reason, if you were looking for BILLY you could usually find him curled up in his forever shining Dodge coupe takin' him his little nap. Once Billy was enjoying his little nap, it took his national anthem, 'Rose of San Antone' to get him back on his feet. His ability to look awake and still be asleep on his feet was the envy of all. After helping to put the squadron in commission, Billy took over the intricacies of the Gunnery Department. Shortly thereafter the arrival of the Aviation Ordnance Officer eased Billy's problems and enabled him to spread his ever welcome drawling good humor. Upon leaving the states, this quality caused many of the 'bull sessions' to be held in Billy's room. His earlier tour as a primary instructor provided the material for many of his tales. Thus, the Bird Dog was forever recounting the wild escapades of the cadets he had instructed and reminding us of his record of never losing a student. Billy called all enemy planes Helen because his every thought revolved around his lovely wife. He had over a hundred pictures of Helen and his daughter Jan, over which he brooded constantly. This slight little Texan held the squadron record for writing the greatest number of letters home. Their marital vows were fifty fifty and Billy felt it included photographs; consequently, he was always asking someone to take his picture—their camera, of course. In years to come Billy will review these words as he sets on his porch down in Texas. He will turn to his nearest listener, blink, and say, "Bull Corn!"

Lt. BILLY M. EASELY
Stanley M. Dupree, ARM 2/C
John G. Murray, AMM 2/C

Lt. (j.g.) ARTHUR C. EULER
Charles H. Card, AOM 3/C
James L. Truax, ARM 2/C

Every now and then the ill winds that continually whistle in and out of the Windy City find course to deposit articles of worth where'er the need is greatest. Such was our good fortune; for when the squadron was still in the throes of adolescence, in blew ART Euler. He graduated at Pensacola after bribing eleven of his thirteen various instructors. Art was so overcome with confidence from this signal achievement that he went to the extreme and decided he was suited to matrimony. Four days after sewing on his gold stripe (one), he reported to Miami ringed both nose and finger. Miami was just one big honeymoon to Art, with the annoying sideline of operational training. Upon his arrival at New Bedford, Ensign Euler was regarded by the flight officer as a Godsend. It wasn't long before Art became a recording genius with a little black book that contained everything the 'Bigs' needed. Dates, laundry marks, flight time, one had only to see Art or the little book. It was on a short jaunt to Brunswick, Maine, for rocket work that Art acquired a suitable nickname. He got this *nom d'amour* from one of the sweet young things which were so numerous in Brunswick's better bars . . . Blue Eyes Euler from that day hence. Art's greatest surprise came one day when he walked up and gave the skipper a terrific whack in the posterior, believing it to be someone else—he claimed. His greatest single triumph, Brunswick excluded, came at Arcata when he took up the duties of signal officer and safely waved two planes in. It was an accomplishment that even Art thought was impossible, as he later confessed to the startled pilots.

Lt. Comdr. JOSEPH F. FILLER
Francis F. Ricketts, ARM 2/C
George M. Tapp, AMM 2/C

JOPLIN JOE Filler, from Missouri was the exec. of the Torpeckers, and a fine one he was, too. He came to the squadron with a little bit of the Missouri mule's stubbornness still clinging to him. Being an "ex-instructor" from NAS, New Orleans, and NAS, Corpus Christi, it was difficult for him to adopt the self-indulging practices of the combat pilot. This condition of mental conflict existed until he went to sea, and from that time on, the transition was an easy one. He could be continually found in his sack on his back in room 225. In fact this state of recline became so habitual that the steward's mates began to think of him as a fixture and dusted him off each day. But Joe's contributions to the nation were not always beneficial to the war effort. It was in Mexico in December, 1944, that he created the international incident that became known as, "The Oh Shaw! Uprising". In this Pan-American frustration he refused to buy the homespun wares of one of Mexico's "little tradespeople". Being unaccustomed to such abrupt denial, the proprietor believed that Joe was questioning the legality of the merchandise. Throughout his duty with the squadron, Joe's wife and daughter occupied a prominent place in his thoughts. He confessed that he was really a family man, with the emphasis on the word family. And when the war ended Joe announced his plans to return with celerity to his wife, his home, and his surveyor's tripod.

Lt. (j.g.) R. BRYANT FOERSTER
Leo. A. Caisse, AMM 3/C
James B. Rickey, ARM 2/C

BRY and a stampeding herd live by the same maxim. If there is anything in the path, either crush it or knock it over; never go around. The damage that this Goliath caused wasn't so much a pre-meditated act as the unswerving determination to reach his objective regardless of the consequences. These innocent acts of minor destruction early earned him the appropriate appellations, Bull and El Toro. El Toro claimed there wasn't a thing in the Navy he couldn't manhandle, and he was forever backing up his claims with evidence. Even a flying truck like the TBF was as a feather in the breeze with Bull in the driver's seat. Many grey hairs were created the day Bull made an over-head gunnery run on a formation— Bull got his share of grey too, for he lived to be reprimanded. This reservoir of voluble outbursts loved to argue on any subject at any time, preferably with Dane. However all of the stored up cliches and tidbits of both the humorous and serious side of life were not wasted in argument. Frequently he could be found in his room, pecking away on his typewriter, putting his thoughts on paper. Bry's greatest obsession was his wife and baby son, and his roommates never talked of them for fear of inviting a harangue that would keep them up the entire night. Of course, they knew he was going to keep them up half the night anyway pounding the keys in a letter home.

Take an adept pilot, add a generous dash of southern drawl, a jigger of adventure, then blend this with a sincere enjoyment of living and an unquenchable thirst; chill with shaved ice and stir well—presto, you have FEARLESS FOSDICK, the favorite son of Greensboro, North Carolina. Frank once wanted to cut people up and pass out pills, so he packed his bags and headed for a pre-med course at Guilford College and from there to the University of North Carolina. While in school, he distinguished himself as an athlete and also put a 'Crewsonian' touch on his approach to the fairer sex. When Frank came aboard at New Bedford, his easy going manner and amiable personality quickly won him friends. He took the junior officers in tow and disseminated valuable information to those näive ensigns who hadn't developed the proper procedures for obtaining maximum allowable sack time. It was while we were operating in New Bedford that Frank met the pretty little redhead that was later to become his wife, with no less than the Skipper as the best man. Before this marriage took place though, Frank was afforded the opportunity for one last fling when the squadron migrated to Hyannis for torpedo exercises. This deep-voiced rebel led the way in social life, and in the twilight hours of his bachelorhood, passed on many wily secrets to his followers. These officers, serving as disciples, have often reflected Frank's thorough tutelage in their professional handling of many trying situations.

Lt. FRANK B. FONDREN, Jr.
Robert J. Hartman, ARM 2/C
William Mallast, AMM 1/C

Ensign JOHN F. GAFNER

Perseverance personified! That was GAFF. He could sit down to a job, and until it was completed exactly the way he wanted it, he never budged. Stubborn—yes, but liked by all. Everyone who knew Gaff liked him, and he never met a person who was not somehow likeable. John was an agrarian soul from Wasco, California, who loved to tinker. Anything that needed fixing, from a paper clip to a tractor, held John's interest until it was once again serviceable. At New Bedford, it was this same mechanical interest that impulsed John's investment in a '35 Chevy. After a complete and painstaking overhaul, the engine purred like a kitten; but to his chagrin, his tires were so weak that he was still unable to go any distance. Another humorous experience with his puddle jumper was the time his engine wouldn't start. In his usual methodical way, Gaff first cleaned out the carburetor, then blew out the fuel line, and finally he removed the gas tank for a cleaning. The explosion that followed was justified; John discovered the car was just out of gas. While stationed at Otis Field, John was married to a saucer blue-eyed girl, Eileen, from New Bedford, Mass. In Maui, he could often be found memorizing his latest letter and mumbling how much homier the war would have been if we had let the Nips invade us. When they were living in Arcata, Calif., John and his wife were constantly amusing everyone with their water fights, and Eileen was always seeking refuge in someone else's apartment. Just before we left Arcata, John pronounced himself as an expectant father.

Ensign FREDERICK A. GAY
Kenneth A. Haley, ARM 2/C
Roy Shane, AMM 3/C

This boy of the booming bass, FRED Gay, drifted into Arcata in the merry month of May, '45. Another Missouri born aviator, he hailed from University City. Before coming to the Navy, Fred attended Washington University of St. Louis. He joined us from VT-24 and CASU 5. After a rendition of 'Hong Kong Blues' with Poe, he was immediately seized by Blu as his singing partner, but to everyone's relief, an opportunity for a duet never arose. Throughout his entire tour, Fred took pride in having his picture taken in sundry poses—maybe it was because he was photogenic. The photograph contribution box for this book was just brimming over with pictures of him. A common saying in the planning room was, "Well, we can always put in another picture of Gay." Fred was the Stinger's H. V. Kaltenborn; each day he presented his views of the news over station W-A-S-P. His broadcasting career reached its height when he released the information on the atomic bomb. With excitement as great as it was, Fred consented to make a special rebroadcast just for the Throttle Benders who were in the sack during the first broadcast. Only once did the Torps see this easy going lad dejected and downcast. After briefings and studying photographs and maps of Wake Island for a week, Fred had the misfortune of drawing a dud on his first strike, and was struck below to the hanger deck. Each night this Missourian could be found in the wardroom keeping up on his lettered love life. It seemed that Fred overstepped the bounds though because a little gal by the name of Jeanne had the measurements for a harness to be put around his neck as soon as he had one foot in the States.

"Boys, I'm homesick; go find me a warm body." Those were his words, and there was nothing immoral in the remark. RUSTY was an ex-embalmer. This mad mortician of Charlottesville, Va., finally traded in his long tails, Homburg hat and solemn look for a gold stripe, white hat and wings at Corpus in September of '44. Rusty was no amateur corpse curer. He spent a three year apprenticeship learning the fundamentals and then took a two year course at the University of Minnesota, polishing his technique. While there he was elected to the presidency of the embalmer's fraternity, Pi Sigma Eta, and to hold this office he was required to drink a 12 ounce tumbler of formaldehyde every other Friday. Always an eye on the post-war market, Rusty wrote regular letters to the U. S. Chamber of Commerce, inquiring where business was deadest. It was at Barbers Point, on Oahu, that Rusty learned just how long the long arm of the law could be. He was put 'in hack' for a week because an MP caught him racing to a football game in Miami when he was in operational training. Rusty was engaged to a northerner from Chicago, but as he explained to his worried family, it was all right for her sympathies were with the South. The fact that Rusty was a *cadet* at nearby Glenview proved that it was true love and not just the uniform. As his primary diversion at sea he played bridge and could often be heard shouting, "Duty Officer, get mah .38; that was mah suit Benny bid."

Ensign RUSSELL P. HALL
Neil G. Martin, AMM 3/C
Raymond E. Hanning, ARM 3/C

AL was best known and described as a rugged individualist. Although he was easy going and friendly, he could handle himself exceptionally well if the going turned rough. His career as a Golden Gloves boxer and the rugged work in the mines of Idaho gave him a noteworthy physique and a forceful personality. To attest his perseverance is the fact that Al worked his way through college entirely on his own. Al is especially remembered for his interest in flying and his flying skill. He gave his time freely in helping the new boys with their instrument work. Not infrequently, Harsh would be delayed in arriving home from the Squadron by becoming intensely engrossed in a discussion of flying. He loved flying and loved to talk about flying. Speaking of love, Al married a sparkling and vivacious blonde from Corpus Christi, Texas. This happy union was blessed with a son, and we know that he will be a living monument to the principles and aspirations of his beloved dad. So a toast to Al, a grand shipmate and a warm friend . . . his memory will remain with every one of us.

Lt. ALBERT T. HARSHBARGER

Ensign CLARENCE R. JOHNSON

"All problems solved for a nominal charge . . . New England my specialty." That was the slogan of BABE Johnson, as he wandered purposely from southerner to southerner, re-enacting the Civil War at each encounter. No battlefield ever got the barrage of invectives that he showered on any rebel who was reluctant to admit defeat. "Why my father's father was the finest carpetbagger that ever set foot in that quagmire of flotsam humanity that we are forced to include as the decaying part of that same great nation to which the State of Connecticut belongs," was one of his milder opening harangues. Johnny loved competition. He was an ardent sportsman and was enthusiastic about participating in any contest, and win or lose, he was proud to be a member of any team that played hard. It was in this same spirit that he carried on what was unofficially the longest continuous cribbage tournament in history, yet always managed to be a few games ahead of his opponent. A great flyer, with a great personality, he joined the Throttle Bender's at Barber's Point in June of '45. His naval career as a pilot was filled with unusual experiences, such as boarding submarines and destroyers. It was through another of his strange adventures that he learned that a jeep carrier's deck is too short on which to land a TBF without a tail hook. This Connecticut Yankee was always up front slugging when the going was tough. The combination of all these facts present a cross-section of the fine character of a fine guy, Babe Johnson.

"Why did you play that card," or, "You should have moved the other checker." Yes, JONESY was at it again. There wasn't a man any place who was a more confirmed kibitzer. Whether it was bridge or cribbage, monopoly or acey-ducey, Bob knew the trickiest methods of playing the game . . . at least, according to him. Bob was born in North Carolina, but, by the time he had reached the ripe old age of three, he had convinced his parents of the need for a change of environment. Hence, they moved to the wilderness of Florida, and there he has since lived in the tropical sunshine, supplemented with a ration of "moonshine" to prevent monotony. When he joined the Throttle Benders in June of '45, Bob took over the navigation department and energetically began teaching classes in elementary navigation to the entire crew. He came to this outfit after quite a gypsy life, having seen duty in VT-1, where he was at sea for twelve months, in VT-10, in VT-17, and finally came to us from VT-100 at Barber's Point. Evidently this transient life appealed to him, for he put in his application for Regular Navy and all the apples that come with it. He was the only fellow in the squadron who regarded Pearl as something more than a water-stop, for Jonesy made plans for a Hawaiian Honeymoon amid the gently stirring palm trees and crystalline surf that have made The Rock so appealing to all aviators. One opinion expressed was that Jonesy was marrying this gal because he figured he could get a cut-rate on the wedding. His bride, Anne, is a minister's niece.

Lt. (j.g.) ROBERT T. JONES
Kenneth L. Morris, AOM 3/C
Edwin B. Johnson, ARM 3/C

LONG JOHN felt as much at home in a TBF as he did on the range, tending his sheep. With either staff or stick, this large, rangy and good looking lad from Hagerman, Idaho, usually had the situation well in hand. He was forever remarking about the wonderful wilds right in his back yard, and of the many times he had to track down wildcats who were disturbing his flock. He admitted the winters were a little too severe for him, and he took time out from his wool works to winter at the University of Idaho for a little 'book larnin.' Having completed a prescribed course in paddle waving at Jacksonville, Fla., Long John received his warmest welcome from Euler. Russ, as he was often called, saw very little stateside duty with us. He was on his nuptial shakedown cruise when the Navy rerouted him to Pearl, without wife. His demure wife, Peg, was forever sending him presents of candy, cookies, and cake to keep him aware that he actually was married and it hadn't been a dream. While at Maui, Long John's nocturnal habits fascinated his roommates; it was here that they exploited his ability to carry on a coherent conversation while sound asleep. It wasn't long before his past adventures became public. His greatest demonstration was to take an empty beer can and crush it in his hands. Only one other Throttle Bender could accomplish this feat, and he had to come from the same state. Every mail call he was forced to defend himself against an Army fighter, as well as Japs. John's olive drabbed brother was always referring to the large gap between an Army captain and a Navy ensign.

Ensign JOHN R. LeMOYNE

The Body Beautiful . . . The American Girl's greatest moment . . . The mighty financier of Torpedo Squadron Eighty Six . . . Power personified . . . This was Gerald E. Louiso. This former Pennsylvania Railroader joined the Navy with a burning desire for adventure and acclaim, and by the time he graduated from Pensacola, LOU felt he was well on his way towards the fulfillment of his dream of a six inch chest expansion, a four figure bank account, and women in every port. Many a light cord has hung limply from its mooring after Lou's ruthless onslaughts have been terminated. As his sparring partner a light cord was perfect—it didn't strike back and his physique could be properly illuminated. The problem of the log books was one that caused Lou much concern. He was so busy supplying the pilots with navigational aids that he just didn't have time to look up data the flight office required from the records. Time and again he begged for a yeoman to take care of this job. His pleas finally became so entreating that his request was granted. Lou then said, "Yes Sir, I'll have MY yeoman get that dope immediately." Lou's decline from paramour par excellence in the abundant days at New Bedford to his ultimate state of neglect, which he attributed to sea duty, was a sad one with which all his fellow pilots were well acquainted. This boastful Barrymore was always averring that Stateside duty was the only requirement that he needed filled to make Crewson look like a small time operator. Through his active social life Lou became well known as a lavish spendthrift. He never failed to give his complete financial support to any and all undertakings of the Throttle Benders. This however, did not account for his hysterics at Maui when, to his utter amazement, he found his budget EIGHT cents on the shy side. Maybe the Gooney Birds stole it!

Lt. (j.g.) GERALD E. LOUISO
Donald H. French, AOM 3/C
Ray D. Taylor, ARM 3/C

Ensign CHARLES N. LUND

"What are you trying to do, pump me?", was a typical expression of SILENT CHARLIE Lund when he wasn't in the mood for conversation. Truly, this fellow received little enjoyment from the favorite Navy pastime of chipping his teeth and beating his gums. This husky lad was born in Reno, Nev., and when he did talk, it was to extoll the merits of his state and its mining possibilities. The hustle and bustle of the big cities never changed his love for the wide open spaces, and many of his weekends were spent in the fresh air of the country. Chuck reported to the squadron at New Bedford a few days after it was commissioned. He thought he left his old nickname of Newt, The Star Gazer, behind, but to his disappointment he found that it had preceded him in the care of several buddies. He soon proved his ability as a pilot in the air, and on the ground he displayed his adeptness in engineering. Blu lost no time in making him an assistant. His reserved attitude gave everyone the confidence that their plane was in competent hands. The Jolly Whaler was frequently visited by Charlie, and it wasn't long before he established himself as a confirmed woman hater. This was an added incentive to the young ladies, and it became a race to see who could be the first one to break his resistance. From all outward appearances, this contest was won by a little girl by the name of Esther. Charlie repudiated all accusations but never provided a satisfactory explanation for his missing ring.

PISTOL Martin, Roy to the fairer sex, is living proof that Kansas had more than salt water taffy to offer the Navy in this war. The name "Pistol," referring to his rapid fire chatter, was thrust upon him early in his cadet career. The Kansas Kid got his first taste of salt water at Pensacola and, finding it somewhat agreeable, went on to Miami for an additional sampling. On a winter cruise in the salty Atlantic he concluded, "As a potion it's good, in motion it's bad." Westward from the States he made the additional statement, as he strained over the forecastle deck, "This trip was to be by boat, instead it will be by rail." Besides his duties in the photographic department, he assumed the responsibility of keeping pace with the contemporary wolves of the squadron. The gypsy life of the Torpeckers made possible such memorable experiences as "Crab Apple" in Boston, "Nantucket" in Pawtucket, and "Juanita" of blanket party fame. At sea, when this casanova was not flying, he could be found baffling his partner, as well as his contestants, in the never ceasing bridge games which prevailed at all hours in the squadron ready room. Contrary to the average combat Navy pilot, he don't smoke, he don't chew, and only holds a very few. The beast in this Mid-Westerner exposed itself whenever the bomb load was marked C.O.D., Tokyo. We all salute you "Pistol," a true friend and an honest gentleman —and a farmer too, by gum.

Lt. (j.g.) ROY J. MARTIN
Guy D. Hatcher, ARM 3/C
Warren W. White, AOM 3/C

It was our great good fortune to have among us the collector of the choicest and rarest bits of scuttlebutt. No one was ever able to determine the devious channels through which CHARLIE Nolan obtained his unlimited supply of information. He was suspected of bribing a steward, who bribed a mess cook, who bribed a mail clerk, who delivered the admiral's guard mail. "I just received the latest dope," was his most frequent greeting —no doubt a check of the morning press would have revealed the same news. His duties as an ordnance officer left Charlie with very little spare time while we were at sea. Many times he was required on deck in the wee small hours to supervise the bomb loadings. This task he performed efficiently between furtive glances at the sky for kamikaze intruders. Last minute orders changing the bomb load was one of the obstacles Charlie was forced to overcome. Just to keep this 'bombcart coolie' from being overburdened with too much sleep, he was kept posted with numerous integrity watches. On these watches Charlie was very sure to impress upon all of the men the importance of fire control. Evidently, Charlie too was once a doubting "Thomas." In his free moments Charlie put many fine friendships to the extreme test by making buddies serve as bridge partners, which game he was endeavoring to master. No one has ever forgotten his hurried trip back to the States from Maui to convince ComAirPac that he was the only man to handle the ordnance problems of VT 86. Though his vacation with his wife, Muriel, was shortlived, his farewell party at the Wailuku Hotel was certainly a memorable celebration.

Lt. (j.g.) CHARLES C. NOLAN, Jr.

CHIEF Ochab was known to be a staunch home town supporter of "Dem Wonderful Bums," and he never wasted any time in asserting that more than just one tree grew in Brooklyn. This junior jaygee, I say again, jaygee, claims Michigan University as his Alma Mater; but Michigan was always shy about making a public acknowledgment of Chief. His athletic activities in the squadron more than once caused onlookers to comment, "By gosh! there's life in the bald, old duffer yet." The Torp's ball club couldn't have been recognized without Chief behind home plate. He most frequently sought diversion at a card table, playing anything from Old Maid to Bridge. He regarded anything milder than a pipe or cigar as a whim of the opposite sex. Chief's theories on relaxation always included a glass of cold beer, a good cigar, and a philosophical discussion. Obe always will remember the ruthless members of the squadron who ordered the removal of his mustache. He contended that any man with his fast dwindling resources of hair should have been granted the small luxury of a mustache. Chief's social life grew as the squadron grew, until at Arcata it reached it's all time all time, and he gained his own resplendent niche in Humbolt's Hall of Fame. It was orders to report back to sea, that gave him a timely avenue of escape from the fair damsels of Humboldt.

Lt. (j.g.) CHARLES OCHAB
Robert C. Wright, AOM 2/C
Robert B. Coad, ARM 2/C

Lt. GEORGE H. PATTOK
Robert D. Fuller, ARM 3/C
Fontaine C. Slater, AMM 2/C

The old man of the outfit was George H. Pattok, better known in the squadron as PAPPY. He graduated from Northwestern University and went on to win his Navy Wings at Corpus Christi, Texas. During a tour instructing the Navy's up and coming birdmen, he acquired a wife, Helen. Upon completion of this hair-thinning duty, he went through operational training at Miami, Florida. He joined the squadron at Quonset, R. I., before it was commissioned. Heading the Torps material and supply department, his versatility in the field of procurement brought repeated exclamations of delight from everyone in the squadron. As a tribute to his ability, there still exists a memo from CAG about the Otis Field Wastebasket Incident. It has been said that this demon of the survey slip, this unscrupulous procurer, this Maharajah of materiel, was making an early accumulation of sundry supplies for his post-war dream of a well stocked store, and even toyed with the feasibility of expanding this dream to a chain. In order to keep harmony in the squadron during this period of acquisition, he guaranteed a district managership to every cooperative pilot. Having an elephantine fondness for cold beer and good cigars, as well as an intense yearning to someday bid and make a grand slam in bridge, this man should go a long ways in procuring a happy and successful life.

The ALABAMA FLASH, William Loyle Poe, was better known as Ed to his squadron associates, deriving the nickname from his satellite, the great poet. Though Ed's poetic achievements did not reach the heights that the poet attained, he avowed that his MARJORIE LEE could surpass all of the merits that had been attributed to Annabel Lee. And no one dared to challenge this assertion. Probably the subject on which he waxed most eloquent was the multitudinous advantages of his home town, Birmingham. After starting a conversation with him, the opening clause of his second remark was sure to be, "Now down in B'ham . . . that's my home town you know . . ." as if anyone that knew him longer than two minutes didn't know. After his health habits had suffered many months of caustic criticism, the scabrous growth on his upper lip blossomed forth into a scraggly, full grown mustache. The suave "savoir faire" he displayed in maintaining this paragon patch showed a perserverance which was in keeping with the highest traditions of the United States Naval Service. As we say farewell to this fine pilot and swell guy and depart for other assignments, we will always remember him strafing anything that looked feasible upon retirement from the main Jap target. So many gun barrels were burned out that the gunnery department anticipated sending a dispatch to Washington requesting: "More gun barrels for Poe."

Lt. (j.g.) WILLIAM L. POE
Richard D. Hornback, AOM 3/C
Harlan G. Shotwell, ARM 3/C

It's a long high fly . . . Scott is going way back . . . back . . . and makes a beautiful catch over his shoulder, retiring the side with no hits, no runs, and not too many errors. Whether it was on a ball field, tennis court, beach, or basketball court, Scott was present to assert his right to the office of athletic director of the Torps. Getting the sack-happy Throttle Benders out for athletics required both tact and brawn, and Scotty was qualified to supply both. SCOTTY claimed to be a Philadelphian but was really just a small town boy, having come from Germantown, Pa. It was while he was exalting himself in athletics at the University of Virginia that his ears started to pick up the distant roar of propellers. And as the storm clouds began to gather, he concluded that he was the type of youth the Navy was crying for in every poster, so he headed for Jacksonville, Fla., and Naval Aviation. When he completed his training, he was ordered to report to Pensacola and was given the arduous task of an instructor in basic training. There he waited 18 months before going to Fort Lauderdale, Fla., for operational training in that monster, the TBF. It was at Lauderdale that he met Ellie, a gal from Oak Park, Illinois. Through the many days overseas Scott's love affair became a prime concern of all, and when we returned to the States the first time, we all looked forward to Scott's wedding. But alack and alas, Scotty returned a bachelor. He again gave us the assurance that he would get his mate by '48 and have an abundance of Scotties.

Lt. LOUIS GEORGE SCOTT
Edward J. Parenti, ARM 2/C
Howard G. Cunningham, AOM 3/C

SPEECHLESS John arrived aboard in May of '45 while we were exploiting the fertile fields of Arcata. His voracious appetite immediately adjusted itself to our little work much play routine which was then in its second week of operation. After several parties everyone discovered that the ordinarily eloquent John had a small amount of difficulty with his enunciation after several jiggered hours had passed. This soft-spoken West Virginian divided his day into two periods: mealtime and sacktime. "A nourishing meal" was his apt comment for any form of food. He liked to eat any type of victual, in any amount, at any time of day or night . . . but especially enjoyed a can of sardines just before retiring at night. One of the Torpecker classics was John's inaccurate reference to himself as a "flyable dud." He gave his most outstanding performance at a rest home in Pearl after our return from the forward area. During his entire stay the only two coherent remarks he made were, "Hi, Boy," and, "Say, Boy." During this same "rest," Shonk met "Medals" Blu in a challenge wrestling bout. John threw him in four seconds, and ten seconds later Blu came down from where he was thrown, with a dull thud.

Lt. JOHN J. SHONK, III
Grant L. Damron, AOM 3/C
Leo H. Burrows, ARM 1/C

"Jun-your!" As the call reverbrated throughout the ready room, we expected to hear in answer, Henry Aldrich's epic, "Coming, Mother," but instead we heard SIMP'S meek, "Yes Sir," that vaguely reminded us of "Yes, Father." Now don't get the idea this young man was a shy, demure individual. No indeed! Simp claimed he could do *anything* that his immediate superiors could do AND do it better. If this was true, why did he make a junior jaygee his God? Simp had been with the Throttle Benders but a short while, when his consistent ability to make contacts while he was on the prowl was recognized. As a result he was appropriately dubbed, "Radar." If you're looking for a covey of "quail" just take Radar along to "home" you in. It had always been a known fact that Simp had a burning desire to see the Golden Gate Bridge, but why he chose the darkest night possible for the occasion was a mystery. It was public fact that there wasn't any transportation back to the city tt that time of night. Whether he went for the beauty of the bridge or the beauty on the bridge was never disclosed. After hearing Simp rave over the merits of the Pine Tree State as a vacation land and a potato country, one would think he was working for the Maine Chamber of Commerce. The most important place in the state, of course, was Oakfield, his home town.

Ensign WILLARD K. SIMPSON
Walter D. Hall, AMM 1/C
William J. Powers, Jr., ARM 3/C

The Rube Goldberg of the Throttle Benders, Jim Staker, was always planning some gadget that could ease his daily tasks. STAKE came to the squadron just before it left the States for Maui in December of '44. From the first day he came aboard Stake demonstrated that genius and insanity are very closely related. The wheels that were constantly whirring around in his creative brain put forth many an idea that increased the versatility of the TBF. But Stake's greatest triumph came when he completed a combination knee pad and plotting board which unfolded into a bridge table, small kitchenette, or portable bar, whichever craving was the most acute. One of his greatest and most talked of moments was a week-end in New York. That was really the time when the country came to the city. During the whole "model" week-end, his most often repeated remark was, "Kansas City was never like this." Stake's little gal, Rosemary, was his greatest single problem and he went to everyone from the chaplain to Mr. Anthony in search of a solution. From the moment he arose in the morning until sleep overtook him at night, Rosemary plagued his every thought. Stake was "eager"—on the athletic field—about the squadron—in his conversation—Stake wanted to get up and go. He always devoted himself wholeheartedly to every undertaking. When a plane was down in the engineering department, it was Stake who investigated. When basketball was mentioned, it was Stake who took up the cry and organized the game. He was a doer not just a talker, but he got his share of vocal exercise, too.

Ensign JAMES M. STAKER

"DAD BLAME IT," he roared, and everyone in the ready room crouched a little lower in their seats, for with these invectives NICK Verano was off on another tirade. Someone must have stolen his candy bar or awakened him from one of his trances, and when this product of the Virginia Hills was riled, heaven help the critter that's done him dirt. Usually Nick was a very mild-mannered person, but on occasions he hearkened to the code of his law-enforcin' father who was once the sheriff of McDowell County, and at those times he felt it his duty to carry on the family tradition and see justice done. The love life of this dark-haired home breaker is an open book to all who care to listen to his tales of ardent wooing. Once, but only once, Nick convinced himself that matrimony had advantages. While in this state of mind, he was saved from that binding contract when the bride-to-be changed her mind. Everyone was disappointed but Nick, who merely shrugged his shoulders and continued to make his home in green pastures. Before his first strike, he was heard to remark that he intended to circle the target at ten thousand feet, and if the flak was too thick, he would return to the ship; if the firing was meager and inaccurate, he would make his drop at eight thousand feet so that he would have plenty of altitude to pull out on retirement. When Nick joined the squadron at Arcata, Calif., he quickly adapted himself to the Throttle Benders' personality and his only complaint was that he always got the most unpleasant tasks in the squadron ground duties—This was hard to understand because Nick was the Junior Ensign.

Ensign NICHOLAS L. VERANO
Harriel D. Adams, ARM 3/C
Donald E. Piepho, AMM 3/C

Lt. GAIL B. YOUNG
Gregory P. Cerro, AOM 3/C
Michael J. Yanulis, ARM 2/C

Better known as SPIDER to his brother birdmen, G. B. Young hails from the oil rich state of Oklahoma—a preview of paradise—so says G. B. He has often been seen and heard extolling the merits of horses and the manner of riding them. He dreams for the future have run the gamut from a small town airport to a dude ranch, all outside of Oklahoma. G. B. came to this squadron married, having gained a wife immediately following his first Pacific tour. He and the Mrs. had Young-uns in June, having purchased two cocker spaniel pups just before Spide sailed. G. B. flew as little as possible, so little in fact, we think of him more as a flight officer than as a pilot. But he can never be accused of not delivering his share of explosives in Tojo's back yard. He performed his duties as schedule maker with great facility, and was showered with acclaim by his fellow Torps. Daybreak and dusk never found Spide on the flight deck; he had a terror that, in the poor light, his sparse frame would be mistaken and lashed down as ship's super structure. His costume for sports brought about his nickname. In his tight crimson trunks surrounded by gangling arms and legs, he reminded everyone of a daddy-longlegs spider. Seizing the name Spider in refuge from his given name of Gail, he proudly displayed a model of his namesake on his flight suit.

CHARLES J. JOHNSON
Aviation Radioman
Second Class
Combat Aircrewman

GILBERT E. AUSTIN
Aviation Machinist
Third Class
Combat Aircrewman

THOMAS O. RUSSELL
Aviation Radioman
Second Class
Combat Aircrewman

KEITH W. GORDON
Aviation Radioman
Third Class
Combat Aircrewman

ROBERT J. GUARIGLIA
Aviation Machinist
Third Class
Combat Aircrewman

RICHARD C. BRYAN
Aviation Radioman
Third Class
Combat Aircrewman

DAVID L. HANCOCK
Aviation Radioman
Third Class
Combat Aircrewman

WILLIAM A. HEMENWAY
Aviation Ordnanceman
Third Class
Combat Aircrewman

THESE ARE THE MEN THAT WORK AN EIGHT HOUR SHIFT;
THREE SHIFTS A DAY

Top Row (*left to right*):

W. E. Kemper, ACMM; J. R. Fulwood, AMM 2/C; I. Werchovsky, ART 1/C; R. E. Howland, AM 1/C; D. R. Ball, Y 3/C; J. G. Jackson, AOM 1/C; J. E. Cowart, ACRM.

Bottom Row (*left to right*):

J. P. Little, AOM 1/C; H. F. Kyer, Y 2/C; G. Brown, AEM 1/C; E. B. Morgan, PR 1/C; R. E. Barber, AMM 2/C; A. B. Jones, AEM 1/C; C. S. Goad, AMM 1/C; J. F. Shimkus, AMM 1/C.

CREW CUTS

IT has often been said that when a group of sailors assemble, there is automatically a representation of just about every phase of good and evil in mankind. So, apparently, no one was surprised, on that dim date back in June of '44, that the crew of the squadron lived up to the aforementioned maxim.

Our immediate boss, Chief Kemper, and his second-in-command, Chief Cowart, held us all in check by introducing the novel eight-muster-a-day system, but nobody in their right mind, not even "Old Buck" or "Jasper" could possibly hope to subdue such wild prairie flowers as Abe, Whitey, The Genius, and Brill when there was always an opportunity to siphon five gallons and head for the Jolly Whaler.

All our initial obstacles were surmounted with the arrival of the pilots and their willing crews along with that picture of sartorial splendour, Chief "if-you-have-any-squawks-turn-'em-into-Jones" Ray. Dillard and Stroud started defying the Flight Surgeon, the stomach pump and the Schenley Corporation, while Deacon Hall appealed to the boys to ease up on the Atlantic and the Whaler for a try at a chess tournament at the U.S.O. But at the moment, everyone was looking for a mascot and Gordon came up with "Torp," a nondescript little terrier who soon won our wholehearted affection.

We moved over to Hyannis, and the squadron began to take shape when the Skipper turned the planes over to the crewmen. However, Foster learned that too much throttle pressure wasn't what the Station C.O. wanted in his lap at morning muster, and "Feets" took a verbal broadside for it.

On our return to New Bedford we acquired the ideal turret gunner, "Why-can't-I-make-first?" Fulwood, who was later to get a thorough checkout, along with Nub Goad, in the intricacies of the TBM hydraulic system by Mr. Dane. Butch Wright and Dick Bryan managed to pull Rickey out of his shell one night but the effects were disastrous and Rick retired the next day, in company with a large number of Alka Seltzer tablets.

Next on our long list of stops was Otis Field, on the Cape, where CAG arrived with his radioman, Mike Yanulis, who received our open-mouthed gapes for his exalted position, until the Commander forsook the lumbering fish for an F4U and Mike was reduced to telling Slater and Cerro that Brooklyn was merely a state of mind. The pilots gave a shindig and asked for volunteer bartenders and after the office door was torn down by the rush to get in and sign up, Abe, Cud, Shotty and Russell emerged victorious. By the time the party was over, Captain Shotwell was piping Commander Aberle out from under the bar. At Otis, Hatcher married his lifelong sweetheart, and the axe fell on Dillard, Conway, Strout, Luell, Pacelli and Crum.

As the days shortened, the leaves disappeared, and the weather grew rainy and cold, rumors flew thick and fast, and word got around that we would soon be heading West. Dupe, Spec, Cowart and Guariglia made one more attempt at dislodging the New Bedford Hotel from its foundations, much to the chagrin of the manager. A day or so later, after five days leave, the Boston and Albany sent over eight kidney crushers and we started for San Diego. Massey was saluted by the good citizens of Springfield, Missouri, on the way, although he was at a total loss to explain just how they knew he was coming. Tyler was hypnotized by a large, black-eyed Dalmatian who sat on the opposite seat with a leer and a decidedly passionate wag in her tail. Charley Card went down for the ten-count in a brief but decisive bout with John Barleycorn.

We said goodbye to the States on December 9th, thus legally earning our sea-pay, bound for Pearl, and ten days later we found ourselves at Kahului, on the beautiful island of Maui. Tom Canty and Roy Shane tried to outdo the SeaBees in various construction jobs and thus acquired their present collection of tools which includes everything but a prime-mover. Johnny Shimkus's nationality had always been a source of conjecture but after seeing him ease into the social circles of Wailuku and its selection of darkskinned post-debs, speculation ceased. Nelson found the environment suitable for flexing his muscles and inaugurated the practice of swinging through the trees every morning after the beer garden had secured. Hartman was finally persuaded by Bill Malast and Mr. Fondren to keep his senses after his "Dear John" letter, announcing the termination of a love idyll which was supposed to be out of this world.

On March first, the Skipper gravely told us that our training days were over and we were on our way to the fleet. A final beer party on the beach gave "Oleo" Egler and Gil Austin an opportunity to make Barney Oldfield look like a piker, when they appropriated a jeep and covered the distance between the picnic area and the barracks in a trifle less than forty seconds and "The Gook," our two fingered Pyle, started a back-to-nature movement by wandering barefooted through the woods in his scivvies. Three days later found us all aboard the U.S.S. Independence where Torp behaved herself in a very unladylike fashion on the forward elevator, before the eyes of the Captain and Exec.

On the thirteenth, we boarded the U.S.S. Wasp at Ulithi, in the Carolines, and our first strike came four days later at Kanoya, on Kyushu. Our reactions to combat were both varied and notable. Caisse told Mr. Foerster just exactly what to do over the air, and Brown's nightmare, after we had been hit, almost cost him a split skull while Iggy Werchovsky reverted to Cossack tactics, riding Barber down the flight deck whenever the Klaxon rang. Hornback proved to be the only man on board who could get tight on Navy jamoke.

Our return to Bremerton brought the good news of sixteen days leave, and Laddie Novak was next to get the marital call, in Chicago, after a rigorous bout with a high, wire fence at the Municipal Airport which was separating him from his wife-to-be. Fulwood never got any further than Parenti's home in Stockton, California and the tales the two of them brought back to Alameda are unprintable.

Our next stop was Eureka, up in the Redwood Country of Northern California, admittedly the wackiest town we had ever seen. Our first casualty was Haley, who lost his shirt playing poker to some of the local belles and even Truax and Bergquist succumbed to the call of the owl and could seldom be found in the barracks at night. Malewsky came back late from leave and was immediately ensconced in the brig but carried his own forty-five and slept with the keys under his pillow. George Bostrom found out that "Jo Ann was a nice girl." Harry Kyer, the squadron workhorse, could be seen almost any time at the Double A, surrounded by an admiring covey of chicks, goggle-eyed at his, "Boy, I've been out there," and when Eureka celebrated the 7th War Loan Drive, O'Tool, Novak and Slater went wild, draping the town's monument to Sutter with reams of Scott's Tissue as we swooped in low over the city.

But good things couldn't last indefinitely, and on June 13th we again embarked on the Wasp with seasoned veterans Buzz Burrows and Mr. Shonk, who had compiled a total of forty missions, along with Grant Damron, their gunner, the youngest in the squadron. "Lucille" Ball, Kyer's right hand man, came also, to help out with the paper work and proved to be a shark at pinochle.

While at Oahu, another officer-crew beer party took place, which was climaxed by Jimmy Myers and Pappy Coad being unceremoniously doused in the cooling tub. Enright and Andy successfully eluded their pursuers and escaped the chilling ordeal. "Shakey" Morris, Martin, Johnson, Hanning, Hancock and Hemenway reported aboard to assume their duties with their pilots.

But it was soon obvious that the war with the Nips couldn't be adequately prosecuted without VT-86, and, with some persuasion, the Skipper finally induced us to return to more serious pursuits, and we went off again on the Wasp to join T.F. 38. Butch Wright assumed the responsibility of Bosun in the crew's compartment and with a large lead persuader managed to make us turn up at G.Q. in the mornings. On the way out, Ricketts received his long over-do "Hero's Medal" from Mr. Bent, inscribed in a very artistic fashion by Pete Howland while Bellinger retired to the back of the Ready Room to go quietly nuts with his drumsticks. Roy Hunter took it upon himself to advise the Marine Complement how he personally sank the Haruna at Kure with eight tons of baloney. However, as we all knew, soon after our arrival over Japan, the Nips realized that "this was too much," so they quit.

Our last mission came when Rigger Morgan, Joe Little, and Mr. Nolan discovered a feasible method for dropping supplies over P.O.W. camps by parachute, and our career in the Western Pacific wound up successfully with some magnificent sight-seeing tours over the Empire.

Time and space, quite naturally, require that this summary of our exploits be brief. Only the lighter side has been mentioned. And this, with the sole purpose in mind, that, as the years pass and you refer upon occasion to this diary, it will enable you to recall, with a grin, your life and times in Torpedo Squadron 86.

IN any officer's guide, high morale is emphasized as the most important single factor to a happy group. There then always follows a number of suggestions for achieving this desired level of morale, such as, intramural contests, USO entertainment, Happy Hours, Officer-Crew beer parties . . . but why go any further than that last item for that is what this is about. We have computed that if all of our used beer bottles were laid end to end on a sidewalk there would have been one helluva lot of cut feet.

The first one was a clambake at a very ultra-refined recreational area which, by the more mundane, was coarsely referred to as Tillie's Acres. No one ever did discover the reason for such a name, but there were some awfully good theories put forward towards the end of the party. When the Squadron had finished this party, Tillie had about ten more Achers and the entire area was a rough reproduction of the northern half of Warsaw after the siege in 1939.

The highlight of the day was a barrel-rolling contest with Fulwood on one side and Parenti, Whitey, and Foster as the other team. Fun was being had by all until a moon-faced character, who claimed to be the proprietor, decided to protect the mahogany woodwork. His pleading did no good, and the boys desisted their revelry only when Luigi, the owner, started cutting his way throught the crowd with a large slavering meat cleaver.

At Maui the great brains of our motley crew formulated another plan of Intestinal Inquisition. Christmas was stealing slowly upon us, and with a festival air Christmas Eve was dedicated to the prolongment of Peace on Earth and everlasting goodfellowship. Instilled with Christmas Spirits and heady from the vast panoramas of tropical resplendency (that are so numerous in Hawaii), we and the pilots gathered on the beach for beer, hamburgers, Christmas Carols, and a USO hula show.

After these two demonstrations, it was decided that these gatherings supplied a maximum amount of entertainment for all hands and the operational losses were low enough to warrant frequent repetition. They became so popular that many select cliques in the squadron were holding clandestine soirées almost every other night. Our ration of bottled brew dwindled at an alarming rate as the tempo and frequency of parties increased. For awhile the supply was so low that several creative minds were frustrated into using Torpedo Alcohol in concocting a deadly punch known as Torpedo Mortis. These experiments were brought to an abrupt and fearful conclusion on the night that Gus "The Gook" Clucas was seen stalking big game amongst the surrounding cane fields and palm trees, armed with nothing more than corn stalks lodged in his shoe (he was wearing only one) and belt.

At Barbers Point, a time-saving procedure was developed. All hands discovered that if the icing tub in which the beer was kept chilled was used frugally, we could eliminate the necessity of barrack's shower and bath. By the end of the evening everyone was happily scrubbed and glowing. Again our losses were negligible. Several of the boys regarded this form of cleansing so highly that they went in innumerable times. The Gook was that night nominated as the Squadron entry in the Miss America Beauty Contest.

And so we say farewell to Torpedo Eighty-Six's social gatherings. We say farewell with the lilting strains of "Aloha" competing with the blaring brass of a Navy band blasting "The Eyes of Texas." We say farewell as one water soaked hamburger and several empty bobbing beer bottles drift over the horizon. May they forever float upon those broad seas into which so many of our proud sons have already thrown so many drained containers.

COMBAT LOG

Preface

AFTER nine months of continuous training Air Group 86, via Atlantic City, Otis, and Maui, went aboard the USS Wasp in Ulithi lagoon on 13 March, 1945. The Wasp was a last minute assignment, consequently there was more than normal confusion attached to our boarding and getting Air Group 61 off. At any rate, we got under way on the following morning. Task Force 58 was off to attack the Nips again.

14 MARCH . . . Sortie from Ulithi lagoon. 1105 . . . launch our first flight. Air and ship's gunnery exercised throughout the day. Launch our night fighters for training flights. Operational losses one water landing and one take-off crash. Both pilots picked up by near-by vessels.

15 MARCH . . . Northerly course. Training continues with pre-dawn launch and additional hops throughout the day.

16 MARCH . . . Ship fuels and replacement airplanes are taken aboard. Approach to enemy homeland necessitates combat air patrols.

17 MARCH . . . Start our run-in on Kyushu. Combat air patrols. Many bogeys on screen, none close the force. Day ends at General Quarters.

18 MARCH . . . Scattered cumulus clouds. Moderate sea. Fleet's disposition Five Victor Dog. Launch position is 75 miles South of Shikoku. Target bears 290 distance 135.

HARUNA

Wasp is under intermittent attack from before dawn until after dark. Wasp accounts for two of the eight planes shot down by disposition. We launch six strikes against Southern Kyushu to Kanoya, Byu, and Ibuski airfields and also against shipping in Kagoshima Bay. Regular patrols over the Task Group. The Air Group shoots down a Judy. Day ends at Torpedo Defense with firing on the port bow. Betty shot down by a task group night fighter.

19 MARCH . . . Many flares herald our approach to the Empire. Judys, Franks, Jills, and Zekes follow soon behind the flares. Altocumulus clouds. Calm sea. Target bears 331 distance 133. Launch our first CAP at 0546 and first strike toward Kure soon after. Wasp is hit by 540 pound SAP bomb at 0709, dropped by a Judy which came out of the overcast almost unnoticed. Air operations resume after fires are extinguished. Wasp shoots down second Kamikaze a few minutes later which crashes into sea close aboard the number two elevator. Entire task force under heavy attack and, on retirement, strikes are launched toward Kanoya. At Kure we hit two carriers, two battleships of the Ise class, one heavy cruiser, a light cruiser, a cargo ship, and a submarine. The Air Group shot down one Helen, one Myrt, one Judy, and two Bettys.

20 MARCH . . . Continue to retire. Launch CAPs and Anti-Sub Patrols to aid in fighting off determined enemy counter attacks. Air Group shoots down one Myrt. Enemy hecklers near task group during the night coming within range. One plane shot down. The day ends in the light of many flares.

21 MARCH . . . Southerly course. Air Group CAP shoots down three Franks during afternoon. In afternoon a large group of Bettys with fighter escort attempt to attack Task Force. Task group pilots shoot down 46 planes, losing one.
22 MARCH . . . Detached from Task Force 58, ordered to return to Ulithi to effect repairs.

Interlude . . . On arrival in Ulithi we learned that the Wasp was to proceed to Pearl for repairs . . . this led to our subsequent return to the States. Our combat narrative begins again when we rejoin the Fleet in July.

11-17 JULY . . . Sortie from Pearl as Task Unit 12.5.3. Destination . . . Wake Island. Conduct CAPs and Anti-Sub Patrols en route.

18 JULY . . . Wake Island bears 355 distance 60. Scattered cumulus. Flying conditions above average. Launch five strikes, three photo missions and regular CAPs and SNASPs. Attack Army and Marine headquarters, Heel Point, and AA positions on Wilkes Island. Anti-aircraft fire moderate and accurate. No planes lost. At dusk change course to Southwest for Eniwetok.

19-20 JULY. At anchor in Eniwetok. Take on provisions.

21 JULY . . . Sortie North with DDs Terry and Benner.

22-24 JULY . . . Routine air patrols. Northwesterly course. Underwater sound contact made by one DD faded.

25 JULY . . . See Minami, Io Shima, and Iwo Jima as we pass close aboard.

26 JULY . . . Northwesterly course. Report for duty with Third Fleet. Receive orders to join Task Group 38.4.

27 JULY . . . Start run-in to our launch position South of Shikoku.

28 JULY . . . Light showers. Flying conditions undesirable. Operate in George Love area. Launch strikes to Kure Harbor and sweeps to Yonago, Miho, Tambaichi, and Hanshin airfields. Our mission to destroy aircraft. Planes were found to be camouflaged and hidden away from the fields . . . many found, strafed, and destroyed. Oil tanks, hangars, and railroads bombed and rocketed. At Kure the battleship Haruna and cruisers of the Oyodo and Tone classes were hit. Mines sighted and destroyed by DDs.

29 JULY . . . Retire and top off DDs. Cruisers and Destroyers leave disposition to bombard

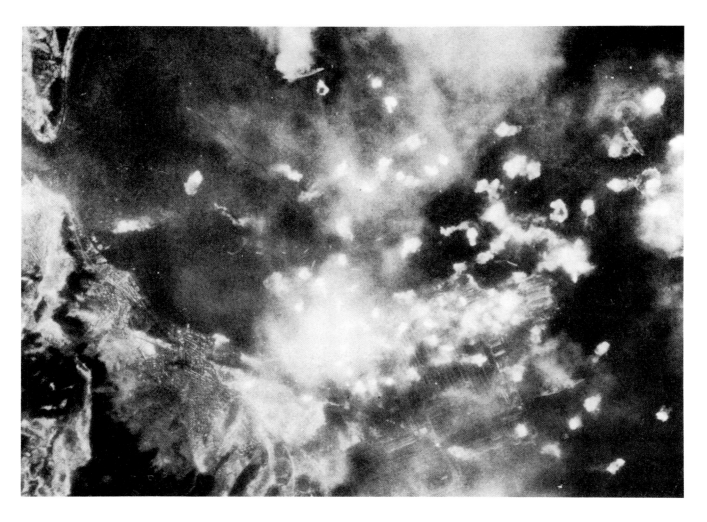

1st KURE RAID, MARCH 19, 1945

WAKE ISLAND

Hamamatsu. Sight more mines. At sunset commence run to North for strikes on Tokyo area.

30 JULY . . . Adverse weather over target. Fog, haze, smoke. Strikes against Tokyo area directed to Maizuru Naval Base and Utsonomiya and Fujisawa airfields. Maizuru . . . hit harbor crowded with war and cargo ships and Naval installations. Airfields . . . revetted planes, hangars, and radar stations hit amid heavy AA. Atami . . . small shipping destroyed.

31 JULY . . . On course South. Typhoon reported 500 miles Southwest.

1 AUGUST . . . Re-arm at sea. Low visibility, heavy swells. Typhoon now 400 miles West.

2 AUGUST . . . Scheduled strikes cancelled. Heavy seas.

3 AUGUST. Gunnery and Air Group exercises as Task Force avoids path of typhoon. At sunset we head Northwest.

4 AUGUST . . . Operate in area 350 miles South of Honshu.

5 AUGUST . . . Scheduled strikes cancelled. Flying conditions impossible.

6 AUGUST . . . Low fog.

7 AUGUST . . . Mines sighted and exploded. In afternoon commence run to North for strikes on Honshu and Hokkaido.

8 AUGUST . . . Scheduled strikes cancelled. Overcast and fog. Many bogeys on screen. Two bandits splashed . . . one by our Air Group.

9 AUGUST . . . Flying conditions average. Operate 150 miles Southeast of Honshu. Target bears 258 distance 173. Launch sweeps toward Yamagata, Yabuki, Koriyama, Harano, and Iwaki airfields. Revetted planes, hangars, installations and several trains hit by our Group. Task Group attacked in afternoon . . . Grace in suicide dive, shot down by Wasp plane and gunners. Crippled plane crashes into water less than 50 feet off starboard beam. Kamikaze attacks continue. Eight more enemy planes shot down by Task Group's CAPs and ship's gunfire. Picket Destroyer hit by Kamikaze.

OYODO—CL

OYODO AT KURE—JULY 28, 1945

10 AUGUST . . . Operate 150 miles East of Honshu. Target bears 232 distance 258. Typhoon in area, but no effects are noted. Launch strikes and sweeps against Mobara, Kisarazu, Harano, Niigata, Shiogama, Koriyama, and Iwaki airfields. Aircraft on runways, oil tanks, and trains smashed with bombs and rockets. AA intense at Niigata. Bogies conspicuous by their absence. Retire to East in late afternoon.

11 AUGUST . . . 350 miles East of Honshu. Receive replacement planes and fuel.

12 AUGUST . . . More mines destroyed. Commence run to Southwest for tomorrow's strikes.

13 AUGUST . . . Light showers. Low, moderate swells. Target bears 280 distance 270. Launch strikes and sweeps against Mito, Mito South, Tatejama, Imba, Katori, Shiroi, Shimoshizu, and Kashiwa airfields. Revetted

aircraft, air installations, factories, and trains strafed, bombed, and rocketed. Bogies around Task Force constantly. 21 enemy planes shot down. Our Air Group gets one Nick and two Graces. Continue to sight mines detonating them as we pass. Retire South at sunset.

14 AUGUST . . . 270 miles Southeast of Japan.

15 AUGUST . . . Cold front. Broken low clouds, light showers. Launch strikes against Tokyo area. Hyakurigahara airfield hit just before the war ends. CincPac issues orders to CEASE OFFENSIVE ACTION AGAINST JAPANESE EMPIRE. Strike recalled . . . remainder of strikes cancelled. Ships hoist personal and battle flags. Six Jap pilots who didn't get the word splashed. Our Air Group splashes Zeke and Judy, the latter being the last plane of the war to attack Third Fleet.

HARUNA—UNDER ATTACK

SUBMARINES AND SUB PENS AT MAIZURU

CONTE VERDE AT MAIZURU   HITS AT KURE, JULY 28, 1945

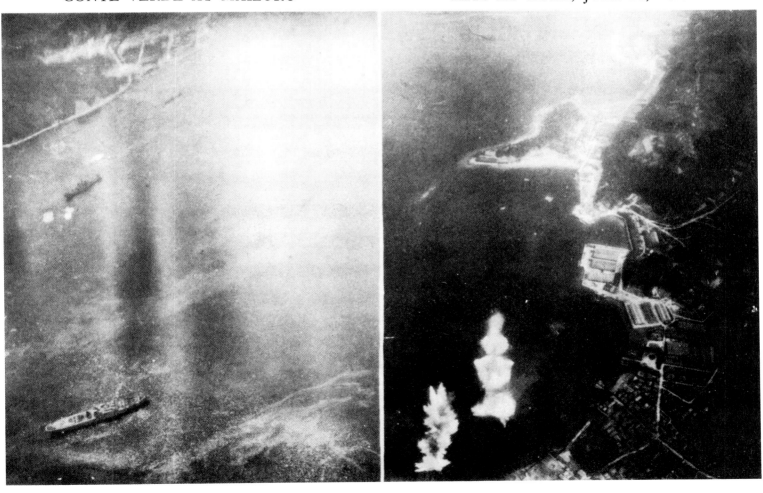

JAP CV IN HIDING BOMBED BY WASP PILOT

SHIZUOKA

NAGOYA HARBOR

DEVASTATED NAGOYA

SACRED MT. FUJIYAMA PHOTOGRAPHED BY
AIR GROUP EIGHTY-SIX PILOTS

A FEW FACTS ABOUT 86

ON 1 September 1945 the Air Group consisted of 194 Officers and 154 enlisted men. The entire Air Group entourage consists of 348 males, 137 wives, 106 children and an unknown quantity of dogs, mistresses and other pets. The personnel consists of 1 Commander, 15 Lieutenant Commanders, 35 Lieutenants, 96 Lieutenant (jg)'s, 47 Ensigns, 11 Chiefs, 46 PO1cs, 52 PO2cs, 39PO3cs and 4S1cs who hail from 45 states and the district of Columbia. California, Missouri, New York and Pennsylvania have contributed 14 Officers each to the group while 13 enlisted men from Pennsylvania gives that state top honors amongst the men. The only states not represented are North and South Dakota and Nevada.

Duty has billeted the Air Group on 15 Air Stations and shipped members aboard 52 different ships, including 3CV's, 9 CVL's, 20 DDs, 1 Minelayer, 2 British DDs, 2 Submarines, crash boats, LCIs, LCMs, ferries and rubber rafts.

A total of 75,591 hours of flight time has been logged by the pilots since the Air Group formed. Approximately 1,083,985 A gasoline coupons would be needed to purchase the gasoline the group has used. This would be enough to drive the old Ford 200 miles a day for the next 1,000 years.

If all our carrier landings had to be repeated, it would take a Landing Signal Officer working night and day, 2 days, 18 hours and 36 minutes to bring the planes aboard at 30 second intervals.

If all the automatic weapon ammunition which was shot was belted together it would be 40.1 miles in length and weigh 1,179,643 lbs. Against the enemy a total of 712,190 lbs. of explosives were dropped at an average of 71,219 lbs. per strike day.

Of the 40 planes damaged by the enemy, 29 were able to return to the ship in their damaged condition while 11 planes were lost. Of the 25 water landings, rescue was affected in 80% of the cases.

The Air Group shot down 19 planes, destroying 70 on the ground, sank or damaged 22 warships and 28 merchant ships.

U.S.S. WASP
CV-18

CAPTAIN WENDELL GRAY SWITZER, USN

COMDR. J. L. THOMAS
AIR OFFICER

COMDR. J. C. CLIFTON
EXECUTIVE OFFICER

PRIMARY FLY CONTROL
CAPTAIN SWITZER
CHAPEL SERVICES

TINTYPE OPERATIONS
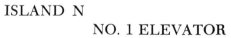

ISLAND N
    NO. 1 ELEVATOR

SHIP'S ORCHESTRA   HAPPY HOUR

THE UNITED STATES SHIP WASP was launched from the Fore River Yards of the Bethlehem Steel Co. in August of 1943. It was placed in commission on 24 November 1943 at the South Boston Navy Yard. Captain C. A. F. Sprague, USN accepted command of the ship in the presence of such notables as Governor Leverett Saltonstall, Mayor M. J. Tobin, Miss Julia Walsh, the sponsor, and Mrs. Franklin D. Roosevelt. After an address by Rear Admiral D. C. Ramsey, USN, Chief of the Bureau of Aeronautics, an informal reception was held in the wardroom.

The WASP was designated CV-18 of the ESSEX Class carrier series. She is 877 feet long and 93 feet wide at mid-ships. She draws 27 feet of water. The flight deck is 83 feet above the keel and is 114 feet wide at mid-ships. The WASP has an allowance of 2571 men and carries almost 3,000 men with her Air Group. Her electrical plant could easily support an American city of 100,000 people and she carries enough food to feed her full complement for over a hundred days. Her four boilers create 150,000 horsepower which can drive her through the water in excess of 33 knots.

In January the WASP was assigned to the Atlantic Fleet. She was degaussed and depermed and then commenced practice operations with her first air group, 14. She got under way for Trinidad in compliance with shakedown operations schedule on 31 January. An anchorage in the Gulf of Paria opposite Port of Spain afforded the crew their first expeditionary liberty. The WASP returned to Boston on 27 February and by 15 March was enroute to the Panama Canal and the Pacific Ocean. She stopped at San Diego long enough to take on a hundred extra planes and 1,000 marine passengers, and tied up at Pearl Harbor on April 3rd. After numerous sorties from Pearl for gunnery ex-

MORNING CATAPULT   HOLD THOSE BRAKES

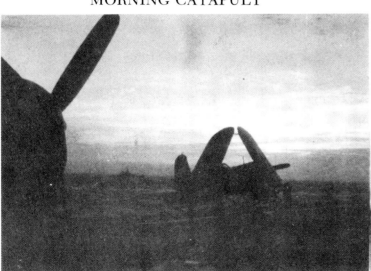

U.S.S. MISSOURI

SECURED

ercises and air group qualifications, the WASP departed for the forward area on 3 May. On 14 May the WASP reported to the Fifth Fleet for duty with Task Force 58 at Majuro Atoll in the Marshalls, recently wrested from the Japanese. This mighty task force got underway to attack the Japanese on 15 May . . . from then on the WASP's cruises helped write history:

19 MAY . . . WASP launched four strikes against Marcus Island.

20 MAY . . . WASP launches two more strikes against Marcus, destroying aircraft, ships and installations.

23 MAY . . . Launched five strikes against Wake.

    On 6 JUNE the WASP in company of Task

Force 58 was off to destroy aircraft and aircraft facilities at Tinian, Rota and Guam and to support landings at the same places.

11 JUNE . . . 201 sorties launched against Tinian town.

13 JUNE . . . Launched strikes against Saipan.

15 JUNE . . . WASP planes strike Rota.

16 JUNE . . . Close support given troops going ashore at Saipan.

19 JUNE . . . WASP shoots down five attacking enemy planes and suffered first casualties from near misses.

20 JUNE . . . WASP participates in historic Battle of Philippine Sea. She is under attack for two days and is at the same time sending

CHANGING COMMAND

MAIL CALL

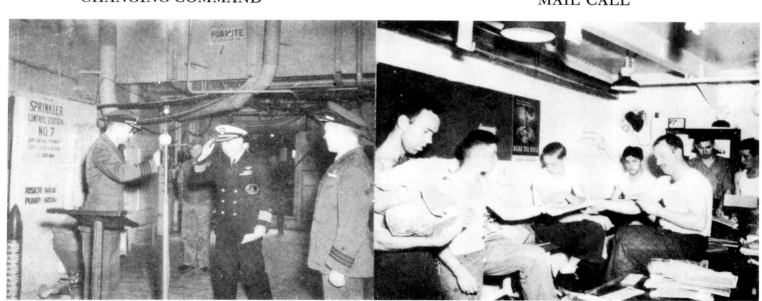

LOOKING AFT   PASSENGERS

numerous sorties against the Jap Fleet in the Philippine Sea.

24 JUNE . . . Pagan Island in the Marianas hit.

On 28 JUNE the WASP entered Eniwetok for stores, provisions and ammunition. Rear Admiral Ralph Davidson comes aboard with his flag.

4 JULY . . . WASP group hits Iwo Jima and from the sixth to the twentieth struck Guam repeatedly.

21 JULY . . . "W" Day . . . Marines land on Guam as WASP group makes supporting strikes.

22 JULY . . . Captain O. A. Weller relieved Admiral A. Sprague.

25-27 JULY . . . WASP launches strikes against Palau, Koror, Babelthaup and Mala-kal.

In AUGUST, the WASP returned to Eni-wetok for more arms and provisions and Vice Admiral J. S. McCain hoists flag as Rear Admiral Ralph Davidson leaves ship.

6 SEPTEMBER . . . WASP returns to strike Palau and Ngesebus and for the rest of the month launched continuous strikes against the southern Philippine area.

21 SEPTEMBER . . . WASP planes are first over Manila Bay.

27 SEPTEMBER . . . the WASP crossed the equator and held the customary polywog initiation much to their dismay and to the delight of the Shellbacks, while en route to Manus in the Admiralties.

In early OCTOBER, the WASP sortied out

AMATEUR NIGHT

LAST KAMIKAZE DIVE ON WASP, AUG. 9, 1945

MAIL

ATHLETICS

of Manus, joined the Third Fleet and started for Formosa, "Nippon's Unsinkable Aircraft Carrier". Strikes were sent against Formosa and Okinawa during the period 8-12 OCTOBER. WASP then moved down to Northern Luzon where strikes were conducted from 18-19 OCTOBER against Jap-held airfields. 25-28 OCTOBER . . . Second Battle of the Philippine Sea . . . Nip fleet is pulverized by WASP and other Third Fleet planes in Leyte Gulf, San Bernadino Straits and off Northern Luzon.

In early NOVEMBER weary Air Group 14 was relieved by 81 and Admiral McCain transferred to the USS HANCOCK.

On 14 NOVEMBER WASP launched strikes against Manila Bay and Nichols Field and on the 19th, Northern Luzon.

From the Fourteenth to the 16th of December the WASP and Task Force 38 loaned air support to the advancing troops in North and central Philippines and then returned to Ulithi for reprovisioning.

In early JANUARY the Third Fleet again headed North striking Formosa and then turned in to the South China Sea. Amid extremely adverse weather, strikes were launched against Hong Kong, Canton, Saigon and Cam Ranh Bay. The fleet stayed in the South Seas for seven long days; however the overcast covered the retiring ships.

On the third of FEBRUARY, Marine Fighter Squadrons 216 and 217 came aboard to increase the Air Group's strength for the forthcoming Empire Strikes.

MARINE GUNNERS

19th LANDING

CONTROL   INTO THE WIND

16 FEBRUARY ... WASP planes are the first to be over the Japanese Capitol. Strikes are very successful in spite of poor weather.
17 FEBRUARY ... WASP launches strikes on Yokahawa.

19 FEBRUARY ... "D" Day at Iwo. The Marines go ashore and are supported by WASP and Fifth Fleet Planes.

In early March the WASP planes strike

Okinawa just before retiring to Ulithi to exchange Air Group 81 for 86. Air Group 86's sorties are covered elsewhere in the book and consequently are not repeated here.

It was during this cruise that Capt. W. G. SWITZER relieved Capt. WELLER on the WASP.

As the peace was being signed in Tokyo Bay, the plankowners of the WASP looked back on 155,822 miles of travels.

The USS WASP and her Air Groups had ... shot down 230 planes ... probably destroyed 21 more planes in the air ... damaged another 50 planes in the air ... sank 114 ships, grossing 228,735 tons ... probably sank 52 more ships weighing 69,500 tons ... damaged 305 other ships. Her Air Groups had flown 6,564 sorties over enemy territory, expending some 1,800 tons of bombs, and 5342 rockets. They had earned a sincere ... WELL DONE.

NAGOYA CASTLE

WASP PILOTS OVER PRISONER OF WAR CAMPS

WE had weathered the typhoon. The flight deck was twenty-five feet shorter, but the Wasp was still operational. We were flying off in a tail-high attitude with no trouble. And there was still a lot of work to be done.

On the morning of the 27th of August, we were launched on a mission to find and photograph prisoner of war camps in the Nagoya area. The launching point was two hundred miles from this one-time important industrial city.

On the way in, the sky was clear with only a few broken clouds, but a solid front of rain walled off the mainland. We flew low on the water to get under this and came within sight of the harbor.

.This was our first flight over Honshu after the cessation of hostilities, and we still weren't sure that they had stopped shooting.

After the front there was a broken cloud layer extending from two thousand up to five thousand feet. We approached Nagoya just above that. The clouds became heavier over the land. The Nips didn't seem to be firing so we turned back out into the bay and let down through the clouds to fifteen hundred feet and flew in over the city under the clouds.

The experience was entirely different from a combat mission. This was the first chance any of us had ever had of seeing the extent of the damage that we had done. Always before we had dropped our bombs and gotten out of there . . . fast. Now we were flying low and slow. Even the smallest targets were discernible.

The first thing we noticed were the people in the streets going about the regular business of an ordinary day. Getting on and off trolley cars, riding bicycles, walking about. Children playing in the school yards. Long-legged animals drawing two-wheeled carts. Always before when we went over they had been out of sight, probably in bomb shelters, and now to see them out in the open was the first definite sign that the war was over.

The destruction of Nagoya was complete and breath-taking. Great blocks completely burned out. Factories gutted and great bomb craters on the airfields that bordered the city, once a world-famous chinaware center.

We were fascinated to the point that we went so low we had to pull up from time to time in order to avoid the chimneys which had once been part of buildings, but which now stood naked and alone.

In a less destroyed part of the city was a great Buddha with its temple. The curled roofs of Japanese homes brought back memories of grammar school geography and meager studies of the curious yellow race.

DESTROYED NAGOYA

CASTLE QUADRANGLE

The people in the streets appeared not to notice us, but we were flying so low that they couldn't keep from looking up occasionally. We could imagine the relief it must have been for them to have us there and for them to know that they wouldn't have to run to a shelter and sit through the whining and explosions of bombs and bullets.

They had moved some of their airplanes back out on the edges of the airfields, and we saw better targets than we had seen for a month. But if the war hadn't been over we knew the planes would still be hidden away from the fields, probably near some great anti-aircraft emplacement where it would be impossible to go low enough to find and destroy them.

Tearing ourselves away from this casual sight-seeing, we began looking for the pris-

oner of war camps. We had charts on which their approximate positions, from meager source materials, had been marked. We looked in those places first. We saw groups of buildings which could have been used to house prisoners, but none of them had the prescribed markings, two large letters, PW. These letters were to be twenty feet high in yellow paint and placed in a conspicuous manner.

Before very long a marked camp was found on the top of a small hill about three miles outside the city. We flew very low over it and the prisoners must have been delirious with joy at seeing the stars on our wings. They took off most of the clothes they had on and waved them vigorously. We could almost hear them shouting they were jumping around so violently. Their great

PRISONER OF WAR CAMP SPOTTED

emotional state was transmitted to us. The great feeling of relief that the war was over returned to us.

We circled the camp for perhaps a half hour, reassuring the prisoners that we had seen them and wishing that we had supplies to drop them. Then we went on to look for others.

We located Nagoya Castle, a reported prisoner of war camp. We orbited low over this, trying to find some marking. The Castle looked like a fort out of the days of the feudal system. Surrounded on three sides by a moat, it was built up in a series of steps and looked as though it might have been used in early times to defend the har-

DROPPING SUPPLIES

bor. The quadrangle was filled with men stripped to the waist playing games . . . what looked like a potato race and something played with the men standing in a circle. We could not identify their nationality, but they were apparently not prisoners. They kept on with their games and paid no attention to us. We finally concluded them to be a part of the Japanese army.

We could find no more prisoner of war camps in the area, and it was time to start back. We actually had to force ourselves to head for home . . . and four hours strapped to the seat of a small plane is an awfully long time.

On the way we flew low over the beaches. People were in swimming, digging for clams in the mud, fishing in small boats. It was like flying along any beach in the States. We came to realize that the war's end was a relief to the Japanese people, too. Although defeated, they could once again go about the process of normal, everyday living. They could go back to their occupations . . . back

INTO THE SUNLIGHT

to their beaches. They could leave their bomb shelters in the daytime.

We left and flew back to the carrier. In the ready rooms we couldn't keep from talking exuberantly about the flight. It had excited us as much as any combat mission. At last we could accept the fact, in its immensity, that the war was really over.

That afternoon we took off again to drop supplies to the prisoners we had found. We carried packages made up by the ship out of supplies that were on hand. These were parachuted down to the grateful men, who stood waving their arms and their clothes. We hoped the packages contained the things that they needed most.

The next day we dropped more supplies and continued our search for more camps in our assigned area, going as far North as Fujiyama. We found no other camps.

By the thirtieth we had established several systems of communication with the prisoners. Morse code and semaphore plus a system of panels by which we dropped them questions and they answered briefly with rough, paneled letters made with parachute silk from our supply drops. We took them everything they asked for, and more . . . small personal packages which we put up ourselves.

This was our last day in the area. We told them we were going to have to leave. The panel message changed. We flew over them low. They lined up in a military formation and saluted. Their panels read, "Men from Bataan-Corregidor Thank Wasp."

No other recognition would we ever need that we had done our job well.

. . . AND AIR GROUP EIGHTY-SIX
FEELS THE SAME WAY . . .
THANK YOU, "WASP".

EDITORS OF THE

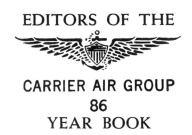

CARRIER AIR GROUP
86
YEAR BOOK

Editor-in-Chief
Robert Camp, Jr., Lt. U.S.N.R.

Assistant Editors
VF
William Sylvester Bahn, Lt. (j.g.) U.S.N.R.
Theodore Roosevelt Ogden, Lt. (j.g.) U.S.N.R.
Theodore Schwartz, Lt. (j.g.) U.S.N.R.

VBF
William Sanford Stevenson, Lt. (j.g.) U.S.N.R.
Frederick Clifford Ford, Jr., Lt. U.S.N.R.
Raymond Vincent Raehn, Lt. (j.g.) U.S.N.R.
Louis Werner II, Lt. (j.g.) U.S.N.R.

VB
Paul B. Brown, Lt. U.S.N.R.
Mac William Henderson, Lt. (j.g.) U.S.N.R.
William G. Mundy, Lt. U.S.N.R.

VT
R. Bryant Foerster, Lt. (j.g.)
Arthur C. Euler, Lt. (j.g.)
Roy J. Martin, Lt. (j.g.)
Charles Clucas, ARM1/c
Harry F. Kyer, Y2/c